TAKING LIBERTIES

TAKING LIBERTIES

National Barriers to the Free Flow of Ideas

ELIZABETH HULL

PRAEGER

New York
Westport, Connecticut
London

Library of Congress Cataloging-in-Publication Data

Hull, Elizabeth.
Talking liberties : national barriers to the free flow of ideas / Elizabeth Hull.
p. cm.
Includes bibliographical references.
ISBN 0–275–93043–2 (alk. paper)
1. Freedom of information—United States. 2. Freedom of movement—United States. I. Title.
KF4774.H85 1990
342.73'0853—dc20
[347.302853] 89–22888

Library of Congress Catalog Card Number: 89–22888
ISBN: 0–275–93043–2

First published in 1990

Praeger Publishers, One Madison Avenue, New York, NY 10010
An imprint of Greenwood Publishing Group, Inc.

Printed in the United States of America

The paper used in this book complies with the Permanent Paper Standard issued by the National Information Standards Organization (Z39.48–1984).

10 9 8 7 6 5 4 3 2 1

To my mother,

Isabel Hull

Contents

Acknowledgments

This book may soon be dated, I am happy to say. Many of the policies I discuss are grim legacies of a long Cold War, and within the next few years several of them may be rescinded if, in the spirit of *glasnost*, relations continue to improve between the United States and the Eastern-bloc countries. More than *glasnost* will be necessary, however, to date my underlying thesis—that at a time when impending crises are increasingly global in nature, it is unrealistic and even foolhardy to keep the First Amendment confined within strict national borders.

In writing this book I received generous support from friends, associates, and institutions. Both the President's Coordinating Council on International Programs and the Research Council at Rutgers University provided travel and operating funds. Mr. Alan Reitman, who retired last year after having served with distinction for 32 years as the associate director of the American Civil Liberties Union, offered sound advice and inspiration.

I am grateful to my colleagues in the Political Science Department at Rutgers-Newark for their ongoing support, and to Rami Shatz for rescuing me on several occasions when my computer "misbehaved." Dr. Kathy Miller deserves particular thanks: She started out as simply my "editor extraordinaire," and ended up in addition as my confidante and crisis manager. Above all I am grateful to my husband Jeff. He sat still while I read him all three drafts of this manuscript, and whenever I paused for breath he'd make me laugh.

Introduction

In its final report, the congressional committee investigating the Iran-Contra affair concluded that "the very premise of democracy is that 'we the people' are entitled to make our own choices on fundamental policies. But freedom of choice is illusory if policies are kept not only from the public but from its elected representatives."[1]

The type of official censorship decried by the congressional committee was the very evil the First Amendment of the U.S. Constitution was designed to prevent. This amendment reads in part: "Congress shall make no law abridging the freedom of speech, or of the press"; and while it serves several individual and communal needs, it serves, above all, the needs of a democratic polity. In such a polity the citizens are sovereign, and the First Amendment guarantees them the two rights necessary to discharge this role: the right to speak "uninhibitedly and robustly" about public affairs,[2] and the right to examine whatever information bears on these affairs.[3]

The U.S. Supreme Court has repeatedly emphasized the First Amendment's crucial role in fostering an informed electorate,[4] and it permits authorities to suppress most types of information only under the most extraordinary of circumstances.[5] As the Court explained when it refused to enjoin publication of *The Pentagon Papers*, speech relating to issues of public concern can be restrained only to prevent an overwhelming danger "so imminent that it may befall before there is opportunity for full discussion."[6]

Ordinarily, then, the government cannot suppress political expression directly; nor can it do so indirectly—by subjecting expression it disfavors to discriminatory treatment, or by saddling it with burdens that are neither essential nor as minimally restrictive as possible.[7] In one case, for instance, the Court threw out a Rhode Island statute authorizing a state commission to impose light sanctions against publications it considered "morally objectionable," because even these "informal sanctions" could inhibit the publications' circulation.[8]

However, in a country committed to the proposition that its citizens should have access to whatever information bears on public affairs, and that endorses with great ceremony international covenants that acknowledge First Amendment rights and that reproves any nation where these rights are abused, the U.S. government nevertheless implements numerous policies that are difficult to fathom and harder still to defend.

Consider, first, whom the United States excludes from its borders. Tomas Borge, Nicaragua's interior minister, was denied permission to visit this country because, as a Department of State official explained, "He intended to make speeches critical of President Reagan's Central American policy."[9] In 1982, Olga Finlay and Leonor Rodriguez Lezcano, Cuban authorities on family law, were similarly prohibited from honoring speaking engagements in the United States because, according to a government spokesperson, a lecture tour "would have been prejudicial to the public interest by providing the two officials with forums for propagating Cuban policies before U.S. audiences."[10]

Borge, Finlay, and Rodriguez Lezcano are in select company: Their names are listed in the Immigration and Naturalization's big, black *Lookout Book,* which reads like a "Who's Who" of international celebrities in the worlds of art, science, and politics.[11] Unless granted a waiver, individuals on this list are forbidden to set foot on U.S. soil for so much as an hour because at some time or another they have subscribed to Marxist tenets, criticized this country's foreign policy, or distributed leaflets advocating a Free Palestine, and have thereby run afoul of one or more provisions of the McCarran-Walter Act.[12]

Since its enactment in 1952, the McCarran-Walter Act has mandated the exclusion or expulsion of any aliens who are or ever have been members or affiliates of anarchist, Communist, or "any other Totalitarian Party"; who advocate the doctrines of world Communism; or whom a consular official "suspects" may be attempting to enter the country "solely, principally . . . or incidentally to engage in activity which would be prejudicial to the public interest."[13]

Next, consider the fate of outspoken Americans who want to travel abroad. Although the Supreme Court once described travel as a constitutional liberty closely related to the rights of free speech and association,[14] in 1981 it indicated in *Haig* v. *Agee*[15] that the Department of State could deny a passport not only to an ex-CIA (Central Intelligence Agency) agent, Philip Agee, whose past actions had caused demonstrable harm, but also to anyone else who "posed a danger to the United States national security."[16] According to Solicitor General Wade McCree, who represented the government during oral arguments in the *Agee* case, "anyone else" might include an American citizen who wanted to visit El Salvador in order to "denounce U.S. policy . . . in supporting [its] junta," or, he implied, any other citizen intent on impugning the United States or its ventures before foreign audiences.[17]

Even individuals who are not outspoken and who simply want to visit Cuba, Vietnam, Cambodia, or North Korea to find out for themselves what's going on, may be denied a passport because, under the Trading with the Enemy Act,[18] the government can declare whole countries off-limits to Americans in order to further national security or foreign policy objectives.[19]

Consider, too, the operation of this country's export control laws, which were originally enacted to prevent Americans from supplying hostile nations with militarily useful hardware.[20] On the theory that the transmission of technological know-how constitutes an export, these laws are now used to prevent scientists from delivering papers, scholars from publishing research, and professors from teaching classes if anyone with access to their information is from China, Libya, or an Eastern-bloc country.[21]

Consider the fate of any film that discusses acid rain, nuclear proliferation, or race relations in a way that government administrators claim "depicts America in an unfavorable light" or constitutes "advocacy."[22] If such a film is imported, Department of Justice agents operating under the authority of the Foreign Agents Registration Act may stamp it "political propaganda" and encumber its distributors with onerous registration and reporting requirements.[23] If it is a U.S. production destined for export, officials at the United States Information Agency (USIA) have in the past and—depending on the results of forthcoming court action—may again in the future deny it the trade concessions it needs to survive.[24]

Consider the fate of Todd Patterson, a sixth-grader attending a New Jersey parochial school, who sought information from the consulates of Eastern-bloc countries as part of a Social Studies project and thereby wound up the subject of a secret, two-inch-thick Federal Bureau of Investigation (FBI) dossier.[25] Consider Edward Haase, who, like the hundreds of other Americans returning to the United States from Cuba, Nicaragua, or the Soviet Union, has his luggage ransacked and his papers confiscated by customs officials.[26] Finally, consider the American people as a whole, who will never know exactly what went on during those crucial first days in October 1983 when the United States invaded the island of Grenada because the U.S. military, with full backing from the Reagan administration, imposed a total news blackout.[27]

These apparently disparate examples have one thing in common: All involve the movement of people or ideas across national borders, and such transborder speech commands little official protection. The executive branch recently argued that "the freedom of speech that [Americans] may enjoy domestically may be very different from that [they] can exercise [in other countries],"[28] and the Supreme Court has held that under most circumstances the First Amendment protects only activity undertaken within U.S. territorial boundaries.[29]

According to the Court, cases involving transborder speech frequently raise larger issues related to immigration policy, national security, and foreign relations; and it maintains that it lacks both the constitutional authority and the institutional competence to deal with these issues. Rather, they are the province of Congress and, especially, the executive branch.[30]

As a consequence of the Court's reticence, then, U.S. Nazis can stage hate marches down the streets of Skokie, Illinois,[31] but Japanese antiwar activists can be denied permission to participate in a United Nations–sponsored peace rally in New York City.[32] Brooklyn- or Boston-based tabloids can proclaim "Revolution Now," but Margaret Randall, a Mexican citizen teaching at the University of New Mexico, can be deported because she once urged the same thing. Rhode Island censors cannot impose even "light sanctions" against constitutionally protected literature,[33] but bureaucrats at the Department of Justice can officially stigmatize a Canadian film dealing with the dangers of nuclear war.[34]

The Supreme Court has only once in its history invalidated a statute that penalized transborder speech. This was in 1965, and the case, *Lamont* v. *Postmaster General*,[35] involved a federal law requiring that "Communist political propaganda" mailed into the United States be detained at the post office until the addressee specifically requests delivery. The Court held that by imposing on addressees the "affirmative obligation" to request delivery—an obligation "almost certain to have a deterrent effect"—the statute violated their First Amendment rights.[36]

After *Lamont*, however, the Court never again challenged the executive's asserted right to regulate anything—people, publications, or motion pictures—that crosses U.S. borders. The closest it came was in a 1972 case, *Kleindienst* v. *Mandel*, involving, as one plaintiff phrased it, a citizen's "right to receive information and ideas."[37] The Court has recognized this right in a number of domestic contexts, throwing out a Georgia law, for instance, that prohibited individuals from possessing obscene material in the privacy of their own homes,[38] and a New York regulation that allowed school authorities to ban any book they found ideologically or morally offensive.[39] The Mandel suit was different, however: It involved a foreigner, a Belgian citizen named Ernest Mandel.

Mandel, a renowned Marxist scholar, was unable to fulfill speaking engagements in the United States because the attorney general denied him a visa. In upholding the denial, the Supreme Court held that while Americans had a First Amendment right to receive information and to hear what the Belgian scholar had to say,[40] this right is not absolute, and in cases involving the admission and exclusion of aliens, it must yield to the attorney general's preemptive right to bar anyone he chooses as long as he cites some "facially legitimate and bona fide reason" for doing so.[41]

In *Mandel* the Court at least professed to balance the right of the individual against the needs of the government. In subsequent cases, however, it dispensed with even this pretense, summarily affirming executive-branch policies whenever individuals or even members of Congress challenged their constitutionality.

Lower courts have been more willing than the Supreme Court to defy the government in cases involving transborder speech, but their decisions are frequently reversed on appeal. In one recent case, *Bullfrog Films v. Wick*, Judge A. Wallace Tashima held that the United States Information Agency could not legitimately deny tariff relief to U.S. films intended for export on the basis of vague and discriminatory standards.[42] In so ruling he made a statement without precedent in federal court history, declaring that, in the absence of some overriding national interest, "the First Amendment protects communication with foreign audiences to the same extent as communication within our own borders."[43] Judge Tashima's ruling was sustained and even applauded by the Ninth Circuit Court of Appeals,[44] but its future looks grim: The Supreme Court will almost assuredly overturn it, and in the process will chastise the lower tribunals for rendering opinions that represent, as former Judge Robert Bork noted in a related case, "judicial incursions into the U.S.'s conduct of foreign affairs."[45]

The Supreme Court's complaisance on such issues is unnecessary because few of the transborder cases it adjudicates involve foreign relations or national security in any but the most speculative and tangential sense. The Court's complaisance is, furthermore, irresponsible, because it allows the government to restrict Americans' access to foreign sources of information.

Americans, like people everywhere, need information from foreign as well as domestic sources, if only because countries are increasingly interdependent, and because problems from drug addiction to ozone depletion are increasingly international in scope. The government urged Judge Tashima to remember that "the world at large is not a First Amendment forum,"[46] but actually the opposite is true: Today's world is indeed a First Amendment forum; the "marketplace of ideas" has become an international arena.[47]

Americans need access to foreign voices for yet another reason: Without it they are increasingly dependent for information upon a notoriously unreliable source, their government. Hodding Carter, assistant secretary of state for political affairs under the Carter administration, suggests that the urge to control information may even be endemic to governments:

> For those who believe that information about public policy—and dissent from it—properly belongs to the people, there is no such thing as a benevolent government. Some are better than others, but all are obsessed with the urge to shield the public from a truthful understanding of what's being done in its name.[48]

The framers of the First Amendment spoke in bold and unequivocal language precisely because they believed, as Hodding Carter believes, that government officials almost by nature seek to control information. They do so not because they are venal, necessarily, or indifferent to the public's best interest, but because they have power, and power intoxicates. Upon its acquisition even normally unpretentious people will in time delude themselves that their privileged insights, coupled with the public's presumed incompetence, justify what they could call "news management," and what others might call "disinformation," or even lies.

Although federal authorities, and in particular, members of the executive branch, may have attempted to manage the news since the republic's inception, until recently their success was limited by technology so primitive that relatively few people relied on Washington for either social services or vital statistics.[49] Since World War II, however, modern presidents have presided over a social welfare state that affects every facet of corporate and private life, and they have at their command a technological apparatus awesome to contemplate. As one consequence, information packaging has become a sophisticated and even institutionalized phenomenon.

Television has provided the president with an "electronic throne" from which he can preempt network programming and appeal directly to the American public. Above all, he and the several thousand bureaucrats who serve him can use computers in ways that until recently seemed the stuff of science fiction: not only to acquire, retrieve, synthesize, and disseminate information, but also to withhold, selectively leak, and otherwise manipulate it in order to mislead the public and create a false consensus. Guatemala and the Bay of Pigs; the bombing of neutral Cambodia and the assassination of Chile's democratically elected president; Vietnam and Watergate, Grenada and the Iran-Contra fiascoes: Each was a morally dubious operation, several were disastrous as well, and all were undertaken in the name of the American people but without their consent or even their knowledge.[50]

Does it really matter if Americans can hear firebrands from Managua or share information with colleagues from Prague? Will they be more enlightened, less easily duped? Not necessarily, but the odds are improved. It is not that foreign sources are any less biased or subservient than their domestic counterparts, but theirs are different biases; they serve different masters, and as a result they can expose Americans to additional information, new ideas, and alternate ways of attending to the human condition.

Notes

1. United States Congress. *Report of the Congressional Committee Investigating the Iran-Contra Affair with Supplemental, Minority, and Additional Views,*" 100th Cong., 1st Sess., H. Rept. No. 100–433 and S. Rept. No. 100–216, Nov. 1987.

2. Justice William Brennan noted in *New York Times* v. *Sullivan* that this country has a "profound national commitment to the principle that debate on public issues should be uninhibited, robust, and wide-open." 376 U.S. 254, 270 (1964). *For discussion see* Chapter 5.

3. *For discussion see* Alexander Meiklejohn, "The First Amendment Is an Absolute," *1961 Supreme Court Review* 245 (1962); Thomas Emerson, "Toward a General Theory of the First Amendment," 72 *Yale Law Journal* 877 (1963).

4. *See Richmond Newspapers, Inc.* v. *Virginia*:

> The First Amendment embodies more than a commitment to free expression and communicative interchange for their own sakes; it has a *structural* role to play in securing and fostering our republican system of self-government. Implicit in this structural role is not only "the principle that debate on public issues should be uninhibited, robust, and wide-open" . . . but the antecedent assumption that valuable public debate—as well as other civic behavior—must be informed. The structural model links the First Amendment to that process of communication necessary for a democracy to survive, and thus entails solicitude not only for communication itself, but for the indispensable conditions of meaningful communication.

448 U.S. 555, 587–88 (1980) (Brennan, J., concurring) (emphasis in original).

Elsewhere in the same case Justice Brennan points out that "the First Amendment goes beyond protection of the press and the self-expression of individuals to prohibit government from limiting the stock of information from which members of the public may draw." 448 U.S. at 576.

See also Mills v. *Alabama*, 384 U.S. 214, 218 (1966) ("A major purpose of [the First Amendment] was to protect the free discussion of governmental affairs"); *Red Lion Broadcasting Co.* v. *FCC*, 395 U.S. 367, 392 (1969) (the goal of the First Amendment is "producing an informed public capable of conducting its own affairs").

Democratic theorists have also emphasized the First Amendment's indispensable role in sustaining a healthy polity. James Madison observed that a "popular Government, without popular information or the means of acquiring it, is but a Prologue to a Farce or a Tragedy, or perhaps both. . . . A people who mean to be their own Governors must arm themselves with the power which knowledge gives." Letter from James Madison to W. J. Barry (August 4, 1822), *reprinted in*

G. Hunt, ed., *Writings of James Madison* (New York: G. B. Putnam and Sons, 1910), p. 9; *quoted in* Note, "The First Amendment Right to Gather State-Held Information," 89 *Yale Law Journal* 923, 932 (1980).

Alexander Meiklejohn, a contemporary constitutional theorist, based his influential First Amendment doctrine on one fundamental proposition: In a democracy, citizens are their own governors. As a consequence, government officials are prohibited from suppressing or otherwise restricting any speech that bears on public affairs:

> When men govern themselves, it is they—and no one else—who must pass judgment upon unwisdom and unfairness and danger. And that means that unwise ideas must have a hearing as well as wise ones, unfair as well as fair, dangerous as well as safe, un-American as well as American. Just so far as, at any point, the citizens who are to decide an issue are denied acquaintance with information or opinion or doubt or disbelief or criticism which is relevant to that issue, just so far the result must be ill-considered, ill-balanced planning for the general good. It is that mutilation of the thinking process of the Communist against which the First Amendment of the Constitution is directed. The principle of freedom of speech springs from the necessities of the program of self-government. It is not a Law of Nature or reason in the abstract. It is a deduction from the basic American agreement that public issues shall be decided by universal suffrage.

Free Speech (New York: Harper and Row, 1949), pp. 26–27.

See also Thomas Emerson:

> The constitutional right to know embraces the right of the public to obtain information from the government. . . . [T]he public, as society, must have all information available in order to instruct its servants, the government. As a general proposition, if democracy is to work, there can be no holding back of information, otherwise, ultimate decisionmaking by the people, to whom that function is committed, becomes impossible. Whether or not such a guarantee of the right to know is the sole purpose of the First Amendment, it is surely a main element of that provision and should be recognized as such.

"Legal Foundations of the Right to Know," 1 *Washington University Law Quarterly* 14 (1976).

5. *See New York Times* v. *United States*, 403 U.S. 713 (1971).
6. 403 U.S. at 725. *For discussion see* chapter 5.
7. *See, for example, Murdock* v. *Pennsylvania*, 319 U.S. 105 (1943) (city ordinance violates the First Amendment that requires Jehovah's Witnesses to secure a license before they can solicit door-to-door); *F.E.C.* v. *Massachusetts Citizens for Life, Inc.*, 107 S. Ct. 616, 626 (1986) (plurality opinion) ("The fact that the statute's practical effect may be to discourage protected speech is sufficient to characterize [it] as an infringement of First Amendment activities").
8. *Bantam Books* v. *Sullivan*, 372 U.S. 58, 67 (1963).
9. E. J. Dionne, Jr., "Barring Aliens for Political Reasons," *The New York Times*, Dec. 8, 1983, p. A–20.
10. Letter, dated October 21, 1983, from Kenneth N. Skoug, Jr., Director, Office of Cuban Affairs, to Thomas H. Holloway, Director, Cornell University, Latin American Studies Program; *cited in Free Trade in Ideas: A Constitutional Imperative* (Report prepared for the Center for National Security Studies, Washington, D.C., May 1984), p. 5. (Report available at the Center for National Security Studies, 122 Maryland Avenue, N.E., Washington, D.C. 20002).

See also Abourezk v. *Reagan*, 592 F. Supp, 880, 887 (D.D.C. 1984); *vacated and remanded*, 785 F. 2d 1043 (D. C. Cir. 1986); *aff'd mem.* 108 S. Ct. 252 (1987) (3–3 per curiam). *For discussion see* Chapter 1.

11. "U.S. Still Blacklists 3000 Canadians for Politics," *The New York Times*, Feb. 1984, p. A–21. *For discussion see* Chapter 1.

12. *For discussion see* Chapter 1.

13. Immigration and Nationality Act of 1952, ch. 477, 66 Stat. 163 (codified at 8 U.S.C. §§1101–1503 (1982).

14. *Aptheker* v. *Secretary of State*, 378 U.S. 500, 517 (1964).

15. 453 U.S. 280 (1981).

16. 453 U.S. at 319 n.9 (Brennan, J., dissenting). *For discussion see* Chapter 2.

17. *Haig* v. *Agee*. 453 U.S. at 319 n.9 (Brennan, J., dissenting).

18. Act of October 6, 1917, ch. 106, 40 Stat. 411 (1917), 50 U.S.C. app. §1 (1968).

19. *For discussion see* Chapter 2.

20. *See, for example*, The Arms Export Control Act of 1976, 22 U.S.C. §§2751–96 (1983); The Export Administration Act, 50 U.S.C. app. §2401 (1983).

21. *For discussion see* Chapter 5.

22. *For discussion see* Chapters 3 and 4.

23. The Foreign Agents Registration Act, 22 U.S.C. §§611–18 (1982).

24. *See* Agreement for Facilitating the International Circulation of Visual and Auditory Materials of an Educational, Scientific and Cultural Character (Beirut Agreement), January 12, 1967, 17 U.S.T. 1579, T.I.A.S. No. 6116, 197 U.N.T.S. 3. *For discussion see* Chapter 4.

25. In 1983, when Todd Patterson was a sixth-grade student in North Haledon, New Jersey, he and other members of his Social Studies class were asked to research a country as part of a project on the United Nations. This assignment sparked Todd's interest in geography and travel, and he thereafter wrote to the embassies of almost every country seeking information for his "encyclopedia of the world."

Shortly after the first of these letters was sent, in the summer of 1983, the FBI started a file on Patterson, which it maintained for at least five years. The agency routinely tracks mail going to and from various countries, although as U.S. Attorney Susan Cassell later explained, Patterson's "flurry of letters" aroused particular concern because they were sent in business envelopes that bore the logo of his father's company, which manufactures technological equipment. Robert Rudolph, "FBI in Legal Battles for 'Kiddie Probe,' " *The Newark Star-Ledger*, Dec. 16, 1988, pp. 1, 18.

In 1987, after discovering the existence of his dossier through the Freedom of Information Act, Patterson sued the agency for illegally maintaining a file on him in contravention of §(e)(7) of the Privacy Act, which, under most circumstances requires that "each agency that maintains a system of records shall . . . maintain no record describing how any individual exercises rights guaranteed by the First Amendment." *See* 5 U.S.C. §552a (e)(7) (1975).

Patterson has been represented by Fred Askin, a professor at Rutgers Law School and an American Civil Liberties Union attorney, who initially asked to have his client's case certified as a "class action" since he is convinced that thousands of files are maintained on "innocent individuals" who never become aware of the fact that they are the subject of an FBI probe. Rudolph, " 'Kiddie Probe,' " pp. 1, 18.

After examining *in camera* the contents of Patterson's file, a federal district court judge wrote an opinion in which he spoke in optimistic terms about Todd's professional prospects and ignored altogether the serious First Amendment issues raised by his case:

> The *in camera* inspection also allows this Court to assure plaintiff [Patterson] that any records maintained by the FBI on him do not reflect negatively on his character or conduct. Accordingly, the Court can assure plaintiff that the law enforcement activity conducted by the FBI in this case should not in any way inhibit him from pursuing any legitimate exercise of his First Amendment rights, including writing letters to countries throughout the world. Furthermore, plaintiff's fear of an aborted or limited public service career arising out of these events is misplaced.

The court encouraged—but stopped well short of commanding—the FBI to expunge Patterson's files, as the agency earlier had offered to do. *Patterson* v. *Federal Bureau of Investigation*, C.A. 88–2319 (D.N.J. 1989).

For discussion see Anthony Lewis, "Test for the Attorney General," *The New York Times*, Jan. 5, 1988, p. A–23; Lloyd A. Carver, Jr., "Youth Sues FBI for Compiling File," *The New York Times* (New Jersey edition), July 10, 1988, p. A–16.

26. *See Haase* v. *Webster*, 608 F. Supp. 1227, 1227–30 (1985); *Haase* v. *Webster*, 807 F. 2d 208 (D. C. Cir. 1986).

27. *For discussion see* Chapter 2.

28. Comment of U.S. Solicitor General Wade H. McCree, Jr., quoted in *Haig* v. *Agee*, 453 U.S. 280, 319 n.9 (1981) (Brennan, J., dissenting).

29. *For discussion see* Chapter 1; *see also* Patrick Allen Flynn, "The Constitution Abroad: The Operation of the Constitution Beyond the Continental Limits of the United States," 32 *Texas Law Review* 58 (1953); Stephen A. Saltzburg, "The Reach of the Bill of Rights Beyond the *Terra Firma* of the United States," 20 *Virginia Journal of International Law* 741 (1980).

30. *For discussion see* Chapter 1.

31. *See, for example, Collin* v. *Smith*, 578 F. 2d 1197 (7th Cir.) (ordinances designed to prohibit Nazi demonstrations violate the First Amendment), *certiorari denied*, 439 U.S. 916 (1978); *Village of Skokie* v. *National Socialist Party of America*, 69 Ill. 2nd 605, 373 N.E. 2nd 21 (1978) (Nazis have the right to demonstrate and display the swastika).

32. *See N.G.O. Committee on Disarmament* v. *Haig*, No. 72 Civ. 3636 (S.D.N.Y. June 10, 1982), *aff'd.* 697 F. 2d 294 (2d Cir. 1982).

33. *See Bantam Books* v. *Sullivan*, 372 U.S. 58, 67 (1963).

34. *For discussion see* Chapter 3.

35. 381 U.S. 301 (1965).

36. 381 U.S. at 307.

37. *Kleindienst* v. *Mandel*, 408 U.S. 753, 760 (1972).

38. *See Stanley* v. *Georgia*, 394 U.S. 557, 564 (1969) ("It is now well-established that the Constitution protects the right to receive information and ideas. . . . This right to receive information and ideas, regardless of their social worth, is fundamental to our free society.") *See also Winters* v. *New York*, 333 U.S. 507 (1948).

39. *See Board of Education* v. *Pico*, 457 U.S. 853, 867 (1982):

This right [to receive information and ideas] is an inherent corollary of the rights of free speech and press that are explicitly guaranteed by the Constitution, in two senses. First, the right to receive ideas follows ineluctably from the *sender's* right to send them. . . . More importantly, the right to receive ideas is a necessary predicate to the *recipient's* meaningful exercise of his own rights of speech, press, and political freedom. (emphasis in the original)

40. *For discussion see* Chapter 1.

41. 408 U.S. at 762–65.

42. 646 F. Supp. 492 (D. C. Cal. 1986), *aff'd.* 847 F. 2d 502 (9th Cir. 1988).

43. 646 F. Supp. at 502.

44. *Bullfrog Films, Inc.* v. *Wick*, 847 F. 2d 502 (9th Cir. 1988).

45. *Abourezk* v. *Reagan*, 785 F. 2d 1043, 1076 (D.C. Cir. 1986) (Bork, J., dissenting).

46. 646 F. Supp. at 503 n.6.

47. *See* Stephen R. Barnett, "United States Regulation of Transborder Speech," 9 *Com/ment* 635, 727 (Summer 1987).

48. Address delivered on September 17, 1984, at the Washington, D.C., Conference "Free Trade in Ideas: A Constitutional Imperative," organized by the American Civil Liberties Union and the Fund for Free Expression, published proceedings at 16. (Available from the American Civil Liberties Union, 122 Maryland Avenue N.E., Washington, D.C., 20002).

49. For an excellent discussion of the government's role in contemporary U.S. society *see* Mark Yudof, *When Government Speaks: Politics, Law, and Government Expression in America* (Berkeley: University of California Press, 1983).

50. *For discussion see* James Goldstone, Jennifer M. Granholm, and Robert J. Robinson, "A Nation Less Secure: Diminished Public Access to Information," 21 *Harvard Civil Rights-Civil Liberties Law Review* 409, 449–56 (1986); Franklyn S. Haiman, *Speech and Law in a Free Society* (Chicago: University of Chicago Press, 1981), pp. 368–408; Morton Halperin, "We Need New Intelligence Charters," 18 *The Center* (May-June 1985), p. 51; Morton Halperin and David N. Hoffman, *Top Secret: National Security and the Right to Know* (Washington, D.C.: New Republic Books, 1977); Arthur Kinoy, *Rights on Trial* (Cambridge: Harvard University Press, 1983), pp. 92, 96, 117–18; Anthony Lewis, "National Security: Muting the 'Vital Criticism,' " 34 *U.C.L.A. Law Review* 1687 (1987); Neil Sheehan, *A Bright Shining Lie: John Paul Vann and America in Vietnam* (New York: Random House, 1988); David Wise, *The Politics of Lying: Government Deception, Secrecy, and Power* (New York: Random House, 1973).

1

Guardians at the Gate: The McCarran-Walter Act and the Exclusion of Controversial Foreigners

> You might well ask yourselves why I, as well as many other intellectuals in Latin America and all over the world, continue to apply for visas to enter your country. I think our answer is very simple: we refuse to play the game of those who would silence the voices of the other cultures of the world in the United States. I, for one, insist on maintaining alive this role of bridge between cultures, of speaking to the Americans on their own home ground, and refusing to be beaten by the ghost of McCarthyism.[1]
>
> Carlos Fuentes

In January 1986, Secretary of State George Shultz addressed an international writers' conference in Manhattan, assuring the assembly that "it has never been the approved policy of the United States to deny visas merely because the applicant wants to say that he disapproves of the U.S. or one of its policies. . . . No denial is ever based on a person's abstract beliefs."[2]

The secretary's words must have astounded Canadian writer Farley Mowat, who believes that he was denied permission to visit the United States because of his vocal opposition to its arms policy.[3] (He can only speculate, since the government refuses to tell him its reasons.)[4] The secretary's statement should also have surprised Nobel prize–winning Colombian author Gabriel Garcia Marquez,[5] as well as former Canadian Prime Minister Pierre Trudeau.[6] Theirs are among the thousands of names that have appeared at one time or another either in the Immigration and Naturalization Service's (INS's) big, black *Lookout Book* (which alerts agents at ports of entry) or in the Department of State's automated visa lookout system (which warns consular officers in U.S. embassies abroad), both of which indicate that these people are officially unwelcome in the United States.[7] Unless granted a waiver, individuals listed in the lookout guides may not set foot in the United States. By virtue of some statement made, some organization joined, or some activity undertaken, they have run afoul of one or more provisions of this country's basic immigration statute, the McCarran-Walter Act.[8]

Passed in 1952 during the Cold War's heyday, the McCarran-Walter Act prohibits aliens from entering the United States for any of 33 reasons. Some reasons are compelling, such as the one that has been used to bar the entry of Kurt Waldheim and other former Nazis;[9] some reasons are, at best, anachronistic, among them those barring "polygamists"[10] and "sexual deviants";[11] and still others are simply indefensible, because they exclude men and women on the grounds of their political beliefs.

§27 of the McCarran Act renders ineligible for a visa any noncitizen whom the attorney general or a consular official "suspects" is attempting to enter the country "solely, principally . . . or incidentally to engage in activity which would be prejudicial to the public interest, or endanger the welfare, safety, or security of the United States."[12] Eight broad categories of excludable aliens are listed in §28, including those who are presently, or who were at any time in the past, members or affiliates of any Communist, anarchist, or terrorist organization, as well as those who, while not members, nevertheless propagate the beliefs of such organizations.[13] Finally, §29 bans any alien who, after entry, "probably would engage in espionage, sabotage, public disorder or other activity subversive to the national interest."[14]

In order to prevent excludable aliens from entering the United States, the act provides that any foreign nationals (except Canadians) must arrive with a visa, which can be secured only be presenting extensive documentation and answering a long series of questions "to the satisfaction" of a consular officer.[15] Under some circumstances an alien can obtain a waiver of excludability, but this is a cumbersome process involving long delays and even more meddlesome questions. After aliens are duly admitted, moreover, they can be deported at any time if they engage in any of the political activity proscribed in §§27–28–29 of the McCarran Act.[16]

The McCarran Act is a bizarre amalgam, listing anarchists and Communists alongside drug pushers, prostitutes, and polygamists as excludable aliens. By virtue of §28, for instance, individuals may be barred if they were anarchists some 10, 20, or even 30 years ago, even if they never advocated violence or were only anarchists of the philosophic sort. As the Canadian writer George Woodcock observed, if Henry David

Thoreau lived today and were an alien, he could be excluded on the strength of his essay *Civil Disobedience*.[17]

The McCarran Act has earned a stream of invective probably unequalled by any other statute in American history, with the possible exception of the Fugitive Slave Law. In vetoing the act in 1952, President Harry S Truman remarked that "seldom has a bill exhibited the distrust evidenced here for citizens and aliens alike."[18] It has been called a "wonderful catalogue of xenophobia,"[19] and described as containing "the most detailed enumeration in the world for the disqualification of aliens who may seek admission to a sovereign nation."[20] Why, then, has a statute eliciting such persistent obloquy managed to survive largely unamended for nearly 40 years?

One reason is that the McCarran Act involves aliens, who would be the chief beneficiaries of any liberal reforms, and officeholders are loath to expend political capital on a group that cannot even vote—especially when so many Americans who can vote perceive the act as a necessary bulwark against foreign invaders. Moreover, many public officials themselves support the McCarran Act for the same reason, which further contributes to its remarkable resilience.

Officials who endorse the McCarran Act defend it as an indispensable and essentially well-administered statute that has been the victim of "bad press." According to Jerome Ogden, assistant secretary of state for visa services, the act is blamed for a type of censorship that no longer exists: While individuals denied admission have "coincidentally" espoused views that were unpopular with the Reagan administration, he maintains that the only reasons they were ever denied entry under §§27–28–29 of the act were for "national security, the prevention of a potentially serious negative effect upon the conduct of foreign relations, or because an alien advocate[d] violence to achieve political ends."[21]

The Reagan administration claimed it did not exclude people on ideological grounds, but even if it did, the Department of State maintains, it was no more guilty than any of its predecessors. In 1977, for example, 877 visa applications were rejected on §§27–28–29 grounds,[22] and this number remained fairly constant through 1985, when the total reached 823.[23] In 1986, of 47,500 people initially deemed ineligible, all but 800 were eventually granted waivers.[24]

Government officials point out that only 8,000 people from 98 countries are currently restricted from entering the United States because of their political views—a number that is extraordinarily small, they maintain, considering that every year millions of foreigners apply for and receive nonimmigrant visas.[25] If the public thinks the number is larger, INS spokesperson Verne Jervis explains, it is because those excluded are often "high-profile" cases and "you only need a few before there is the vague impression that hundreds are being kept out."[26] Jerome Ogden adds that several celebrated cases, involving such well-known personalities as Graham Greene, Yves Montand, and Carlos Fuentes, "have taken on a life of their own in visa folklore," even though each individual eventually received permission to visit the United States.[27]

Furthermore, administration officials do not believe that the exclusionary provisions are unnecessarily vague or encompassing. Michael Newlin, deputy assistant secretary of state for consular affairs, points out that certain provisions, such as §27, which bars aliens whose presence might be "prejudicial to the public interest," or §29, which bans anyone whose "activity [is] subversive to the public interest," cannot be drawn more precisely without denying the executive branch the flexibility it needs to handle unanticipated dangers.[28]

Exactitude is simply not possible, Newlin continues, when decision-makers must grapple with many imponderables, assess intelligence reports and fragmentary information, and attempt to predict the reactions that an individual's entry may trigger, both here and abroad.[29] Senators Alfonse D'Amato (New York) and Malcolm Wallop (Wyoming) agree: Testifying at a congressional hearing in 1986, they pointed out that if the language of the exclusionary provisions were significantly tightened—to outlaw only those linked to overt criminal behavior, for instance—the government would be paralyzed in its efforts to outlaw whole categories of people no less pernicious because they do not throw bombs or run drugs.[30] Should Soviet doctors who engage in psychiatric torture be allowed to come here, simply because they pose no direct threat to Americans' own security? Should leaders or even functionaries from states where human rights are systematically abused be admitted just because Americans' own interests are not directly imperiled?[31]

Most of the McCarran Act's supporters suspect that its critics are, at bottom, left-wingers, who are incensed less by the exclusionary principle itself than by the occasional rejection of an individual who shares their political biases. John Corry, reviewing a television documentary on the McCarran Act for the *New York Times*, observed that when the Carter administration barred Ian Smith, prime minister of what was then Rhodesia, there was a dearth of liberal opposition, and when the Reagan administration excluded Robert D'Aubuisson, the leader of the far right in El Salvador, only Senator Jesse Helms seemed upset.[32] Corry doubts that the Nicaraguan government would allow the ultraconservative former White House spokesperson Patrick Buchanan to speak in Managua, and he wonders whether this would disturb someone like Arthur Miller, the playwright and human rights activist. (Miller, in response, pointed out that for decades he has struggled for "the rights of all opinions to be heard everywhere," and would attempt to persuade the Nicaraguan leaders to allow Buchanan to speak).[33]

Those who defame the McCarran Act are considered not only left-wing but even unpatriotic by some of its stalwarts. Illinois Senator Paul Simon recounts an experience during the 99th Congress, when he introduced a proposal (similar to one he is currently cosponsoring) that would prohibit the exclusion of anyone solely on the basis of their political beliefs. He raised this proposal as an amendment to a larger immigration reform bill, and watched it lose almost two to one. As Simon tells it, "We have a Republican table and a Democratic table. You go down and you read the summary of the amendment, and the Republican summary of my amendment said, "the Simon Amendment wants to admit anarchists and Communists to the U.S."[34] Even his staunch supporters have warned Senator Simon to "back off" from this "no-win" issue.[35]

Finally, many government officials believe that even temporary admission to the United States is a privilege, that just as no family is obliged to invite its detractors to dinner, so no nation is obliged to welcome its critics. New Mexico Senator Pete Domenici apparently shares this view. He recently refused a request by the president of the University of New Mexico to intercede on behalf of Margaret Randall,[36] a faculty member and a Mexican national who was then battling the INS in its efforts to deport her.[37] Noting Randall's frequent and often fervent denunciation of U.S. policy, Senator Domenici explained that "the question is not whether Ms. Randall is free to express her views or to visit her family, but whether Ms. Randall is entitled to the privilege of emigrating to the United States and of becoming an American citizen."[38]

The McCarran Act's assailants naturally find the government's arguments self-serving and unpersuasive. New York University law professor Burt Neuborne and civil rights attorney Steven Shapiro respond that although most people will eventually receive a visa, they must be prepared to tolerate long delays and to undergo the ideological grilling that securing a waiver entails.[39] Morton Halperin, Washington director of the American Civil Liberties Union, contests the claim that recent presidencies have all been the same, maintaining instead that the Reagan administration's use of the McCarran Act represented not a continuation of former practices but a "radical departure."[40] It may have been no worse than others in terms of the sheer numbers excluded, Halperin contends, but these exclusions represented a much more self-conscious and ultimately more successful attempt to shape public policy.[41]

The Reagan administration did, in fact, enlist the McCarran Act in its campaign to shape public policy—a disturbing phenomenon regardless of whether its practices represented the "radical departure" Halperin claims. Before 1980, individuals were barred primarily because they were either members of Communist organizations or because they posed objective threats to the nation's security. Notwithstanding its protestations to the contrary, the Reagan administration excluded scores of influential people because they opposed its arms control policies, for instance, or its conduct in Central America. It finessed these exclusions by subverting the spirit if not the letter of the McGovern Amendment on the one hand (see below), and both the spirit and the letter of the McCarran Act's §27 on the other.

The United States and the Soviet Union are both bound by the Helsinki Agreement of 1975, Basket Three of which obligates them and the other signatories to respect and promote the free passage of persons and information into and out of their territories.[42] Troubled that this country was violating the Helsinki Accords by excluding too many people on ideological grounds, Congress in 1977 passed the McGovern Amendment to the McCarran-Walter Act.[43] The McGovern Amendment provides that any alien barred under §212 (a)(28)—which proscribes the entry of anyone who is a member or affiliate of a Communist or anarchist party—will be granted a waiver by the attorney general unless the secretary of state finds and certifies both to Congress and to the attorney general that such admission would be contrary to the security interests of the United States.[44]

The McGovern Amendment, then, was intended to prevent anyone being banned under §212 (a)(28) unless such persons could reasonably be expected to harm the national security in some objective—as opposed to hypothetical—way. The amendment has not fulfilled its promise, however, because administration officials have discovered in it a loophole of mammoth proportions. As Barbara Watson, assistant secretary of state for consular affairs, explains, the amendment does not apply to "applicants ineligible on grounds other than, or in addition to, mere organization membership."[45] According to this interpretation, the McGovern Amendment thus provides an exemption only for party members, not for those who, instead of or in addition to party membership, believe in or propagate views that are considered politically objectionable. This interpretation produces an anomalous result: The chief totem of the Communist Party may receive a waiver, but not his neighbor the Marxist theoretician, or his cousin the armchair anarchist.

The McGovern Amendment has not fulfilled its promise for another reason: it applies only to aliens barred under §212 (a)(28) of the McCarran Act—scarcely an impediment once officials discovered §27, which provides for the exclusion of "aliens who the consular officer or the attorney general know or have reason to believe seek to enter the United States solely, principally, or incidentally to engage in activities which would be prejudicial to the public interest, or endanger the welfare, safety, or security of the United States."[46] To administrators this provision must seem providential: The exclusions it mandates can be neither reviewed nor appealed, and its language is so expansive that scarcely anyone eludes its reach.

Despite its expansive language, however, §27 was intended to apply only to those aliens who were likely to engage in espionage, sabotage, or other activities that might jeopardize national security; the key word was *activities*. This provision was used as its authors envisaged, for instance, when it served to exclude a Libyan student who wanted to study aircraft maintenance in the United States—a useful military skill that would be foolish to foster in a potential enemy.[47] Before the McGovern Amendment was enacted in 1977, in fact, §27 was seldom used for other than its intended purpose.[48] Since the early 1980s, however, it has been recruited time and again to ban aliens whose presence could by no stretch of the imagination serve to harm national security.

In 1983 the government prohibited Nino Pasti from visiting the United States to deliver a lecture to a disarmament group in Boston. Pasti, a former NATO (North Atlantic Treaty Organization) General and member of the Italian Senate, was a vociferous critic of the placement of Pershing II missiles in Europe. This criticism was his undoing: The general was denied a visa because, as then Under Secretary of State for Political Affairs Lawrence Eagleburger explained:

> The timing of Pasti's proposed visit coincided with the initial deployment of Cruise and Pershing II missiles in certain NATO countries—a particularly delicate period for U.S. foreign policy, and a period during which the Soviet Union was employing every propaganda tool at its disposal in an effort to frustrate the deployment.[49]

Tomas Borge, the interior minister of Nicaragua, was denied a visa under §27 because, a government spokesperson explained, he intended "to make speeches critical of President Reagan's Central American policy."[50] Dario Fo, an Italian playwright, was banned under §27 on two recent occasions because, as another official pointed out, he "never has a good word to say about the United States."[51] Furthermore, in 1982, 315 aliens hoping to participate in demonstrations scheduled to coincide with the United Nation's special session on disarmament were denied admission under §27,[52] probably less because they posed any danger than because, as Eagleburger explained, "We have absolutely no obligation to let Tommy Bulgaria or anyone else from Soviet-front groups come here, participate in demonstrations, get on air time and do the government's work for it."[53]

§27, then, provided the Reagan administration with a useful tool in its campaign to manipulate public debate. In the effort to inhibit political opposition, however, government officials can rely on several McCarran

Act provisions in addition to §27, and they have recently done so with uncommon aggressiveness against one particular group: the Palestinians.

In 1987 Congress instituted a brief grace period during which aliens could be neither excluded nor deported on the basis of their political beliefs or associations: Specifically exempted, however, was any member, affiliate, or representative of the Palestinian Liberation Organization (PLO).[54] In 1988 Congress also mandated the closure of both the PLO's Observer Office in New York City—a move that a federal judge has halted at least temporarily on the ground that it violates the United Nation's Headquarters Agreement[55]—and its Information Office in Washington, D.C.[56] Finally, in December 1988, the Department of State refused to grant a visa to Yasir Arafat, chairman of the PLO, thereby denying entry for the first time in the United Nation's history to an individual specifically invited by the organization's General Assembly.[57]

In its treatment of the Palestinians, the INS has been as harsh as either Congress or the State Department, as illustrated by the "round-up" it orchestrated early in the morning of January 27, 1987, in Los Angeles, California.[58] Immigration agents arrested at gun-point seven Jordanians and the Kenyan-born wife of one of them; they were handcuffed and shackled, and thrown in jail, where they were kept for two weeks in solitary confinement. In making these arrests the INS acted on information supplied by the FBI, whose agents had undertaken a long-term investigation of suspected Palestinian sympathizers.[59] The FBI was unable to link these individuals to anything unlawful, but it had reported to the INS its suspicion that they might be affiliated with the Party for the Liberation of Palestine (PFLP), or at least that they subscribed to its journal.[60] (The PFLP, which is a Marxist organization dedicated to the creation of a Palestinian state, gained considerable notoriety in the 1970s when it claimed responsibility for a series of airline hijackings.)

At a detention hearing on February 16 the INS accordingly charged the "Los Angeles Eight"—some of whom had been in the United States as long as 15 years—with the deportable offense of being affiliated with an organization that advocates the doctrines of world Communism.[61] The Immigration Service's sole evidence against them, however, was its assertion that in addition to belonging to a Marxist organization, they had contributed to its journal—a journal that is freely available in libraries and book stores throughout the country.[62] The immigration judge, considering this insufficient grounds for further detention, ordered the defendants released pending a deportation hearing.[63]

At this point INS officials changed their strategy: Now they sought to deport six of the Palestinians for simple visa violations, such as accepting employment without authorization, and the other two for offending that provision of the McCarran Act that mandates the expulsion of any alien who advocates "the unlawful damage, injury, or destruction of property."[64] The Palestinians countersued, charging the government with an array of constitutional offenses; they won, if only temporarily and only in the central district of California, where Federal District Judge Stephen Wilson's order is controlling.[65]

In his opinion, issued on January 26, 1989, Judge Wilson declared major provisions of the McCarran Act "unconstitutional on their face"—including those that allow the deportation of an alien who advocates or is affiliated with organizations that advocate world Communism, totalitarian dictatorship, or the unlawful destruction of property.[66] Citing relevant precedent, Judge Wilson pointed out that the Supreme Court allows the government to penalize only those who advocate "imminent lawless action" that is likely to succeed.[67] The McCarran Act's objectionable provisions, however, are "substantially overbroad":[68] They penalize not only those who are "preparing a group for violent action and steeling it to such action,"[69] but also noncitizens such as the Palestinians, who, by espousing their beliefs or by donning PFLP buttons, are engaging in the sort of political expression the First Amendment was designed to safeguard.[70]

While the government always retains the right to deport aliens engaged in harmful activity unrelated to speech, Judge Wilson said, it cannot, as here, try to use its immigration powers to regulate the dissemination of ideas, or to deprive aliens admitted to this country of what he claimed was their right to full protection under the First Amendment.[71] This right would clearly be meaningless, he continued, if on the basis of speech or political associations they could be banished from the country.[72]

On appeal *American-Arab Anti-Discrimination Committee* v. *Meese* will probably be overruled or substantially modified, since it represents a radical departure from most related rulings by higher tribunals. Judge Wilson's opinion is nevertheless significant, because this Reagan appointee is the first member of the federal judiciary to outlaw on constitutional grounds major provisions of the McCarran-Walter Act.

In deference to what it claims are the political branches' "plenary powers" over issues involving the nation's borders and its foreign relations,[73] the Supreme Court has not once in its history upset on constitutional grounds major legislative or executive policy that discriminates against noncitizens.[74] This is true even when the policy serves, as Judge Wilson said, to prevent certain ideas from entering society.[75] As a consequence, although it declared as far back as 1945 that noncitizens residing in the United States enjoy the same First Amendment rights as citizens, the nation's highest court offers aliens little support when they are denied a visa or banished from the country because they subscribe to *Pravda* or sport PFLP buttons.[76]

In practice, then, resident aliens enjoy only limited rights and nonresident aliens enjoy virtually no rights to speak their minds in the United States, but the Supreme Court indicated in an important 1972 case that U.S. citizens have at least some constitutional right to hear what they have to say. This case, *Kleindienst* v. *Mandel*, involved Ernest Mandel, a Belgian journalist and a well-known Marxist theoretician, who was invited to speak at Stanford and a number of other universities.[77] The Justice Department refused to grant him a visa, however, on the ground that persons who advocate the doctrines of world Communism are excludable under §28 of the McCarran Act. Several of the journalist's intended hosts then sued the attorney general, alleging that by excluding Mandel he had interfered with their First Amendment "right to hear."

Yes, said the Court, Americans are entitled to receive as well as to disseminate information, and yes, they do have a constitutional right to hear what Mandel has to say.[78] However, this right is not absolute, and it must yield to any "facially legitimate and bona fide government interest."[79] Whenever the government asserts a facially valid justification, moreover, this ends the matter: The Court will neither probe any further nor balance the government's interest against the First Amendment rights of those "who seek personal communication with the applicant."[80]

Americans' right to hear foreign speakers is thus swallowed up in a vast exception: They may hear whomever they want provided the government grants its permission. Government officials, in turn, can effectively deny permission to whomever they choose, since the Supreme Court suggests that it will accept as "legitimate and bona fide" almost any reason they cite. (*Mandel* itself is illustrative: The attorney general claimed the Belgian scholar was excluded because on a prior visit he had violated travel restrictions imposed by the Department of State; the Court accepted this justification, even though it conceded that Mandel had never been apprised of these restrictions.)[81]

Americans can still read Mandel's books, watch him on transatlantic television, or play his tapes, so does it matter if they cannot hear him in person? According to the Court, it matters—but not very much. Although the Court recognized that there may be "particular qualities inherent in sustained, face-to-face debate, discussion and questioning [that made it] loath to hold [that] the existence of other alternatives extinguishes altogether any constitutional interest" in having direct access to a speaker's ideas,[82] it nevertheless emphasized that this constitutional interest was subordinate to the "plenary congressional power to make policies and rules for the exclusion of aliens."[83]

What the Court gives, it thus takes away again: Americans are entitled to direct contact with a foreign speaker, but only if Congress and the attorney general approve. In so ruling the Court effectively denies Americans personal access to many provocative thinkers, and for members of the scientific and academic communities, the consequences are serious. In 1952, Victor Weisskopf, vice-chairman of the Federation of American Scientists, spoke before a congressional hearing. For members of these communities, he said, there is no substitute for face-to-face interchange in order to confront ideas directly and "to challenge and ferret out details":

> It is obvious to anyone who knows scientific life that the personal exchange of ideas is a most important way of productive work. The mere reading of foreign literature can never replace the personal give and take, seminars, discussions, and actual collaboration. International exchange of ideas and discussion is indispensable because details of scientific research are never written down in the actual publications. Frequently, only conversations can reveal a special technique or a special instrumental design which foreign scientists have used to make their experiment work. Only their presence can help our own scientists to put these experiments into use for discoveries for the development of our program.[84]

Even for ordinary people—who are not members of the scientific or academic communities—reading a book or watching a speaker on closed-circuit television is not at all the same thing as a face-to-face meeting.

Since 1972 lower courts have adjudicated several cases theoretically governed by *Mandel*, but, unlike the Supreme Court, they have been willing to probe and even to reject reasons cited by the government for excluding or deporting an alien.[85] The case decided by Judge Wilson is illustrative, as is *Allende* v. *Shultz*.[86]

The plaintiff in the *Allende* case was Hortensia Allende, the elderly widow of the former president of Chile. She was unable to fulfill speaking obligations in the United States because the Department of State found her inadmissible under both §27 and §28 of the McCarran Act, and her American sponsors thereupon sued the secretary of state on the ground that he had violated their First Amendment rights. The State Department countered that Allende's presence would be "prejudicial to the conduct of foreign affairs of the United States," in part because she was an active member of the World Peace Council, an instrument of Soviet foreign policy.[87] Allende had also participated in three international conferences between 1977 and 1981 during which she criticized the United States, pressed for disarmament, and advocated women's rights. The Department of State concluded that her involvement in these conferences, independent of her membership in the World Peace Council, constituted a "facially legitimate and bona fide" reason to deny her a visa under §27 of the act.[88]

In March of 1987, a federal district judge held that Allende was clearly covered by §28 since her participation in international conferences was incidental to her membership in the World Peace Council.[89] Since §28 encompasses exclusions based on membership in Communist-dominated groups, the government could not validly claim that her membership in such a group also justified her exclusion under §27. In any event, the government failed to establish a "facially legitimate and bona fide" reason why Allende's ineligibility should not be waived under the McGovern Amendment, which provides that aliens barred solely because of membership in Communist organizations must ordinarily be granted a visa.[90]

The First Circuit affirmed the lower court's ruling in April 1988, and decided a second issue as well.[91] The State Department had argued that by prohibiting the admission of aliens who would engage in "activities prejudicial to the public interest," Congress also intended to bar those whose mere presence in the United States could prove harmful, quite apart from their actual or intended behavior.[92] The First Circuit disagreed, holding that under §27 the government lacked the authority to exclude aliens unless their actual "activities" could prejudice United States interests.[93] It concluded that Allende's "prejudicial activity" was, in fact, her proposed speeches, for which she could no longer be barred because Congress had recently enacted a statute temporarily prohibiting the exclusion of aliens solely on ideological grounds.[94]

In *Abourezk* v. *Reagan*,[95] a related case involving four aliens who had also been denied permission to speak in the United States, the Court of Appeals for the District of Columbia issued an opinion that was similar in two respects to the First Circuit's ruling in *Allende*: It prohibited the government from circumventing the McGovern Amendment by using §27 to exclude aliens who were members of organizations proscribed under §28, and it also prohibited the barring of foreigners on the ground that their mere "presence" could harm the public interest.[96]

Judge Robert Bork dissented in *Abourezk*, lamenting that the majority opinion "begins, albeit cautiously, a process of judicial incursion in the United States' conduct of its foreign affairs."[97] He maintained that the plaintiff's asserted First Amendment rights must yield to the executive's exclusive power to conduct foreign policy,[98] and he noted that in the recent case of *Zemel* v. *Rusk*[99] the Supreme Court had affirmed the president's right to prohibit U.S. citizens from traveling to Cuba—which "is certainly no less serious constitutionally than preventing that country's citizens from coming to the United States."[100]

Judge Bork's dissent is significant because it parallels the logic increasingly used by the Supreme Court in striking down lower court efforts to curb executive authority, particularly in any area involving noncitizens; as a consequence, even the slim victories achieved in *Abourezk* and *Allende* may be negated if these cases reach the High Court on appeal. Any protection accorded the First Amendment rights of aliens, at least insofar as the exercise of these rights affects U.S. citizens, is consequently less likely to come from the judiciary than from Congress, where a decades-long effort to amend the McCarran Act may yet prove successful.

Should this effort ultimately succeed, improved relations between the United States and the Soviet Union will be partly responsible, there being now at least a tentative truce in the Cold War that spawned and then sustained the McCarran Act. More than 30 national organizations, including the American Bar Association, will also deserve credit, as will several influential legislators who, in the twilight hours of 1987, at last won a skirmish in their long campaign to amend the act.[101]

The skirmish began during a last-minute session in which legislators were attempting to pass several omnibus spending bills before adjourning for the Christmas holidays.[102] The Senate Foreign Relations Committee was considering the State Department Authorization bill, which had passed the House much earlier and which would provide the Department of State with some eight billion dollars for the next two years. Knowing that the State Department cannot spend a cent without congressional approval, and that President Ronald Reagan could therefore scarcely risk a veto, New York Senator Patrick Moynihan seized the moment: He attached an amendment that prohibits government officials from denying or imposing restrictions on visas, or deporting people on the basis of "past, current or expected beliefs, statements, or associations" which "if engaged in by a United States citizen in the United States would be protected under the Constitution."[103]

Ironically, several members of Congress hesitated to support this amendment because it removed many of the McCarran Act's most objectionable features and they feared that it might frustrate their efforts to rewrite the act in its entirety.[104] They ultimately accepted the Moynihan proposal, however, on the condition that it incorporate a novel caveat: In order to sustain pressure in Congress for wholesale reform, they provided that the Moynihan Amendment would "self-destruct" on March 1, 1989. The amended authorization bill then passed both houses of Congress, and, as Moynihan had predicted, President Reagan had little choice but to sign it.[105] Thus, on December 20, 1987, with virtually no fanfare, the McCarran-Walter Act underwent temporary and imperfect, but nonetheless major, reform.

As applied, however, the 1987 amendment, which Congress extended in October 1988 for another two years,[106] has brought about no fundamental change: The Department of State continues to require anyone seeking a visa to answer a long series of questions about past and present political beliefs and associations (although it insists that this information is used solely to detect actual or potential lawbreakers),[107] and it continues to operate on the assumption that it is as free as ever to exclude aliens on the basis of political ideology when "necessary to protect important internal security or foreign policy interests of the United States."[108]

The 1988 extension differs in one significant respect from its predecessor: It no longer protects resident aliens from deportation or exclusion on ideological grounds.[109] Margaret Randall, who has been fighting deportation for half a decade, is among the many affected by this change.[110] In February 1988, the Department of Justice informed her that as a consequence of the new legislation, it would abandon its efforts to expel her;[111] once the legislation was amended, however, it resumed its campaign.[112]

The 1988 extension, in fact, creates a perverse situation: Aliens accepted for permanent residence, who are generally eligible to become citizens after residing for five years in this country, may again be deported for espousing their political beliefs, while nonimmigrants—those residing in the United States only temporarily—can say almost anything they choose without fearing reprisals. This undercuts a basic principle underlying U.S. immigration policy, which is that as aliens become increasingly established in the community, their rights enlarge correspondingly.

The 1987 and 1988 amendments are, as intended, only stopgaps until the McCarran Act can be substantially overhauled. Almost every year since 1983, a bill effecting such an overhaul has been introduced in Congress—usually by Massachusetts Representative Barney Frank, who, more than any other legislator, has agitated for reform.[113] Each year Frank and his cosponsors expect their efforts to succeed, moreover, because key congressional and executive officials finally agree on the central issue—that aliens should not be barred solely on the basis of their political beliefs. These key players agree on little else, however, and as a result each year the sponsors are predictably disappointed when their attempts at reform are frustrated.

Administration officials are adamantly opposed to any expansion of judicial review, for instance, while the reformers consider it essential to prevent the executive branch from excluding people on grounds never sanctioned by Congress.[114] Moreover, administration officials believe that not only terrorists should be barred from the country, but also, as a Department of State adviser put it, "all their accomplices in the international terror network,"[115] as well, including those who "advocate or teach" or are affiliated with organizations that "advocate or teach" the propriety of certain violent acts.[116] Barney Frank and his cohorts fear this language sweeps so wide as to ensnare even individuals like the Los Angeles Eight, whose only offense was their political affiliation.

The major point of dispute, however, involves the extent to which the executive branch should retain authority to bar aliens for "foreign policy" reasons. On one side are those who maintain that *activities* should be the operative word: No one should be barred whose activities do not present an actual threat to public safety or security. On the other side are executive officials who believe that the United States must retain its authority to exclude anyone whose presence might have "adverse foreign policy consequences"—a deposed dictator, for instance, such as the shah of Iran.[117]

These differences may delay, but they probably will not destroy, congressional efforts to enact comprehensive reform. As long as the delay continues, however, everyone loses, because, as Mexican writer Carlos Fuentes observed, the McCarran Act "belong[s] to the realm of sado-masochism."[118]

Conclusion

Fuentes is right: The McCarran Act is indeed sadomasochistic policy, subjecting innocent people to needless humiliation, and the country itself to widespread derision. Dario Fo, a popular Italian playwright, tells of the reaction throughout Western Europe when he and his wife, actress Franca Rama, were denied visas in 1980.[119] Editorial writers likened the United States to a banana republic, while newspapers featured a long-running comic strip depicting the nation as a pitiful colossus quivering with fear at the sight of the two Italian entertainers wading onto its shores.[120] The McCarran Act exposes the United States not only to ridicule, but also to widespread resentment. As Fuentes observed, more than anything else the act "damages the image of the U.S. in intellectual circles abroad" because it makes the country seem not only timid, but also two-faced.[121]

In the fall of 1985, the Soviet Union refused to allow certain Americans to attend the Moscow Book Fair. A few months later, South Africa refused to admit nine U.S. representatives from the National Council of Churches because of its alleged ties to the "terrorist" African National Congress. In 1987 Hungary forbade Janos Kis, a distinguished philosopher, to visit the United States for a one-year teaching stint at the New School in Manhattan.[122] In each instance, U.S. commentators castigated these countries for violating both the Helsinki Accords and basic human rights. While they are perhaps obliged to protest the misdeeds of South Africa, Hungary, or the Soviet Union, some humility is in order here, since this country practices much the same kind of exclusionary politics. Just as Hungary refused to let Kis teach at the New School, the Department of State tried its hardest to prevent Dennis Brutus, a poet raised in South Africa, from teaching at Northwestern University.[123] The United States has sought, as well, to keep Cosmo Pieterse, a Namibean poet and playwright, from taking a teaching post at Ohio University,[124] and Angel Rama, an Uruguayan literary essayist, from accepting an appointment at the University of Maryland.[125]

When this country engages in what writer Garry Wills calls "preemptive ideologizing"—namely, "the attempt to thwart an enemy by strenuously imitating him"—it only diminishes its own moral authority.[126] Hodding Carter, assistant secretary of state for political affairs in the Carter Administration, made this point: "We cannot, as we have, point fingers at Moscow for refusing to let a Nobel Laureate, Andrei Sakharov, out, if we refuse to let another Nobel Laureate, Colombian author Gabriel Garcia Marquez, in, as we have done."[127]

America's ill-wishers exult when it behaves like the countries it censures. They have, for instance, made much of its treatment of Tom Ronse, a Belgian journalist who, in fall 1986, was detained overnight in Newark, New Jersey, because immigration officials had discovered in his baggage "some typewritten stuff in English which espoused Communist doctrine."[128] After his release, Ronse was told to return to immigration headquarters on October 3, by which time officials would have investigated his material to determine whether or not it warranted his exclusion.[129] *Tass*, the Soviet government news agency, crowed. Comparing Ronse's treatment to that accorded Nicholas Daniloff, a U.S. correspondent who was detained in Moscow, Tass reported that "this incident demonstrates anew the real worth of 'freedom' in the United States, and the readiness of Washington to attack even a citizen of an allied country if he professes views not to the Administration's liking."[130]

On October 3, 1986, about the same time immigration agents were, in Ronse's words, "being kind of harsh on me,"[131] they were being even harsher on another foreign journalist, Patricia Lara. Lara, a Colombian, had come to the United States to attend a banquet given at her alma mater, Columbia University, to honor writers who had promoted—ironically, as it turned out—"inter-American understanding and freedom of information."[132] Her name appeared in the INS's *Lookout Book*, however, so rather than enjoying the evening at Columbia University, Lara spent that night and the next four nights in a maximum security cell in lower Manhattan. During this time she was denied so much as a shower until officials from the Colombian embassy interceded. Finally, after a perfunctory hearing, she was expelled from the country. She received a hero's welcome upon her return home, and newspapers throughout Latin America compared her to Nicholas Daniloff.[133]

Elliott Abrams, then secretary of state for inter-American affairs, later explained on the television program "Sixty Minutes" that Lara had ties to M–19, a notorious terrorist organization in Colombia.[134] He may well be right, although Colombian officials staunchly deny his charge,[135] and Abrams himself produced no evidence to corroborate it (engaging instead in what *New York Times* columnist Anthony Lewis termed a "hit and run attack").[136] The issue, however, is not the personal history of Lara or Ronse, nor, certainly, the right of any country to exclude actual malefactors from its border. The issue is, rather, the international standing of the United States, which is invariably diminished when the country appears hypocritical, waving the banner of free expression and pillorying countries like Nicaragua when they abuse First Amendment rights, and then unceremoniously expelling anyone whose viewpoint it finds offensive. Among its allies this country's standing is further eroded, moreover, when in detaining their nationals it appears to manhandle or otherwise abase them.

The experiences of Lara and Ronse are atypical; few foreigners are actually abused in this way. Nearly every person who visits the United States is subjected to demeaning treatment, however, since no one can set foot on these shores without first convincing government officials that he or she is politically and morally worthy to receive a visa.[137] The United States is the only democratic country in the world that refuses to admit anyone who does not pass a test for ideological and moral fitness. Not only the physicist wishing to settle in the United States but also the parents hoping to show their children the Statute of Liberty and the grandmother invited to visit her family in Cincinnati must first attest to the fact they have never been prostitutes, anarchists, drug smugglers, or purveyors of Communist dogma.[138]

The initial, and crucial, decision whether to grant a visa is usually left to the discretion of consular officers, who can deny admission to anyone they even suspect might threaten the public interest. They are not required to support their findings or even to record the actions they take,[139] and since they operate within vague and open-ended standards, INS spokesperson Duke Austin concedes that "there's a strong motive for a bureaucrat to deny an application when it's not a clear yea or nay."[140]

An alien denied a visa on grounds other than §27 can frequently obtain a waiver—described by Carlos Fuentes as "a form of sufferance: a discretionary whim"—but doing so requires perseverance and guile.[141] One must answer copious questions, enumerating and explaining past friendships, associations, and even innocent activities that may have taken place decades earlier. Former Canadian Prime Minister Pierre Trudeau used to require a waiver, for instance, because his name appeared in the INS's *Lookout Book* as a result of his attendance at an economic conference in Moscow.[142] When his fellow compatriot, the distinguished poet and painter Barker Fairly, sought to visit the United States, he also required a waiver, even though he was 97 years old, because his former wife had once been a Communist.[143]

Aliens denied immigrant visas, which entitle them to permanent residence in the United States, can obtain waivers of ineligibility only by demonstrating "to the satisfaction of a consular officer" either that their memberships in proscribed organizations were not voluntary or that they qualify as defectors—namely, individuals who have terminated membership at least five years earlier and have thereafter actively opposed the organizations and their principles.[144] Canadian writer and editor George Woodcock was once told that he might obtain a waiver if he were willing to say, "I'm not an anarchist at any time and I deeply regret I ever was one."[145] (He declined the opportunity, deeming the process "too much like the recantation formula of the Holy Inquisition" for his taste.)[146]

Herbert Agar wrote an article for the *Saturday Review of Literature* in which he described the ordeal confronting scientists in the bid for a waiver. Let us, he says,

> picture a famous European man of science, or of letters, who has been invited to a conference in the United States by his American colleagues. He goes to our embassy in his own country to seek a visa. He is given forms to fill out which are an insult and an absurdity: an insult because they seem to presuppose that he is a potential enemy who has to prove his innocence; an absurdity because he is asked to testify on the spot, to exactly what he thought, or wrote, or believed, forty years ago. He is then interviewed by a harassed consular official, again on the assumption that a distinguished foreigner (honored, requested, and awaited by his American confreres) is probably a fraud, and that he must somehow reassure us that he has not been lying. Finally, his papers go forward to Washington. There, in a land of abused and overworked bureaucrats, the dreary forms and timid reports are
>
> upwhirled aloft
> Fly o'er the backside of the world far off
> Into a limbo large and broad, since called
> The Paradise of fools.
>
> Emerging at last from the Miltonic chaos, the papers return to their point of origin. And the great man receives his visa several months after the conference to which he was invited has come to an end.[147]

Agar wrote in 1953, but 34 years later, his sentiments were echoed (if in less picturesque language) by representatives from the American Association for the Advancement of Science, who complained to a congressional committee that the exclusionary provisions discourage many distinguished scientists from visiting the United States.[148] According to U.S. author William Styron, they are similarly discouraging to international literati. Speaking before the writers group PEN America, Styron described the eagerness of his friend Gabriel Garcia-Marquez to visit the United States. Nonetheless, for many years Garcia-Marquez would not come "because some personage in an American embassy in whatever country it was . . . asked him if he was a Communist, asked him if he had ever been a homosexual, asked him all the[se] humiliating things. . . . I think this is . . . one of the basic flaws of the ideological exclusions. . . . It submits men of good will, men who pose no possible danger to our society, to our humiliation."[149]

Many travelers—scientists, men and women of letters, and ordinary people—simply will not come. Many members of the British Association of University Teachers will not visit the United States, for instance, because, as a spokesperson explained, "They consider it anathema to be forced to attest to their political views and affiliations."[150] Jaime Garcia Torres will not come. He is the most distinguished publisher in Mexico and director of Latin America's largest publishing house, but as Carlos Fuentes observed, Garcia-Torres "will not even apply for a visa to avoid the ordeals inherent to cultural communication with the United States."[151]

Of course the United States needs restrictive immigration laws to bar the entry of anyone with a serious criminal record or a genuine link to terrorist or seditious activity. The objectionable provisions of the McCarran Act are not those focused on such legitimate threats, but the broad, all-encompassing ones that ensnare in their nets Chilean widows, Italian generals, and Mexican journalists who may not favor capitalism, the Contras, or the deployment of cruise missiles. Government officials claim these sweeping provisions promote national security, and even the international opprobrium they invite might not be an intolerable price to pay if they did, indeed, serve that end. The irony is that they do not serve, and may even frustrate, the attainment of this goal: Many of the McCarran Act's exclusionary provisions have become censors' tools, and whereas national security is rarely enhanced by censorship, it is almost invariably enhanced by an educated citizenry with access to people of many and varied points of view.[152]

Notes

1. *Quoted in* E. McIntire, "The Denial of Visas under Sections 212 (a)(27) and (28), the Ideological Exclusionary Clauses, of the Immigration and Nationality Act: A Documentation of Nine Cases Prepared for Congressman Barney Frank" (August 15, 1983), p. 21. (Unpublished report available from the Office of Congressman Barney Frank, 1030 Longworth Building, Washington, D.C., 20515).

2. Statement before PEN International Conference in New York City, *quoted in* Mehren, "Is PEN Mightier than the State?" *The Los Angeles Times*, January 15, 1986, Part 5, p. 1.

3. Susan Benda and Morton H. Halperin, "Forbidden Writers—The Foreign Threat in Literary Garb," 47 *College English* (Nov. 1985), p. 690.

4. Mowat later received a partial explanation from an anonymous source, who told the author that he had been designated *persona non grata* after a 1968

newspaper article quoted him as saying that he was prepared to retaliate against American B–52 bombers with a .22 rifle when they engaged in training runs over Newfoundland. Mark Schapiro, "The Excludables," *Mother Jones* (January 1986), p. 30.

Shortly after this incident took place, the Immigration Service offered Mowat a one-time-only waiver in order for him to visit the United States to complete a scheduled publicity tour for his book *Sea of Slaughter* (Boston: Atlantic Monthly Press, 1986). (Mowat indicated that he would accept the offer only if he received a personal apology from President Reagan and a complimentary, first-class flight into the United States aboard Air Force One. Ibid.)

Mowat has detailed his experiences with the United States Immigration Service in a book entitled *My Discovery of America* (New York: Atlantic Monthly, 1985).

5. *For discussion see* McIntire, "The Denial of Visas," p. 20.

6. "U.S. Still Blacklists 3,000 Canadians for Politics," *The New York Times*, Feb. 19, 1984, p. B–21.

7. *See* "40,000 Barred from the U.S.," *The New York Times*, April 28, 1987, p. A–28. Canadian author George Woodcock recounted how in 1983 he was denied entry to Honolulu during a 24-hour stopover on his way to Australia because the immigration officer then on duty found his name under "W" in the *Lookout Book*: It was "a literal black book, heavy and thick. I have seen nothing like it since I entered Egypt by boat at Alexandria twenty years before, during Nasser's paranoiac reign." *See* his "On Being 'Inadmissible,' " 31 *New York Review of Books* (Sept. 27, 1984), p. 43.

8. Immigration and Nationality (Walter-McCarran) Act, ch. 477, 66 Stat. 163 (1952) [codified at 8 U.S.C. §§1101–1524 (1982)].

So many international notables have been barred from the United States under the exclusionary provisions of the McCarran Act that Susan Benda and Morton Halperin, legislative analyst and director, respectively, of the Washington office of the American Civil Liberties Union, observed that "one may well assume that foreign writers omitted from the list suffer a disappointment not unlike that felt by those Americans who considered themselves strident liberals but failed to turn up on President Nixon's enemy lists." Benda and Halperin, "Forbidden Writers," p. 692.

9. *See* "Waldheim Barred from the U.S.: Role in Nazi 'Persecution' Is Cited," *The New York Times*, April 28, 1987, pp. A–1, A–28.

10. 8 U.S.C. §1182 (a)(11).

11. 8 U.S.C. §1182 (a)(4).

12. 8 U.S.C. §1182 (a)(27).

13. 8 U.S.C. §1182 (a)(28). Specifically, subsection (28) provides for exclusion of:

(A) Aliens who are anarchists;

(B) Aliens who advocate or teach, or who are members of or affiliated with any organization that advocates or teaches, opposition to all organized government;

(C) Aliens who are members of or affiliated with (i) the Communist Party of the United States, (ii) any other totalitarian party of the United States, (iii) the Communist Political Association, (iv) the Communist or any other totalitarian party of any State of the United States, of any foreign state, or of any political or geographical subdivision of any foreign state, (v) any section, subsidiary, branch, affiliate, or subdivision of any such association or party, or (vi) the direct predecessors or successors of any such association or party, regardless of what name such group or organization may have used, may now bear, or may hereafter adopt: *Provided,* That nothing in this paragraph, or in any other provision of this chapter, shall be construed as declaring that the Communist Party does not advocate the overthrow of the Government of the United States by force, violence, or other unconstitutional means;

(D) Aliens not within any of the other provisions of this paragraph who advocate the economic, international, and governmental doctrines of world Communism or the establishment in the United States of a totalitarian dictatorship, or who are members of or affiliated with any organization that advocates the economic, international, and governmental doctrines of world Communism or the establishment in the United States of a totalitarian dictatorship, either through its own utterances or through any written or printed publications issued or published by or with the permission or consent of or under the authority of such organization or paid for by the funds of, or funds furnished by, such organization;

(E) Aliens not within any of the other provisions of this paragraph, who are members of or affiliated with any organization during the time it is registered or required to be registered under section 786 of Title 50, unless such aliens establish that they did not have knowledge or reason to believe at the time they became members of or affiliated with such an organization (and did not thereafter and prior to the date upon which such organization was so registered or so required to be registered have such knowledge or reason to believe) that such organization was a Communist organization;

(F) Aliens who advocate or teach or who are members of or affiliated with any organization that advocates or teaches (i) the overthrow by force, violence, or other unconstitutional means of the Government of the United States or of all forms of law; or (ii) the duty, necessity, or propriety of the unlawful assaulting or killing of any officer or officers (either of specific individuals or of officers generally) of the Government of the United States or of any other organized government, because of his or their official character; or (iii) the unlawful damage, injury, or destruction of property; or (iv) sabotage;

(G) Aliens who write or publish, or cause to be written or published, or who knowingly circulate, distribute, print, or display, or knowingly cause to be circulated, distributed, printed, published or displayed, or who knowingly have in their possession for the purposes of circulation, publication, distribution, or display, any written or printed matter, advocating or teaching opposition to all organized government, or advocating or teaching (i) the overthrow by force or violence, or other unconstitutional means of the Government of the United States or of all forms of law; or (ii) the duty, necessity, or propriety of the unlawful assaulting or killing of any officer or officers (either of specific individuals or of officers generally) of the Government of the United States or of any other organized government, because of his or their official character; or (iii) the unlawful damage, injury, or destruction of property; or (iv) sabotage; or (v) the economic, international, and governmental doctrines of world Communism or the establishment in the United States of a totalitarian dictatorship;

(H) Aliens who are members of or affiliated with any organization that writes, circulates, distributes, prints, publishes, or displays or causes to be written, circulated, distributed, printed, published or displayed, or that has in its possession for the purposes of circulation, distribution, publication, issue, or display, any written or printed matter of the character described in subparagraph (G) of this paragraph.

8 U.S.C. §1182 (a)(28).

14. 8 U.S.C. §1182 (a)(29). §29 provides for the exclusion of the following:

aliens with respect to whom the consular officer or the Attorney General knows or has reasonable ground to believe probably would, after entry, (A) engage in activities which would be prohibited by the laws of the United States relating to espionage, sabotage, public disorder, or in any other activity subversive to the national security, (B) engage in any activity a purpose of which is the opposition to, or the control or overthrow of, the Government of the United States by force, violence, or other unconstitutional means, or (C) join, affiliate with, or participate in the activities of any organization which is registered or required to be registered under section 7 of the Subversive Activities Control Act of 1950.

15. Richard D. Steele, *Steele on Immigration Law* (Rochester, N.Y.: The Lawyers Cooperative Publishing Co., 1985), pp. 115–16, 126, 370, 375–78.

16. 8 U.S.C. §1251 (a)-(f) (1982). Most aliens who seek to enter the United States are screened twice—first, by a U.S. consul in their own country, who issues them their visas, 8 U.S.C. §1104 (1982); and second, by immigration officers at United States points of entry. 8 U.S.C. §1103.

"Exclusion" takes place either when aliens are refused visas in the first place, or when they have been issued visas but are nevertheless denied entry when they reach the United States border. "Deportation" occurs when the government removes an alien who is already present in the country. *For discussion see* Mitchell C. Tilner, "Ideological Exclusion of Aliens: The Evolution of a Policy," 2 *Georgetown Immigration Law Journal* 1, 3 n.7 (Summer 1987).

17. Woodcock, "On Being 'Inadmissible,' " p. 43.

18. 98 *Congressional Record* 8082 (1952) (veto message of President Harry Truman).

19. TRB, "Something to Declare," 189 *The New Republic* (Oct. 17, 1983), p. 8.

20. Jack Wasserman, *Immigration Law and Practice*, 3d ed. (Philadelphia, Pa.: American Law Institute, American Bar Association Committee on Continuing Professional Education, 1979), pp. 1–10.

21. Jerome Ogden, " 'Ideological Grounds' Are a Myth," *The New York Times*, Jan. 10, 1987, p. 15.

22. David Shipler, "Seeking Visa Denials as Plan to Manipulate Debate," *The New York Times*, Nov. 12, 1986, p. B–6.

23. Ibid. Interpreting figures provided by the Department of State or the Immigration and Naturalization Service can be confusing since an individual can be denied a visa for several different reasons, and each ineligibility is cited in the statistics. *See* Ogden, " 'Ideological Grounds,' " p. A–15.

24. Robert Pear, "U.S. May Back Some Changes in Aliens Law," *The New York Times*, Aug. 12, 1986, p. A–14.

25. Benda and Halperin, "Forbidden Writers," p. 695.

26. R. Lacayo, "Placing a Lock on the Borders," 128 *Time* (Dec. 29, 1986), p. 68.

27. Ogden, " 'Ideological Grounds' Are a Myth," *The New York Times*, p. A–15.

28. United States Congress. Commission on Security and Cooperation in Europe, "Questions and Answers for the Record for Deputy Assistant Secretary of State for Consular Affairs Michael Newlin," in Hearings before the Commission on Security and Cooperation in Europe, on Implementation of the Helsinki Accords, 96th Cong., 1st Sess., 9 *U.S. Visa Policies* (April 5, 1979), p. 24 (hereinafter cited as *Helsinki Hearings*).

The Commission on Security and Cooperation in Europe, an independent agency established by Congress, held hearings on February 6, 1986, to examine how U.S. visa policies affect implementation of the Helsinki Accords. In the past, the commission focused on the failure of Soviet-bloc countries to comply with the accords, and this hearing was therefore unusual in that it concentrated on U.S. behavior.

29. U.S. Congress, "Questions and Answers for Newlin," pp. 50–52.

30. Senator Alfonse D'Amato (New York), opening statement, *Helsinki Hearings*, p. 4; Malcolm Wallop (Wyoming), statement, *Helsinki Hearings*, pp. 8–9.

31. *Helsinki Hearings*, p. 10. Besides, they assert, the Russians are worse. Senator D'Amato described the many ruses employed by the Soviet Union either to prevent Americans from visiting that country altogether or to encumber these visits with so many restrictions as to render them meaningless. "So . . . we have little, if anything, to apologize for." Ibid.

32. John Corry, " 'The Visa War' and Free Speech," *The New York Times*, Jan. 6, 1987, p. C–18.

33. *Quoted in* Frances Fitzgerald and Rose Styron, "Letter to the Editor," *The New York Times*, Jan. 14, 1987, p. A–26.

34. *Helsinki Hearings*, p. 20.

35. Ibid.

36. "Writers Protest Deportation Case," *The New York Times*, Nov. 16, 1986, p. A–27.

37. *For discussion see* David Cole, "Deportation of a Poet," 246 *The Nation* (June 25, 1988), p. 892.

38. "Writers Protest Deportation Case," p. A–27.

39. Burt Neuborne and Steven R. Shapiro, "The Nylon Curtain: America's National Border and the Free Flow of Ideas," 26 *William & Mary Law Review* 719, 723 (1984–1985).

40. *Quoted in* Committee on Immigration and Naturalization Law, Association of the Bar of the City of New York, "Visa Denials on Ideological Grounds: An Update," 8 *Seton Hall Legislative Journal* 249 (1985).

Steven R. Shapiro, a staff attorney for the American Civil Liberties Union, makes the same point: "[the Reagan administration] has used visa denials as a very conscious policy, a blatant attempt to manipulate debate." *Quoted in* Shipler, "Seeking Visa Denials," p. B–6.

See also Jamie Kalven, "U.S. Visa Policy: The Machinery of Exclusion," 43 *Bulletin of Atomic Scientists* (May 1987), p. 28.

41. Committee on Immigration and Naturalization Law, "Visa Denials," p. 249.

42. "Conference on Security and Cooperation in Europe: Final Act," 37 *Department of State Bulletin* 323 (August 1, 1975), *reprinted in* Richard B. Lillich, ed., *International Human Rights Instruments: A Compilation of Treaties, Agreements, and Declarations of Special Interest to the United States* (Buffalo, New York: W. S. Hein, 1983), §470.1.

43. Pub. L. No. 95–105, tit. 1, §112, 91 Stat. 848 [codified as amended at 22 U.S.C. §2691 (1982)].

44. 22 U.S.C. §2691. Congress, disturbed by the fact that other signatories were not emulating its liberal gestures, and worried that the new waiver pro-

visions would force the United States to admit leaders of the Palestine Liberation Organization (PLO) [*see* 125 *Congressional Record* 8345 (1979) (statement of Ill. Rep. Edward Derwinski)], soon revised the McGovern Amendment by specifically excluding from its coverage both PLO members and the nationals of non-complying signatories. Solarz Amendment, Pub. L. No. 96–60, tit. 1, §109, 93 Stat. 397, 397–98 (1979) [codified at 22 U.S.C. §2691 (21)(c) (1982)]. The Solarz Amendment is unnecessary, however, since PLO members who might undertake terrorist activity are already excludable under §29 of the McCarran Act. *See supra* note 14.

45. Testimony of Barbara Watson, *Helsinki Hearings*, p. 50.

46. 8 U.S.C. §1182 (a)(27).

47. *See El-Werfali* v. *Smith*, 547 F. Supp. 152 (S.D.N.Y. 1982).

48. *For discussion see* Neuborne and Shapiro, "The Nylon Curtain," pp. 751–54.

49. *See* Complaint for Injunctive and Declaratory Relief, *Cronin* v. *Shultz*, Civ. No. 83–3895 (D.D.C. 1983).

50. E. J. Dionne, "Barring Aliens for Political Reasons," *The New York Times*, Dec. 8, 1983, p. A–20.

51. Erika Munk, "Cross Left," *The Village Voice*, June 2, 1980, p. 86.

52. *See N.G.O. Committee on Disarmament* v. *Haig*, No. 82 Civ. 3636 (S.D.N.Y. June 10, 1982), *affirmed without opinion*, 697 F. 2d 294 (2d Cir. 1982) (N.G.O. is an acronym for "nongovernmental organizations"). The secretary of state determined that the aliens, most of whom were Japanese students affiliated with the World Peace Council, were inadmissible under §28 of the McCarran Act, but nevertheless recommended that the attorney general grant them a waiver under the McGovern Amendment. The attorney general refused, however, and the district court subsequently agreed with him that the aliens' affiliation with the World Peace Council—"an organization found to be an instrument of Soviet policy"—was a legitimate reason for a denial. Ibid. It also accepted his claim that the exclusions were in the public interest and promoted national security. The court, significantly, refused even to examine the government's classified evidence to ascertain its validity.

53. Steven Burr, "Immigration and the First Amendment," 73 *California Law Review* 1889, 1917 (1985).

54. Representatives of Communist labor organizations are also excluded from coverage on the rationale that they are mere puppets of the state, whose admission, moreover, could be interpreted by other countries as U.S. approval of their actions.

55. Claiming the PLO was "a terrorist organization and a threat to the interests of the United States," which should not benefit from operating in this country, Congress passed, and on December 22, 1987, President Reagan signed, the Anti-Terrorism Act requiring the PLO to shut its United Nations Observer Mission within 10 days. *See* Anti-Terrorism Act of 1987, §§1002–4, 22 U.S.L.A. §§5201–5203; Robert Pear, "P.L.O. Told to Shut Mission in 10 Days," *The New York Times*, March 12, 1988, p. A–4. When the measure became law, then Attorney General Edwin Meese accordingly ordered the mission shut, despite State Department reservations that the closing would violate the United Nations Headquarters Agreement, under which the organization established its base in New

York City. *See* Philip Shenon, "U.S. to Order P.L.O. Mission Closed," *The New York Times*, Feb. 27, 1988, p. A–3.

The Headquarters Agreement, a treaty that was adopted in 1947 by a joint resolution of Congress, requires the United States, as the organization's host country, to refrain from "impos[ing] any impediments [to] official travel and United Nations business undertaken by member delegations or guests." Ibid. The PLO has had a United Nations Observer Mission since 1974, when the General Assembly invited it to establish one.

When the Anti-Terrorism Act was challenged in court, Federal District Judge Edmund L. Palmieri held that under the 1947 Headquarters Agreement the United States must allow PLO representatives "access to the presence in the vicinity of the United Nations": "The P.L.O. Mission to the United Nations is an invitee of the United Nations under the Headquarters Agreement," he said, "and its status is protected by that Agreement [because] it remains a valid and outstanding treaty obligation of the United States." *United States* v. *Palestine Liberation Organization*, 690 F. Supp. 1243 (1988) (opinion withdrawn from publication).

Judge Palmieri hastened to add, however, that the Headquarters Agreement superseded the Anti-Terrorism Act only because in drafting the latter Congress did not explicitly state that it intended to overrule the treaty. Ibid. Congress, of course, could take such action at any time.

In a separate ruling, Judge Palmieri said the Anti-Terrorism Act may legitimately serve to prohibit PLO activities in the United States outside the United Nations. Ibid. *For discussion see* "Judge Rules P.L.O. Can Retain Office," *The New York Times*, June 30, 1988, pp. A–1, A–5.

56. Both the State and Justice departments determined that the 1982 Foreign Missions Act vested the Department of State with authority to alter the status of the PLO's Information Office from that of a "foreign agent" to that of a "foreign mission," a move that would place it within the State Department's jurisdiction. On September 15, 1987, Secretary of State George Shultz accordingly declared the office a "foreign mission" and ordered it closed. *See* Elaine Sciolino, "Ousting the P.L.O.," *The New York Times*, Sept. 24, 1987, p. A–24.

Charles A. Redman, a State Department spokesperson, maintained that the decision was a demonstration of "U.S. concern over terrorism committed and supported by organizations and individuals affiliated with the P.L.O." Ibid. The move prompted consternation among many observers, however, who pointed out that no one affiliated with the Information Office had ever been associated with terrorist activity. *For discussion see* Sherille Ismail, "The American Who Was Given a 'Mission,' and Then Denied Free Speech," 14 *First Principles* (May 1989), p. 12. Rather, they contended, the office merely disseminated information about Palestinians to the U.S. public. Ibid.

Secretary of State Shultz had himself earlier opposed the closing for reasons he cited in a November 23, 1987, letter to New York Representative Jack F. Kemp: "[The Palestinian Information Office] regularly files reports with the Department of Justice on its activities as an agent of a foreign government, complies with all other relevant United States laws and is staffed by Americans or legal resident aliens, [and] it is entitled to operate under the protection provided by the First Amendment of the Constitution." Ibid.

On December 2, 1987, a federal district court upheld the secretary's action. *Palestine Information Office* v. *Shultz*, 674 F. Supp. 910 (D.D.C. 1987), and on August 6, 1988, its decision was sustained by a panel of the U.S. Court of Appeals for the District of Columbia. *Palestine Information Office* v. *Shultz*, 853 F. 2d 932 (D.D.C. Cir. 1988). According to the appellate court, "this is a case about the President, acting pursuant to express authorization from Congress, ordering a foreign mission to close because its activities were deemed inimical to America's interests." 853 F. 2d at 945.

For discussion see "Palestinians Lose in a U.S. Court," *The New York Times*, Aug. 6, 1988, p. A–2; "Rebuff to Palestinians Is Upheld," *The New York Times*, Dec. 3, 1987, p. A–13.

Attorneys for the American Civil Liberties Union, who represented the Palestine Information Office, maintained that the government was violating the plaintiffs' First Amendment rights. The court of appeals responded, however, that PLO advocates were "as free today as they were before the order to express whatever ideas they wish and to associate with whichever individuals they wish. . . . They are not free, however, to set up an office that functions as a foreign mission when the State Department finds that the national interest requires otherwise." 853 F. 2d at 939, 941.

Hasan Abdel Rahman, the director of the Information Office, questioned the court's logic. As his lawyer explained:

> This reassurance is both hopelessly vague and substantially empty. . . . [I]f Rahman retains his right as an individual to advocate on Palestinian issues, then he retains his right to rent an office, purchase equipment and work with others who share his political commitment. Yet, the moment he opens an office, he risks the possibility of closure under the Foreign Missions Act.

Ismail, "The American Who Was Given a Mission," p. 11.

57. When it signed the United Nations Headquarters Agreement, the United States agreed to impose no obstacles to the transit to and from New York City of an individual invited by the organization, and to grant that individual a visa promptly. The State Department nevertheless refused to issue a visa to Yasir Arafat, who had been invited to address the General Assembly during the debate on Palestine originally scheduled for early December 1988 in New York City. Robert Pear, "Shultz's 'No' to Arafat," *The New York Times*, Nov. 28, 1988, pp. A–1, A–12.

The Department of State maintained that it acted properly in denying Arafat a visa because he leads a terrorist organization. United Nations officials and many diplomats countered, however, that numerous leaders who routinely attend the United Nations are engaged in wars and various armed struggles that unavoidably involve covert activities against their enemies. *For discussion see* Paul Lewis, "Arab Officials Say Votes Are in Hand to Move U. N. Talks," *The New York Times*, Nov. 28, 1988, pp. A–1, A–12. UN officials pointed out that "[a] lot of people come here with blood on their hands, [but] we're in the business of healing disputes, not making them worse." Ibid. *See also* Alan Crowell, "Arabs Denounce Exclusion of Arafat," *The New York Times*, Nov. 28, 1988, p. A–13; Steven Lohr, "European Nations Assail Decision by U.S. to Deny a Visa to Arafat," *The New York Times*, Nov. 28, 1988, p. A–13. Some officials also observed that by denying Arafat a visa Secretary of State Shultz acted to discourage—and even punish—him at the very time he had been laboring at a meeting in Algiers to move the PLO in a constructive direction. As one UN representative said, "How can we play a part in ending the Israeli-Palestinian conflict if we're not willing to listen to one side?" Anthony Lewis, "Include Us Out," *The New York Times*, Dec. 1, 1988, p. A–35.

On December 2, 1988, the United Nations General Assembly voted overwhelmingly to move its current session to Geneva so that Arafat could address it, and accordingly, for the first time in the organization's history it left New York City in order to protest the actions of the host country. Paul Lewis, "U. N. Votes to Move Session to Geneva," *The New York Times*, Dec. 3, 1988, p. A–1.

58. *For discussion see* Daniel Jussim, "Terrorizing the Constitution," *Civil Liberties* No. 360 (Spring 1987), pp. 1, 3; Judith Cummings, "Judge Frees 8 Aliens Linked by U.S. to Radical Palestinian Groups," *The New York Times*, Feb. 18, 1987, p. A–16; Lena Williams, "9 Aliens' Arrests Laid to Politics," *The New York Times*, Jan. 29, 1987, p. A–10.

Two days later, immigration authorities seized an eighth Jordanian while he was taking a final examination, and dragged him away. That same day, January 28, an armed agent also seized an American citizen of Palestinian origin and spirited her away to an unknown location where she was tethered to a metal pole and otherwise brutalized by unidentified officers in an attempt to coerce her into testifying against the eight Palestinians. Anthony Lewis, "Yearning to Breathe Free," *The New York Times*, Feb. 13, 1987, p. A–35.

59. Jussim, "Terrorizing the Constitution," p. 3.

60. Ibid.

61. Ibid., p. 1.

62. Ibid., p. 3.

63. Leonard Weinglass, one of the attorneys for the defendants, is convinced that even without any link to the PFLP his clients would have been marked for expulsion simply because they are passionate advocates of a Palestinian state. To bolster his thesis, Weinglass elicited testimony during a recent federal trial from Edgar Chamorro, a former leader of the Nicaraguan rebels, who told Judge Ingrid Hyrcenko on May 8, 1987, that he had plotted for four years in Miami to bomb key Nicaraguan ports, airports, and installations without any fear of being deported. In fact, Chamorro said, he and other Miami-based opponents of Nicaragua's Marxist-led government were actively financed and otherwise supported by the Reagan administration through the CIA. Weinglass's point in introducing this testimony, of course, was to contrast the support provided for this group's unlawful endeavors with the treatment accorded the Palestinians. Judith Cummings, "Nicaraguan Testifies for Arabs Facing Deportation," *The New York Times*, April 9, 1987, p. A–7.

64. Judith Cummings, "Charges Dismissed against Palestinian Supporters," *The New York Times*, May 12, 1987, p. B–7. In another article Cummings quoted William Odencrantz, western general counsel to the INS, who explained that the department had dropped the subversion charges against six of the defendants only because deporting them for routine visa violations was easier: "To use a football analogy," he said, "we don't care how we score our touchdown, by pass or by run, we just want to get them out of the country." "Foes in Subversion

Case Clash Over Whether U.S. Has Proof," *The New York Times*, April 25, 1987, p. A–6.

After the arrest of the Palestinians in the spring of 1987, some reporters suspected that an "alternate policy" might exist, and accordingly began investigating whatever internal memoranda they could unearth from both the Immigration Service and the Department of State. They discovered more than they had bargained for. Judith Cummings, "Arrest of Palestinians in Los Angeles to be Reviewed, U.S. Aide Says," *The New York Times*, Feb. 17, 1987, p. A–19.

Reporters discovered the existence of a so-called "Contingency Plan," proposed by the investigative division of the INS, that consisted of several related studies and recommendations. According to one recommendation, immigration officials should "target" specific individuals on the basis of information supplied either by other governmental agencies or by intelligence sources; once targeted, these individuals should be charged with violating those provisions of the McCarran Act that authorize the deportation of anyone who, after entry, advocates sabotage or the overthrow of the U.S. government by unconstitutional means. Stephen Engelberg, "Greater Access to Terrorism Data Is Sought for Immigration Agency," *The New York Times*, Feb. 6, 1987, p. A–16; *See also* Lewis, "Yearning to Breathe Free," p. A–35.

A second proposal advises officials to charge targeted aliens with multiple offenses in order to provide a "fallback" position in case any single charge fails; and a third proposal recommends a major change in the Executive Order on Intelligence Activities in order to provide what would be unprecedented authorization for the FBI and the CIA to disclose intelligence information to the INS, including any information gathered abroad by the CIA. Engelberg, "Access to Terrorism Data," p. A–16.

According to a related study, prepared by the INS in May 1986, "the Service will likely be required to concentrate its counterterrorism efforts against particular nationalities or groups known to be composed primarily of certain nationalities, most probably those citizens of states known to support terrorism." Ibid. The study listed eight examples: seven Arab countries and Iran. Lewis, "Yearning to Breathe Free," p. A–35.

Another document encouraged the adoption of new visa restrictions that would bar aliens "likely to be supportive of terrorist activities within the United States." Engelberg, "Access to Terrorism Data," p. A–16. Finally, the INS investigators who wrote the Contingency Plan urged that it be implemented immediately and in a way calculated to bypass both Congress, which might balk at the recommended changes, and the normal administrative rule-making procedure, which involves public comment and long delay. Ibid.

Doug Stormer, the chief defense lawyer for the Palestinians, is convinced that a definite connection exists between the memoranda and the arrest of his clients. Cummings, "Arrest of Palestinians," p. A–19. Immigration officials, however, while acknowledging the existence of "contingency planning," deny that any plan has been endorsed. Engelberg, "Access to Terrorism Data," p. A–16. According to John F. Shaw, the assistant INS commissioner of investigation in Washington, D.C., contingency planning had been undertaken in response to "concerns" of the Department of Justice about "acts planned in foreign countries, so we would be fully apprised and take proper precautions." Cummings, "Arrests of Palestinians," p. A–19.

Mr. Shaw was probably referring to the concerns expressed in the INS's May 1986 study, which predicted that sooner or later the United States would face a situation similar to the one that occurred in 1979 when, in response to the seizing of the U.S. hostages in Teheran, the Carter administration sought the expulsion of all Iranian students living in the United States who had violated any of the terms of their visas. Engelberg, "Access to Terrorism Data," p. A–16. As the study notes, INS machinery was altogether incapable of determining even the identities of the Iranian students, let alone which among them were out of status. *For discussion see* Elizabeth Hull, *Without Justice for All: Constitutional Rights of Aliens* (Westport, Conn.: Greenwood Press, 1985), pp. 65–70.

65. *American-Arab Anti-Discrimination Committee, et al.* v. *Meese*, No. 87–02107–SVW (C. D. Cal. Jan. 26, 1989) (LEXIS, Rutgers Law School Library, Newark, New Jersey).

66. Ibid.

67. Ibid.

68. Ibid.

69. Ibid., *citing Noto* v. *U.S.*, 367 U.S. 290, 297–98 (1961).

70. Ibid.

71. Ibid. The judge stressed the relationship between the First Amendment and a vigorous democracy:

> The First Amendment serves our national interest not only by preserving individual rights to speech but by ensuring that all speech from whatever source is protected. The maintenance of the "uninhibited marketplace of ideas," crucial for our democracy's prosperity, requires that each idea be afforded the same protection whether espoused by a citizen or an alien within this country.

Ibid.

72. Ibid. Judge Wilson contested the government's argument that in the deportation context resident aliens were not entitled to full First Amendment protection:

> It is impossible to adopt for aliens a lower degree of First Amendment protection solely in the deportation setting without seriously affecting their First Amendment rights outside that setting. Under a lower First Amendment standard, and without the constitutional protection against ex post facto laws, the Government could conceivably pass a law allowing for the deportation of aliens for statements made several decades earlier. An alien would have no way of knowing whether his or her speech would someday become a ground for deportation and consequently would be chilled from speaking at all.
>
> Simply stated, the Government's view is that aliens are free to say whatever they wish but the Government maintains the ability to deport them for the content of their speech. To state the proposition is to reject it. As Justice Murphy wrote over forty years ago:
>
> > Any other conclusion would make our constitutional safeguards transitory and discriminatory in nature. Thus the Government would be precluded from enjoining or imprisoning an alien for exercising his freedom of speech. But the government at the same time would be free, from a constitutional standpoint, to deport him for exercising that very same freedom. The alien would be fully clothed with his constitutional rights when defending himself in a court of law, but he would be stripped of those rights when deportation officials encircle him.

Ibid., *citing Bridges* v. *Wixon*, 326 U.S. 135, 162 (Murphy, J., concurring). "Since aliens enjoy full First Amendment protection outside the deportation setting," Judge Wilson concluded, "we decline to adopt a lesser First Amendment test for use within that setting." Ibid.

Another case involving the First Amendment rights of Palestinians arose after the Department of State refused to grant PLO member and United Nations representative Zuhdi Labib Terzi permission to participate in a debate about Mideastern politics with law professor Alan Dershowitz in Cambridge, Massachusetts. The State Department permits Terzi to live in the United States because of his United Nations status, but prohibits him from traveling outside New York City unless his mission is strictly social. *Harvard Law School Forum* v. *Shultz*. 633 F. Supp. 525, 527 (D. Mass. 1986). The State Department refused to grant Terzi a waiver to participate in the debate because, it explained, his appearance would constitute political activity on behalf of the PLO and thus "undercut our policy of not lending legitimacy to that organization." Ibid. *See* Thomas J. Antonini, Michael L. Fantozzi, and Lynn Marie Pruss, "*Harvard Law School Forum* v. *Shultz*: When Exclusion of Aliens under the Immigration and Naturalization Act Conflicts with the First Amendment Rights of United States Citizens," 14 *Journal of College and University Law* 153 (Summer 1987).

The Harvard Law School Forum and Professor Alan Dershowitz challenged the secretary's action. They won the first round in the chambers of District Court Judge Walter Skinner, who contended that the secretary's reason for denying Terzi permission to travel to Cambridge was "bona fide" but not "legitimate" because it was "directly related to the suppression of a political debate" with U.S. citizens:

> It may well be that the public interest will, in some respect, be adversely affected by affording a forum to a P.L.O. representative whose policies are in conflict with those of the United States and indeed anathema to many citizens. The public interest in preserving free and open debate on precisely such subjects, however, must be regarded as of overwhelming priority, as mandated by the First Amendment and as being at the heart of our survival as a free people.

633 F. Supp. at 531.

Judge Skinner enjoined the secretary's action, but on April 25, 1986, his order was stayed by a three-judge panel of the First Circuit Court of Appeals. At this point Terzi refused to participate any longer, and after taking a vote the forum resolved to make no further efforts to arrange a debate, even if travel permission were ultimately granted the PLO representative. The First Circuit accordingly vacated the case as moot. No. 86–1371 (First Cir. June 18, 1986).

73. The Supreme Court's logic in a 1904 case, *U.S. ex rel. Turner* v. *Williams* has never been repudiated:

> Repeated decisions of this court have determined that Congress has the power to exclude aliens from the United States; to prescribe the terms and conditions on which they may come in; to establish regulations for sending out of the country such aliens as have entered in violation of law. . . .
>
> Whether rested on the accepted principle of international law that every sovereign nation has the power, as inherent in sovereignty and essential to self-preservation, to forbid the entrance of foreigners within its dominions, or to admit them only in such cases and upon

such conditions as it may see fit to prescribe; or on the power to regulate commerce with foreign nations, which includes the entrance of ships, the importation of goods, and the bringing of persons into the ports of the United States, the act before us is not open to constitutional objection.

194 U.S. 279, 289–90 (1904).

See also Harisiades v. *Shaughnessy*:

It is pertinent to observe that any policy toward aliens is vitally and inextricably interwoven with contemporaneous policies in regard to the conduct of foreign relations, the war power, and the maintenance of a republican form of government. Such matters are so exclusively entrusted to the political branches of government as to be largely immune from judicial inquiry or interference.

342 U.S. 580, 587–88 (1952).

As late as 1977 the Supreme Court reaffirmed these earlier cases:

The conditions of entry for every alien, the particular classes of aliens that shall be denied entry altogether, the basis for determining such classification, the right to terminate hospitality to aliens, the ground on which such determination shall be based, have been recognized as matters solely for the responsibility of Congress and wholly outside the power of this Court to control.

430 U.S. 787, 796 (1977).

For discussion see Hull, *Without Justice for All*, pp. 32–38, 46–59, 62–78.

74. *For discussion see* ibid., pp. 32–35, 46–52, 53–59, 62–78, 147–54.

75. *American-Arab Anti-Discrimination Committee et al.* v. *Meese*, No. 87–02107–SVW (C. D. Cal. Jan. 26, 1989).

76. *Bridges* v. *Wixon*, 326 U.S. 135, 148 (1945) ("Freedom of speech and press is accorded aliens residing in this country.")

77. 408 U.S. 753 (1972).

78. Ibid. at 762–65. Earlier the district court had elaborated on this point: "The concern of the First Amendment is not with a non-resident alien's individual and personal interest in entering and being heard, but with the rights of the citizens of the country to have the alien enter and to hear him explain and seek to defend his views; that . . . is of the essence of self-government." *Mandell* v. *Mitchell*, 325 F. Supp. 620, 631 (E.D.N.Y. 1971).

See also Board of Education v. *Pico*, 457 U.S. 853, 867 (1982) ("The right to receive ideas is a necessary predicate to the *recipient's* meaningful exercise of his own rights of speech, press and political freedom.") (emphasis in original).

Martin v. *City of Struthers*, 319 U.S. 141, 143 (1943) (individuals have a constitutional right to receive door-to-door solicitation).

79. 408 U.S. at 770.

80. Ibid.

81. Ibid. 778 (Marshall, J., dissenting).

82. Ibid. at 753, 765.

83. 408 U.S. at 769.

84. Statement of Victor Weisskopf, vice chairman of the Federation of American Scientists, *Hearings before the President's Commission on Immigration and Naturalization*, 82nd Cong., 2nd Sess. 408 (1952).

85. *See, for example, Harvard Law School Forum* v. *Shultz*, 633 F. Supp. 525 (D. Mass. 1986); *for discussion see supra* note 72.

86. 605 F. Supp. 1220 (D. Mass. 1985).
87. Ibid. at 1224.
88. Ibid.
89. Ibid. at 1220.
90. Ibid. at 1224.
91. 845 F.2d 1111 (First Cir. 1988).
92. 845 F.2d at 1117.
93. Ibid.
94. Ibid. at 1121.
95. 592 F. Supp. 880 (D.D.C. 1984), *vacated and remanded*, 785 F. 2d 1043 (D. C. Cir. 1986), *affirmed mem.*, 108 S. Ct. 252 (Oct. 19, 1987) (3-to-3 decision with justices Harry Blackmum and Antonin Scalia not participating).
96. 785 F. 2d at 1054, 1056–58. *Abourezk* v. *Reagan* was a consolidated case involving four aliens who had been invited by U.S. journalists, religious groups, and universities to speak at various forums throughout the country: Tomas Borge, Nicaragua's interior minister; Nino Pasti, an Italian peace activist, one-time senator, and NATO general; and Olga Finlay and Leonor Lezcano Rodriguez, Cuban experts on family law. All four were members of organizations that the Department of State claimed were instruments of the Communist Party, and accordingly could have been barred under §28 of the McCarran Act. They were barred instead under §27, however, which mandates the exclusion of those aliens who seek to enter the United States in order to engage in activities "prejudicial to the public interest." 785 F. 2d at 1047.

The government made no attempt to prove that the four would actually engage in "prejudicial activities." In its various briefs it simply maintained that their mere presence would in some unspecified way harm U.S. interests; its statements were similar to the one made by John Hughes, a Department of State spokesperson, who hypothesized that Tomas Borge was excluded because he "would have used [his speaking engagements] as a platform for the same kind of rhetoric we have seen before." Stuart Taylor, Jr., "U.S. Rights Group Assails Denial of Visas to 2 Latins," *The New York Times*, Dec. 1, 1983, p. A–16.

Plaintiffs, U.S. citizens who had invited the aliens to the United States, raised three important points that the Circuit Court of Appeals for the District of Columbia systematically addressed when it heard *Abourezk* in March 1986. First, plaintiffs maintained that §27 authorized the government to deny visas only on the grounds of national security or public safety, not for "foreign policy" reasons. The court, however, reasoned that §27's broad language and legislative history commanded no such narrow reading. 785 F. 2d at 1053.

Second, plaintiffs claimed that by using the term "activities" as opposed to "entry" in §27, Congress intended to bar only those aliens whose conduct, rather than mere presence, would prejudice the public interest. The court agreed, holding that the word activities would be superfluous and even misleading if the government could exclude aliens on the basis of mere entry. Ibid. at 1057. However, since the legislative history was ambiguous on this point, it remanded the issue to the district court for a clarification of congressional intent. Ibid. at 1056.

Finally, plaintiffs claimed that the government had circumvented the Mc-

Govern Amendment by using §27 to exclude aliens who were members of §28 organizations. Again the court agreed:

> When an alien is a member of a proscribed organization, so that subsection (28) applies, the government may bypass that provision and proceed under subsection (27) only if the reason for the threat to the "public interest[,] . . . welfare, safety, or security" is independent of the fact of membership in or affiliation with the proscribed organization.

Ibid. at 1058 (citations omitted). The court stressed the fact, however, that the government retained broad latitude to exclude aliens who had "affiliations with hostile governments" independent of any Communist Party affiliations, or who would engage in activities "prejudicial to the public interest while here." Ibid. at 1060.

On October 19, 1987, the Supreme Court voted three-to-three to affirm the lower tribunal. 108 S. Ct. 252 (per curiam) (Justices Blackmum and Scalia did not participate). Its affirmance is of limited significance, however, since none of its evenly divided rulings establishes a national precedent. *Abourezk* is controlling in the District of Columbia, however, where virtually every case involving a visa can be brought since the Department of State is located there.

Even the Supreme Court's opinion was not the last word in this protracted case. The justices remanded *Abourezk* v. *Reagan* to the district court for clarification and disposition of certain issues, and the lower tribunal ultimately held that with the exception of Borge, the State Department had unlawfully excluded all the speakers solely because of their membership in proscribed organizations. Borge may also have been excluded on the grounds that he intended to visit this country as an official representative of a foreign government considered hostile by the United States, but since the record was unclear on this point the court ordered the State Department to admit the Nicaraguan Interior Minister along with the other plaintiffs. *Abourezk* v. *Reagan*, No. 83–3739 (D.D.C. June 7, 1988). (LEXIS, Rutgers Law School Library, Newark, N.J.).

97. 785 F. 2d at 1076.

98. Ibid. at 1063.

99. 381 U.S. 1 (1964); *for discussion see* Chapter 2.

100. 785 F. 2d at 1075.

101. These 30 organizations comprise the Coalition for Free Trade in Ideas, which seeks the elimination of any official restraint on constitutionally protected expression. The coalition is staffed by members of the American Civil Liberties Union and the Fund for Free Expression. Benda and Halperin, "Forbidden Writers," p. 696 n.12.

102. *See* Linda Greenhouse, "The Law on 'Excludable Aliens': Stay Tuned," *The New York Times*, Jan. 1, 1988, p. A–36; Susan Benda, "Ideology No Longer a Basis for Visa Denials," 13 *First Principles* (Feb.-March 1988), p. 9.

103. Jonathan Fuerbringer, "Senate Bars Denial of Visas on Political Grounds," *The New York Times*, Dec. 17, 1987, p. A–27.

104. Greenhouse, " 'Excludable Aliens,' " p. A–36.

105. Foreign Relations Authorization Act, FY 1988 and 1989, Pub. L. No. 100–204, §901, 101 Stat. 1339 (Dec. 22, 1987); (amended Oct. 1, 1988) n.2.

106. Pub. L. No. 100–204, §901, 101 Stat. 1339 (Dec. 22, 1987); (amended Oct.

1, 1988) n.2. *See* editorial, "A Half Step Toward Free Speech," *The New York Times*, Oct. 29, 1988, p. A–28.

107. "Letter to Interested Parties" from Susan Benda, legislative analyst for the American Civil Liberties Union, April 11, 1988, p. 2. (The letter is available from the American Civil Liberties Union, 122 Maryland Avenue N. E., Washington, D.C., 20002.)

108. Ibid.

109. David Cole and Lucas Guttentag, "Free Speech Takes Step Backward in Ideological Exclusion Law," (Letter to the editor), *The New York Times*, Nov. 11, 1988, p. A–24.

110. *See Randall* v. *Meese*, Civ. No. 85–3415 (D.D.C. Oct. 23, 1985); *In the Matter of Randall*, No. A11 644 708 (I.&N. Dec./Aug. 28, 1986); *Randall* v. *Meese*, C. A. No. 85–3415 (D.D.C. 1987). When the district court heard Margaret Randall's case in 1987, it rested its decision entirely on the fact that she came under the purview of §212 (a)(28)(G) of the McCarran Act and was therefore properly subject to deportation. The court summarily dismissed her First Amendment claims:

> Insofar as plaintiffs allege that their right to association with Randall's ideas would be affected by her deportation they go beyond the jurisdiction of this Court. That Randall may be deported and thereby will not share her ideas with citizens of this country because of her physical absence is a consequence of deportation and not reviewable by this Court. Additionally, any pattern or practice of the INS to curtail information by denying visas is also not applicable to the matters before this Court.

C. A. No. 85–3415 n.5. *For discussion see* David Cole, "Deportation of a Poet," 246 *The Nation* (June 25, 1988), p. 892.

111. Linda Greenhouse, "U.S. Ends an Effort to Deport Teacher on Basis of Ideology," *The New York Times*, Feb. 5, 1988, p. A–11.

112. Cole and Guttentag, "Free Speech Takes a Step Backward," p. A–24.

After the State Department Authorization Bill was amended in 1988, few political, legal, or administrative options remained for Margaret Randall. At this point, however, relief came from an unexpected tribunal and on unexpected grounds: On July 27, 1989, the Immigration and Naturalization Service's highest appeals panel ruled that Randall, a native New Yorker, should never have been subject to deportation proceedings in the first place. According to the panel, when she applied for Mexican citizenship in 1967 she was living in Mexico, married to a native of that country, and unable to secure employment without becoming a Mexican citizen. Her decision was thus motivated by "economic duress," *not* a desire to sever ties with the United States, and, as a consequence, she never forfeited her American citizenship. "Writer Wins Long Fight to Halt Deportation," *The New York Times*, July 28, 1989, p. A–11.

113. *See for example*, H.R. 4509, 98th Cong., 1st Sess. (Nov. 18, 1983); H.R. 5227, 98th Cong., 2d Sess. (March 22, 1984); H.R. 1119, 100th Cong., 1st Sess. (Feb. 18, 1987); H.R. 1719, 100th Cong., 1st Sess. (March 19, 1987); H.R. 3293, 100th Cong., 1st Sess. (Sept. 16, 1987); H.R. 3713, 100th Cong., 1st Sess. (Dec. 8, 1987); H.R. 4427, 101st Cong., 1st Sess. (March 8, 1989).

Since 1983 scores of senators and representatives have either introduced or cosponsored bills to amend the McCarran Act. *See* Carlos Ortiz Miranda, "Rethinking the Role of Politics in United States Immigration Law: The Helsinki Accords and Ideological Exclusion of Aliens," 25 *San Diego Law Rev.* 301, 321–26 (1987–1988). Although none of these bills has ever reached a vote by the full House or Senate, on March 8, 1989, Massachusetts Representative Barney Frank introduced H.R. 4427, which he predicted would be passed before the end of the year. Barney Frank, "Letter to Constituents," March 24, 1989. (Available from the office of Representative Barney Frank, 1030 Longworth Building, Washington, D.C., 20515).

Frank's bill prohibits government officials from deporting or excluding anyone solely on the basis of his or her "beliefs, statements, or associations." It also eliminates as grounds for exclusion homosexuality, former mental illness, and polygamy (the last being a ground flagrantly ignored by consular and immigration officials, as evidenced by the steady stream of wealthy Saudis who visit the United States each year for medical treatment). Linda Greenhouse, "House Gets a Bill to Ease Visa Law," *The New York Times*, Feb. 19, 1987, p. B–6. Under H.R. 4427, significantly, officials are also prohibited from denying visas to individuals solely because they are either affiliated with the PLO or representatives of Communist trade unions.

What Frank's bill eliminates, as he explained in reference to similar legislation that he had earlier introduced, "are those general charges to the leadership of this country to say 'we don't like your opinions and you are staying out of here, we don't like what you say,' " *Helsinki Hearings*, p. 13. His bill vests government officials with broad authority, however, to ban anyone whose activities represent more than a speculative threat to the public health or national security—drug peddlers, for instance, or people with criminal records, or Nazi or terrorist ties. *See* American Civil Liberties Union, "Key Issues Re: House Bill Amending the McCarran-Walter Act—General Overview of H.R. 4427," American Civil Liberties Report, April 25, 1988, p. 3. (Report available from the American Civil Liberties Union, 122 Maryland Avenue N.E., Washington, D.C., 20002.)

In order to gain support from the George Bush administration, Frank's bill contains some "compromises": it allows the executive branch to exclude individuals, for instance, under the following circumstances:

> [When their presence in the United States could] violate or conflict with a treaty or other international agreements to which the U.S. is a party; convey the impression that the U.S. recognizes or supports a foreign government that it doesn't (this would apply only to government officials, not private citizens); or convey the impression that the U.S. supports a group which it doesn't support (this would apply only in relation to an alien member of the group who is a candidate for elected office and who is seeking to enter this country in a period prior to the election, or to a member of a group which purports to be a "government").

Representative Barney Frank, "Letter to Constituents," March 24, 1989.

114. On June 23, 1987, Judge Abraham Sofaer, legal adviser to the Department of State, testified before the House Subcommittee on Immigration, Refugees, and International Law. Although he pledged to work with other government officials to develop proposals that would eliminate political ideology or past or present membership in proscribed organizations as grounds for exclusion, he made clear that the administration would never support any bill that would

expand judicial review of visa decisions. "Testimony of Abraham D. Sofaer, Legal Adviser, Department of State, before the House Subcommittee on Immigration, Refugees, and International Law," June 23, 1987, pp. 1–2, 11 (hereinafter cited as Sofaer Testimony). Decisions involving foreign affairs are matters of national policy, he said, and as such are the province of the executive branch, subject to congressional oversight. Courts lack any standard by which to assess the importance of foreign policy interests, the judge continued, and, moreover, litigation would force the government to reveal sensitive intelligence sources in order to prove its case. Ibid.

115. Sofaer Testimony, p. 6.

116. Ibid. During his June 1987 testimony before the House Subcommittee, Judge Sofaer stated that the administration would never support any proposed legislation that would prevent government officials from continuing to bar anyone who "advocates or teaches" the propriety of certain violent political acts. Sofaer Testimony, p. 6. Neither will the administration endorse any legislation that does not continue to bar representatives of state-run Communist labor organizations, or that prevents it from dealing with people from Communist countries whose activities in the United States could adversely affect national security—by resulting in the transfer of sensitive technology, for example. Sofaer Testimony, pp. 6–7.

The administration must accordingly have the discretion either to bar these people outright, Sofaer continued, or to offer them only restricted visas. (For instance, he said, the United States might allow a computer scientist from East Berlin to attend a university conference, but prohibit him from visiting Silicon Valley. Sofaer Testimony, p. 7.)

117. In his June 1987 testimony, Judge Sofaer stressed the fact that the administration must retain the right to exclude anyone whose admission could have potentially adverse foreign policy repercussions—a right, he pointed out, available to virtually every other nation in the world. Sofaer Testimony, p. 8.

Diane Dillard, former public affairs officer in the State Department's Bureau of Consular Affairs, also maintained that the executive branch must retain its discretion to bar certain people for "foreign policy reasons." Marvine Howe, "U.S. Denial of Visas over Politics of Foreigners: The Battle is Heating Up," *The New York Times*, July 28, 1985, p. A–16. Dillard cited as examples Libyans and Iranians seeking to acquire certain militarily useful technological skills, Sikhs who advocate the overthrow of the government of India, or Armenian and Cretan extremists. Ibid.

118. Carlos Fuentes, "McCarran-Walter Sadomasochism," *The New York Times*, Oct. 6, 1984, *reprinted in* Benda and Halperin, "Forbidden Writers," p. 696. His remarks continued:

> It is hard to imagine that the institutions of this Republic, its democratic edifice, its vast economic and military and moral power, can be endangered by Graham Greene, Gabriel Garcia Marquez, Dario Fo, Mrs. Salvador Allende. Experience has taught us that it is the application of the exclusionary clause that endangers the Republic, mocks democracy, demoralizes the true friends of the United States, and offers undeserved aces to the Soviet Union.

Ibid.

119. Statement made at the September 17, 1984, Washington, D.C., confer-

ence "Free Trade in Ideas: A Constitutional Imperative," organized by the American Civil Liberties Union and the Fund for Free Expression, published proceedings at 96; (hereinafter cited as Free Trade in Ideas Conference) (proceedings available from the American Civil Liberties Union, 122 Maryland Avenue N.E., Washington, D.C., 20002).

Fo and Rama eventually received visas, although the State Department never gave any explanation for its reversal. Mel Gussow, "U.S. to Give Visa to Fo, Controversial Writer," *The New York Times*, Oct. 31, 1984, p. C–19.

120. Free Trade in Ideas Conference, p. 96.

121. Ibid., p. 54.

122. Ronald Dworkin, Susan Sontag, et al., "Letter to the Editor," *The New York Times*, July 22, 1987.

123. Free Trade in Ideas Conference, pp. 79–84.

124. Center for National Security Studies, "Free Trade in Ideas: A Constitutional Imperative." Report prepared by the Center for National Security Studies, a Project of the American Civil Liberties Union, May 1984, pp. A–7, A–9 (hereinafter cited as Free Trade in Ideas Report) (copies available from the Center for National Security Studies, 122 Maryland Avenue N.E., Washington, D.C., 20002).

125. Ibid., pp. A–10, A–12.

126. Garry Wills, "Introduction" to Lillian Hellman, *Scoundrel Time* (Boston: Little, Brown, and Co., 1976), p. 7.

127. Free Trade in Ideas Conference, p. 20. Jack MaCrae III, the editor-in-chief of the publisher Holt Rinehart and Winston, noted that when he talked about greater freedom of expression in the Soviet Union, South Africa, and South Korea, officials from these and many other countries immediately responded with, "What about your own ideological restrictions on foreigners?" Marvine Howe, "U.S. Denial of Visas over Politics of Foreigners: The Battle Is Heating Up," *The New York Times*, July 28, 1985, p. A–16.

128. Dennis Hevesi, "Belgian Writer Held at Newark Airport as a Suspected Communist," *The New York Times*, Sept. 27, 1986, p. A–34.

129. Ibid.

130. Ibid.

131. Ibid.

132. *For discussion see* Anthony Lewis, "Is There No Decency?" *The New York Times*, Dec. 1, 1986, p. A–21; "Patricia Daniloff," 243 *The Nation* (Nov. 1, 1986), p. 428; Patricia Lara, "When Visa Officials Shut America's Gate," *The New York Times*, Jan. 10, 1987, p. A–15; Dennis Hevesi, "Latin Reporter, Here to Attend Awards, Is Held," *The New York Times*, Oct. 15, 1986, p. B–5.

133. Lara, "America's Gate," p. A–15.

134. Lewis, "Is There No Decency?" p. A–21.

135. Ibid.

136. Ibid. *See also* editorial, "Aliens' Rights and Citizens' Confidence," *The New York Times*, Jan. 7, 1987, p. A–22.

137. *For discussion see* Jamie Kalven, "U.S. Visa Policy: The Machinery of Exclusion," 43 *Bulletin of Atomic Scientists* (May 1987), pp. 21, 25–27.

138. The United States is, in fact, one of the few democratic countries in the world that requires a visa at all, let alone one based on political acceptability,

and U.S. citizens are spoiled. Accustomed to receiving a passport after simply establishing their identity, and then breezing off to London, Vienna, or Bonn, most of them would be outraged if, as a precondition for visiting Vienna, for instance, they had to undergo anything like the ideological third degree their country inflicts on others.

139. *See* Steele, *Steele on Immigration Law*, pp. 24, 35–37, 115–16, 370–78.

The President's Commission on Immigration and Naturalization, *Whom We Shall Welcome* (Washington, D.C.: U.S. Government Printing Office, 1953), questioned whether consular officials are adequately equipped to make such decisions:

> Issuance or denial of a visa frequently involves complicated legal problems of eligibility. . . . Yet . . . only 3 percent of the consular officers are attorneys. Consular officers are required to decide . . . complicated security issues, occasionally involving knowledge of foreign political, economic and social movements, and a host of other issues involving technical knowledge and the wise exercise of discretion. And yet, the visa-issuing consular officers are generally junior and subordinate officers in our consulates, and assignment to visa-issuing duties is not always regarded as a desirable post within the Foreign Service.

Ibid., p. 146.

The negative decisions of consular officers are theoretically subject to review by a supervisory consul. These supervisors, however, frequently serve more than one consulate, or are themselves overburdened with casework. In either case, they lack the time necessary to subject these decisions to more than perfunctory review. *For discussion see* U.S. Commission on Civil Rights, *The Tarnished Golden Door: Civil Rights Issues in Immigration* (Washington, D.C.: U.S. Government Printing Office, 1975), p. 50.

The State Department may also review consular decisions, but only with regard to questions of law. Factual determinations remain within the absolute discretion of the consular officer. 22 C.F.R. §42.130 (c) (1982). Moreover, parties adversely affected by consul's action cannot seek redress in the federal courts, since the judiciary has repeatedly held that administrative determinations in this area are final unless judicial review is authorized by explicit statutory language. *See, for example, Ulrich* v. *Kellogg*, 30 F. 2d 984 (D. C. Cir. 1929); *Estrada* v. *Ahrens*, 296 F. 2d 690 (5th Cir. 1961).

For discussion see James W. Mohr, "Opening the Floodgates to Dissident Aliens," 6 *Harvard Civil Rights–Civil Liberties Law Review*; "Judicial Review of Visa Denials: Reexamining Consular Nonreviewability," 52 *New York University Law Review* 1137 (1977).

140. Jane Gross, "For Finnish Woman, Struggle for a U.S. Welcome," *The New York Times*, Sept. 15, 1986, p. B–4.

When Patricia Lara was detained on October 16, 1986, she was jolted not only by the brusqueness of her treatment, but also by its sheer unexpectedness—after all, a mere six months earlier she had sailed through inspection at the same airport in New York City. Dennis Hevesi, "Latin Reporter, Here to Attend Awards, Is Held," *The New York Times*, Oct. 15, 1986, p. B–5. Her experience is not an uncommon one, and illustrates the type of capricious treatment aliens can receive even after they have secured a visa and arrived at a U.S. port of entry. There, like Lara, they can be barred from the country because their names suddenly appear or reappear in a *Lookout Book*, or because immigration agents "have reason to believe" that for one reason or another their presence offends some provision of the McCarran Act. *See supra* note 139.

141. Free Trade in Ideas Conference, p. 62.

142. Woodcock, "On Being 'Inadmissible,' " p. 43.

143. Ibid.

144. 8 U.S.C. §1182 (a) (28)(1). INS spokesperson Duke Austin explains that current law does not explicitly state the steps necessary to demonstrate active opposition to an outlawed party, and adds that "you can cleanse yourself of that exclusion, but it's not an easy thing." Gross, "Finnish Woman," p. B–4.

145. Woodcock, "On Being 'Inadmissible,' " p. 43.

146. Ibid. Leszek Kolakowski, a fellow at Oxford University and a part-time professor at the University of Chicago, left his native Poland in 1968 and is now among the world's foremost authorities on, and critics of, Marxist theory. He points out that whenever former members of the Communist Party apply for permanent residence, they must sign a statement indicating in effect that they were compelled to join the party as a means of survival. Free Trade in Ideas Conference, p. 69. Such a statement is always a lie, he said, because the 90 percent of the population that does not join manages to survive. By making this request, immigration officials thereby yield a strange selection: "They like people who lie to them, and they punish those who tell the truth: one wonders why the system should be beneficial to America." Ibid. (The system *does* in fact reward "people who lie"; Senator Paul Simon (Illinois) noted that immigration agents told Kolakowski to "just lie, tell them you weren't—don't mention that you were a Communist at one time." *Helsinki Hearings*, p. 20.)

147. Herbert Agar, "A Prayer For the New President," 36 *Saturday Review of Literature* (Jan. 17, 1953), p. 8.

148. Letter from William D. Carey, executive officer of the American Association for the Advancement of Science, to Senator Alfonse D'Amato (New York), Chair, Commission on Security and Cooperation in Europe, Feb. 12, 1986, *reprinted in Helsinki Hearings*, Appendix 7, pp. 85–86. Carey wrote the following:

> The AAAS would once again like to express its concern about this restrictive policy. The exclusion of individuals on the basis of political ideology is a violation of the free circulation of ideas and free travel of individuals, rights guaranteed in the Helsinki Final Act, to which the U.S. is a signatory. Moreover, because of the extensive requirements for obtaining special permission to visit, scientists have been discouraged from applying for such permission. The advancement of science in the U.S. and abroad requires the free exchange of ideas, publications, and personal meetings and interactions without regard to political ideology. We are not aware of cases in which these restrictions have affected scientists wishing to visit the U.S. in recent years. However, we remain deeply concerned that such restrictions are part of U.S. law and we believe they should be eliminated.

Ibid. *See also* Statement of John Edsall, chairman of the American Association for the Advancement of Sciences' Committee on Scientific Freedom and Responsibility, *Helsinki Hearings*, pp. 88–92.

149. United States Congress, Committee on the Judiciary, "Exclusion and Deportation Amendments of 1983," Hearing before the Subcommittee on Immigration, Refugees, and International Law of the Committee on the Judiciary,

98th Cong., 2d Sess. 130–31 (June 28, 1984) (testimony of William Styron, on behalf of PEN American Center).

150. Testimony of Arthur Helton, *quoting* letter dated Feb. 8, 1980, from Professor Tom Bottomore, University of Sussex, to Sophie Silberberg, executive director, Fund for Free Expansion, *cited in* Hearing on Exclusion and Deportation Amendments of 1983, June 24, 1984, 98th Cong., 2d Sess. H.R. 4509 and H.R. 5227, at 138 (Washington, D.C.: U.S. Government Printing Office, 1984), p. 138.

151. Free Trade in Ideas Conference, p. 62.

152. As Bernard Malamud said in reference to the exclusion of Dario Fo and Franca Rama: "The free exchange of ideas among nations and individuals does not endanger our national security but strengthens it. The denial of [nonimmigrant] visas . . . is a denial of the opportunity to enrich the intellectual and artistic life of our country." Statement of Bernard Malamud, President, PEN American Center. In PEN American Center "News Release," May 22, 1980 (available from Fund for Free Expression, 36 West 44th Street, New York, N.Y. 10036).

2

The Border as Barrier: Federal Restrictions on the Freedom of Movement

> Travel abroad, like Travel within the country... may be as close to the heart of the individual as the choice of what he eats, or wears, or reads. Freedom of movement is basic to our scheme of values.[1]
>
> Justice William O. Douglas

"The right to go out of [the] Kingdom and to return safely and securely" was recognized as long ago as 1215, when England's King John signed the Magna Carta,[2] and as recently as 1989, when 35 nations meeting in Vienna agreed to respect the right of every person "to leave any country, including his own, and return to his country."[3] Travel is thus a historically and near-universally recognized right, one the United States has agreed to safeguard and promote when signing various international covenants, and thus it is particularly surprising that not a single reference is made to this right in the U.S. Constitution.[4] Certainly the framers were aware of its importance, travel being a right so engrafted on English common law that William Blackstone defined personal liberty itself as "consisting in the power of locomotion, of changing situations, or of moving one's person to whatever place one's inclination may direct."[5] The colonists, moreover, had alluded to the importance of travel even in the Declaration of Independence, charging therein that by restricting migration to the American colonies King George III had "endeavored to prevent the population of these States."[6]

Why, then, is there such an omission? The record is sketchy, but the Supreme Court has suggested that perhaps the framers considered the right to travel to be implicit in other rights that were specifically guaranteed.[7] At any rate, while the Court held as early as 1849 that Americans have a fundamental right to travel among the various states of the Union[8]—such freedom of movement being essential to the country's federal system—this omission surely contributed to the Court's unwillingness for over a century to declare that they had a similar right to travel across national borders.[9]

Americans fared reasonably well without the Court's solicitude, however. Although Congress passed an act in 1856[10] and another in 1926 granting the secretary of state the power not only to issue passports but to grant, deny, or condition them in any way he saw fit,[11] citizens could ordinarily travel abroad even without these documents, since, as Zechariah Chafee recalled in 1956, neither the United States nor most other countries required them:

> Until less than forty years ago this right [freedom of movement] was completely enjoyed by American citizens. To jump on a steamer in Boston and go to Liverpool was as easy as boarding a night-boat for New York. During the horse and buggy age, in which I was happily brought up, a passport was unknown except for Baedeker's remark that it might help you get permission to look at a private collection of paintings. The only country which required a passport was Czarist Russia, and few Americans wanted to visit that despotic regime.[12]

This era of easygoing travel ended in 1952, when Congress passed the Internal Security Act, which for the first time in U.S. history made it a criminal offense to leave the country without a passport.[13] Two years earlier, furthermore, Congress had made the receipt of a passport explicitly contingent on an applicant's political ideology, by forbidding members of "Communist organizations" that were registered with the attorney general to leave the United States.[14] Shortly thereafter, the Department of State adopted regulations prohibiting foreign travel not only to members of the Communist Party, but also to anyone who had any association with them.[15] By 1952 the secretary of state, armed with an arsenal of open-ended statutes and regulations, was denying passports virtually at will. Unless a court intervened, moreover, individuals denied passports were accorded no notice, no hearing, no opportunity to review the evidence, and no explanation whatsoever beyond the claim that their travel would not be in "the best interests of the United States."[16]

J. Henry Carpenter, a widely respected theologian, having urged "high-level negotiations" between the United States and the Soviet Union, was in 1948 denied permission to visit Japan.[17] The formidable

Ruth B. Shipley, then director of the Passport Division, explained: "Dr. Carpenter knows the answer for our refusal of a passport. It is his political activities."[18] In 1954 the eminent playwright Arthur Miller was prohibited from visiting Brussels to attend the opening of one of his plays; the reason given was that his trip was not in "the best interests of the United States."[19] Nobel prize–winning scientist Linus Pauling was barred from traveling abroad,[20] as was Howard Fast, the writer.[21] New York Congressman Leo Isaacson was denied a passport in 1948 because he intended to participate in a conference supporting the Greek rebels, whose victory the U.S. government opposed.[22] In 1950 the Department of State told singer and actor Paul Robeson that since he would probably speak out against colonialism if he went abroad, and thus "meddle in United States foreign policy," his visit would not be "in the best interests of the United States."[23]

Men and women were denied passports because they were acquainted with "Iron Curtain" ambassadors,[24] because they had favored Attorney General Tom Clark's nomination to the Supreme Court,[25] and because they had attended peace conferences.[26] One prominent writer, who had been commissioned by a consortium of U.S. newspapers to report on land reform programs in Europe, was denied a passport on the grounds that nothing "constructive" could be expected from his writings (he then promised to write "constructively," but Shipley held firm).[27]

In time the State Department's free wheeling antics became even less defensible: The United States had agreed when it signed the Helsinki Accords in 1975 to relax its travel restrictions,[28] Cold War paranoia had at least marginally subsided, and Watergate had exposed the dangers of an unleashed executive. As a consequence, in 1978 Congress passed two acts that sharply restricted the situations in which the president could prevent foreign travel.[29] This action trailed by two decades a related move by the Supreme Court, which in a 1958 case had responded to the State Department's excesses by proclaiming a constitutional right to travel.[30]

The 1958 case involved Rockwell Kent, a member of the Communist Party and an artist of some note. Kent had planned to travel to Helsinki in order to attend a conference sponsored by the World Council of Peace, but the conference was over long before he ever reached Europe because the Department of State refused to grant him a passport. Kent in turn sued the State Department, and although his case eventually became a landmark, it raised a simple issue of statutory interpretation: Did Congress, in enacting the Passport Act of 1926, intend to vest the secretary of state with authority to deny passports to members of the Communist Party?

The Supreme Court said "No," and in a move without precedent, proclaimed international travel an important component of that liberty protected by the due process clause of the Fifth Amendment. Justice William O. Douglas, speaking for the majority in *Kent* v. *Dulles*, stated that "travel abroad, like travel within the country . . . may be as close to the heart of the individual as the choice of what he eats, or wears, or reads. Freedom of movement is basic to our scheme of values."[31]

The Passport Act of 1926 speaks in broad terms, authorizing the secretary of state to issue passports under such rules as the president may prescribe. Nevertheless, Justice Douglas continued, "where activities or enjoyments, natural and often necessary to the well-being of an American citizen, such as travel, are involved, we will construe narrowly all delegated powers that curtail or dilute them."[32] Thus, travel may be restricted, but such restrictions must be authorized by Congress, not by some unaccountable bureaucrat. Such authorization need not be explicit, however, provided that Congress is aware of and acquiesces in executive action. Did Congress, in fact, acquiesce in the State Department's policy of denying passports to members of the Communist Party? Disregarding wartime measures that it deemed irrelevant, the Court concluded that the Department of State had routinely withheld passports from only two classes of people: noncitizens and criminals.[33] In contrast, the Court could unearth only an occasional and often ambiguous case involving Communists—not nearly enough to comprise a pattern, let alone one to which Congress could knowingly have acceded. The Department of State policy was consequently declared unconstitutional, and Rockwell Kent received his passport.

Although the Court established in *Kent* v. *Dulles* that administrative agencies cannot unilaterally prevent people from traveling on the basis of their political beliefs, it sidestepped another, and ultimately more important, question: Was Congress free to do so? Six years later, in *Aptheker* v. *Secretary of State*, the Court answered the question by saying "It depends."[34]

Aptheker involved a congressional statute that made it a criminal offense for any member of the Communist Party to apply for or use a passport.[35] The Court, after characterizing travel as "closely related" to the rights of speech and association, found this statute unconstitutional on its face.[36] The Court recognized the importance of its objective, but found its method of implementation to be unnecessarily broad because it lumped together everyone who belonged to the party, both those who did and did not pose dangers, and penalized them all indiscriminately.[37]

One year after *Aptheker*, the Supreme Court again reaffirmed the importance of travel while at the same time sustaining executive action that substantially restricted this right in *Zemel* v. *Rusk*.[38] Admittedly, this case involved a crisis situation, and its facts were distinguishable from those in *Kent* and *Aptheker*, but when viewed in light of subsequent developments, it nevertheless signaled a retreat from the earlier opinions.

On January 3, 1961, the United States broke diplomatic relations with Cuba, and shortly afterwards the Department of State announced that U.S. passports would no longer be validated for travel there. In December 1962, two months after the Cuban missile crisis, Lewis Zemel, explaining that he wanted to visit Cuba in order "to satisfy [his] curiosity . . . and become a better informed citizen," sued the Secretary of State and the Attorney General for denying him permission to do so.[39]

The Supreme Court upheld the ban, but stressed that only a bona fide emergency—in this case the Cuban missile crisis—could justify it. Speaking for the majority, Chief Justice Earl Warren explained that the passport restrictions were "supported by the weightiest considerations of national security."[40] Although Warren reiterated that travel is a "liberty" protected by the Fifth Amendment, he made clear that it is not an absolute right, but rather one that can be abridged to the extent necessary to promote important governmental interests.[41] The State Department's travel ban promoted just such an interest, he concluded, because it could hobble Cuban efforts to export the Communist revolution.[42]

Even to further an important governmental interest, however, executive officers cannot restrict travel without at least implied congressional permission. In *Zemel* the Court found what had been missing in *Kent*: congressional acquiescence in a consistent administrative practice.[43] The executive branch had frequently imposed area-wide bans for national security and foreign policy reasons, and the Court was unaware of a single instance in which legislators had balked.

As the Court noted, the executive branch had indeed imposed numerous travel bans without meeting any concerted resistance from Congress.[44] At various times since World War II it has forbidden Americans to visit Iran, many Arab nations, and most Communist-bloc countries. In 1965, when *Zemel* was decided, the State Department was refusing to validate passports to North Korea and North Vietnam as well as to Cuba. According to executive branch officials, these restrictions not only provide them with diplomatic artillery,[45] but they also protect Americans from dangerous situations and prevent them from "complicating" sensitive foreign policy maneuvers.[46]

Area-wide travel bans, however, are extraordinarily susceptible to abuse. While they may, indeed, safeguard American lives or diplomatic negotiations, they also enable those in power to insulate their foreign policy adventures from public scrutiny. Congress suspected, in fact, that the executive branch often imposed area bans for the same reason it revoked passports, namely, to advance partisan rather than national security interests, and accordingly, in 1978 it amended both the Travel and the Passport acts in order to eliminate criminal penalties for traveling without a passport and to prohibit the president from imposing area restrictions unless the safety of Americans was endangered.[47] Some four years later, however, the Reagan administration, with the Supreme Court's collaboration, had succeeded in enfeebling both acts.

The Reagan administration, relying on the Trading with the Enemy Act (TWEA), a 1917 statute, managed to circumvent the newly amended Passport Act.[48] TWEA was enacted during World War I, and among its provisions, §5(b) vested the president with broad powers to deal with the current crisis. Unlike most other wartime expedients, however, TWEA was never rescinded; instead, the act was extended to cover peacetime as well as wartime emergencies, resulting in a major inflation of presidential power. Under TWEA's authority, for instance, in 1942 President Franklin D. Roosevelt proclaimed a national holiday and closed all U.S. banks,[49] and, by the end of World War II, his administration, citing "national emergencies," had promulgated a total of 470 orders.[50]

Roosevelt's successors also relied on TWEA. President John F. Kennedy cited the act when he imposed an embargo on Cuba after the missile crisis.[51] He also prohibited Americans from engaging in any property transactions with Cuban nationals, thereby effectively preventing them from traveling to the island. The terms of this boycott remained essentially unaltered until March 1977, when President Jimmy Carter made one significant change by permitting Americans to spend the money necessary to visit Cuba.[52]

Meanwhile, Congress, sobered by revelations of the Watergate scandal in particular, was attempting to curb the vast discretionary powers exercised by modern presidents and to regain that authority over foreign affairs that had been "slipping through its fingers."[53] Amending TWEA was among its first moves. Since the executive branch had repeatedly invoked §5(b) of the act in order to regulate activities never contemplated by its drafters, in 1977 Congress provided that thereafter the emergency powers authorized by this provision could be exercised only during wartime.[54]

At the same time TWEA was amended, the International Emergency Economic Powers Act (IEEPA) was enacted.[55] IEEPA grants the president exceptional powers during peacetime crises, but requires that before exercising these powers, he must first declare a national emergency and consult with Congress. Rather than requiring the president to declare a new national emergency in order to extend §5(b) policies already in operation, however, Congress inserted a grandfather clause in the amended TWEA providing that he could continue exercising "the authorities conferred upon the President by §5(b) . . . which were being exercised with respect to a country on July 1, 1977, as a result of a national emergency declared by the President before such a date."[56] The ambiguity of this grandfather clause has been responsible for repeated clashes between legislators and administration officials.

In 1982, after Americans had been permitted to travel to and from Cuba for five years without restriction, the Reagan administration abruptly adopted measures that effectively put an end to such visits. The secretary of the treasury did not ban travel outright, but like his predecessors in the Kennedy administration, he issued regulations threatening Americans with criminal sanctions if, while visiting Cuba, they paid for any transportation-related expenses such as food and lodging.[57] Shortly thereafter, individuals and nonprofit groups who wanted to visit Cuba for "educational, political, and religious reasons" filed suit, maintaining that the regulations were not promulgated according to procedures established under either the amended TWEA or IEEPA.[58] Although the First Circuit Court of Appeals agreed, the Supreme Court did not.[59]

Chief Justice William Rehnquist, speaking for the majority in *Regan v. Wald*,[60] reasoned that the grandfather clause allows the president to continue exercising "authorities . . . which were being exercised with respect to a country on July 1, 1977."[61] Since President Carter was exercising "authorities" on this date by exempting travel-related transactions from other trade restrictions then in force, President Reagan consequently inherited the general authority to continue regulating trade with Cuba and could lawfully reimpose travel-related restraints.

The Court brushed aside the constitutional issues, declaring that the plaintiff's First Amendment rights were in no way offended because the ban applied to every American, in contrast to the regulation found objectionable in *Kent*, which applied only to members of the Communist Party. Neither were the plaintiffs' travel rights impermissibly restricted. When assessing the constitutionality of governmental policy affecting travel, Chief Justice Rehnquist explained that the Court would maintain its "classic deference to the political branches" and invalidate their policies only when they furthered no important governmental interest.[62] The travel ban certainly furthered important interests, he concluded, because it deprived Cuba of hard currency and thereby hampered its efforts to pursue "objectives inimical to U.S. foreign policy."[63]

While the Court claimed to be displaying its "classic deference to the political branches," in fact it was deferring to only one branch, the executive. Congress passed the IEEPA in order to curb executive powers in foreign affairs that had been steadily accumulating since the enactment of TWEA in 1917. The Court, however, managed to transform both the amended TWEA and the IEEPA from the restrictive statutes they were intended to be into broad grants of authority to the executive. As one commentator observed, by concluding that IEEPA authorized the president to impose new restrictions without following the procedures carefully prescribed in the act, "the Court defers not to Congressional mandate but to the President's disavowel of that mandate."[64]

In *Kent, Aptheker,* and *Zemel,* the Court had declared travel to be a component of the liberty protected by the due process clause of the Fifth Amendment. Ordinarily, when dealing with important liberties, the Court employs what it calls "heightened scrutiny," allowing the government to abridge these liberties only to further important interests, and even then only when the means employed are substantially related to those interests.[65] In *Wald,* however, the Court subjected the disputed regulations instead to the most minimal scrutiny—such scrutiny as it typically employs when reviewing legislation that poses no threat to individual liberties, whereby any means not patently irrational are tolerated.[66]

The Court, therefore, simply accepted the government's contention that because Cuba was attempting to destabilize Central America, it was imperative to deprive it of hard currency. It neglected to examine the legitimacy or even the logic of the method chosen, however, to pursue this supposedly important end. Consider the fact that although it was effectively prohibiting Americans from visiting Cuba in order to deprive the Castro regime of needed dollars, the administration conceded that no more than eight million dollars annually had actually been spent by U.S. residents traveling to Cuba[67]—a sum dwarfed by the hundreds of millions of dollars in hard currency that multinational affiliates of U.S. corporations were allowed to continue spending there each year.[68] Since the amount of money transferred by individual travelers was minimal—indeed microscopic—alongside the vast sums U.S.-based corporations were channeling into the Cuban economy, the suspicion persists that the disputed regulation was not intended to restrict dollars at all, but rather the American public's right to travel.

Although Congress amended the Passport Act in order to circumscribe the conditions under which the president may impose area-wide travel restrictions, by virtue of the Supreme Court's ruling in *Regan* v. *Wald* the president can still declare whole countries "off limits" to American citizens simply by prohibiting them from paying any travel-related expenses to and from these countries. Congress also passed the Travel Act in order to facilitate freedom of movement, but in a 1981 case entitled *Haig* v. *Agee,* the Supreme Court again colluded with the executive branch to frustrate this goal.

In 1968 Philip Agee terminated his 11-year contract with the CIA, and 4 years later he launched a broad campaign against the agency. As he explained during a London press conference, he intended "to expose CIA officers and agents and drive them out of the country where they are operating."[69] Louis Wolf, coeditor of *Covert Action Information Bulletin* and the magazine *Counterspy*, collaborated with Agee, and between 1975 and 1979 they published the names of several CIA operatives, one of whom was assassinated shortly thereafter.[70]

Meanwhile, the CIA, long distressed by Agee's actions, had gained monumental new worries: On November 4, 1979, Iranian students seized 52 American hostages on the grounds of the American embassy in Teheran. The students were threatening to try the captives for espionage, and, according to a rumor Agee later denied, he had agreed to serve as a juror.[71] The specter of its renegade agent performing this role finally goaded the CIA into action, and in December 1979 it persuaded Secretary of State Cyrus Vance to revoke Agee's passport. Vance claimed as authority a Department of State regulation adopted in 1966 empowering the secretary of state to revoke or restrict a passport upon determining that the holder's activities abroad were "causing or . . . likely to cause serious damage to the national security or foreign policy of the United States."[72]

Agee forfeited his right to an administrative hearing and immediately brought suit, charging that the 1966 department regulation exceeded the authority granted the secretary of state under the Passport Act of 1926. He also claimed that the revocation of his passport violated his right to travel, as well as his First Amendment right to criticize government policies. The Supreme Court disagreed with him and with the lower tribunals that had upheld his claims.[73] Chief Justice Warren Burger, speaking for the majority in *Haig* v. *Agee*, canvassed at length the charges against *Agee*, and then examined the language of the Passport Act.[74] Although this act does not expressly authorize the revocation or denial of passports for national security reasons, in previous cases such as *Kent* and *Zemel* the Court had held that congressional acquiescence in executive policies "substitutes for" explicit authorization.

Had Congress, in fact, "acquiesced" in the disputed policy? Although the chief justice cited three instances in which passports had been revoked on national security grounds without apparent objection from Congress, he acknowledged the paucity of this sample. He concluded, however, that requiring a "longstanding pattern" would be irrelevant in cases where, as here, there had been few occasions when a passport holder's activities abroad had actually threatened national security. In his attempt to establish congressional acquiescence, however, Chief Justice Burger relied less on the three instances in which passports were revoked than on legislation passed in 1978 amending both the Passport and the Travel Acts. As he explained, these amendments constitute "weighty evidence of congressional approval of the Secretary's interpretation, particularly that in the 1966 regulations."[75]

Having established to his satisfaction the legitimacy of the 1966 regulation, Burger briefly addressed the constitutional questions raised in this case. He observed that "the freedom to travel abroad with a 'letter of introduction' in the form of a passport . . . is subordinate to national security and foreign policy considerations," and is thus subject to reasonable governmental regulations.[76] Measures designed to safeguard the security of foreign intelligence operations are certainly reasonable, Burger continued, and he suggested that the freedom to travel abroad commanded far less protection than the freedom to travel within the United States, "which is virtually absolute."[77]

Chief Justice Burger then examined Agee's First Amendment claims, concluding that since his disclosures were made with the express purpose of obstructing intelligence operations, they were beyond constitutional protection. The revocation of Agee's passport was based not on his general criticism of CIA policy, but on his "repeated disclosures of intelligence operations and the names of intelligence personnel."[78] Such disclosures fall into the category of speech that is "clearly not protected by the Constitution."[79] In any event, Burger added, the revocation of Agee's passport would inhibit his action, not his speech, since he remained as free as ever to criticize the government.[80]

Agee is a disturbing opinion for many reasons, not least because the majority displayed, as Justice William Brennan pointed out in his dissenting opinion, an almost wanton disregard for accuracy when reviewing both the historical record and the pertinent legislation.[81] The Court cited three instances in which passports were revoked for reasons of national security, attempting to prove that by not reacting to such revocations, Congress thereby signaled its approval. However, as Daniel Farber pointed out in his exhaustive critique of the *Agee* decision, these few and "scattered" cases hardly establish a "consistent pattern."[82] In one instance the action was not even taken pursuant to the regulation challenged in *Agee*, and in two instances passports were denied for reasons having nothing to do with national security.[83] Since each of the three cases was an obscure one, moreover—the most notable among them meriting only brief mention on page 16 of the *New York Times*[84]—Farber concluded that "to infer Congressional approval under these circumstances is to surpass bounds of credibility."[85]

Furthermore, the claim that passports had been revoked in only three instances because citizens traveling abroad rarely threatened the national security is inaccurate at best. During the period the Court drew upon for its examples, scores of Americans posed dangers: Some, like former Attorney General Ramsey Clark and actress Jane Fonda, traveled to Hanoi during the Vietnam War to support the Viet Cong;[86] others visited Teheran during the hostage crisis in order to attend a conference on Iranian grievances against the United States. Surely these people posed more serious dangers than the individuals cited by the Court, and clearly

Congress was more aware of their actions—indeed, legislators castigated them daily—yet none had their passports revoked.[87]

The Court maintained also that over a 30-year period, Congress had evinced strong support for travel restrictions imposed on national security grounds. Such a statement plays havoc with reality. Administration officials on a regular basis, and President Dwight D. Eisenhower himself on at least two occasions, asked Congress to grant the executive branch authority to revoke passports on such grounds, but the legislators steadfastly refused.[88] Agee's attorneys repeatedly raised this point, and the Court repeatedly chose to ignore it.

Agee raised two issues of vital importance to an understanding of the First Amendment: One was the point at which speech merges into action, and the other, the extent to which the government may discipline those whose speech it abhors. The Court addressed these issues in the most cursory way, explaining that Agee was being punished for his action rather than his speech; that because his speech threatened national security it was not protected by the Constitution anyway; and finally, that even if he could no longer use a U.S. passport, he remained as free as ever to criticize the government.

The Court was right on one point: that by directly endangering the lives of intelligence agents, Agee's words forfeited First Amendment protection. The Court has long held that certain classes of speech are not shielded by the Constitution, among them obscenity,[89] "fighting words,"[90] and speech that poses a "grave and immediate danger to the security of the United States."[91] However, the majority did more than reaffirm the government's traditional right to curb incendiary speech—it suggested that simply by invoking national security, the government could restrict the travel rights not only of those who, like Agee, posed genuine risks, but of anyone who merely criticized the administration's foreign policy. The majority thereby endorsed a view of governmental prerogatives that Solicitor General Wade H. McCree, Jr., representing the executive branch in oral arguments before the Supreme Court, advanced during an extraordinary colloquy with Justice Brennan:

Question: [Solicitor] General McCree, supposing a person right now were to apply for a passport to go to Salvador, and when asked the purpose of his journey, to say, to denounce the U.S. policy in Salvador in supporting the junta. And the Secretary of State says, I just will not issue a passport for that purpose. Do you think that he can constitutionally do that in light of our previous cases?

McCree: I would say, yes, he can. Because . . . [t]he President of the U.S. and the Secretary of State working under him are charged with conducting foreign policy of the Nation, and the freedom of speech that we enjoy domestically may be different from that we can exercise in this context.

Brennan: Clearly the reach of the Secretary of State's discretion to deny a passport on national security or foreign policy grounds is potentially staggering.[92]

"Potentially staggering," indeed! According to the solicitor general, the executive can deny passports to individuals who are vocal in their opposition to the administration's Latin American policy, for example, or its stance on apartheid. The *Wall Street Journal* observed that in *Agee* the chief justice "raised the possibility that Americans mightn't have free speech rights when they are abroad."[93] The holding goes even further, however, suggesting that Americans may not exercise free speech rights even at home without possibly forfeiting their right to travel.

The chief justice also asserted that "to the extent the revocation of his passport operates to inhibit Agee, . . . it is an inhibition of his action, rather than speech. Agee is as free to criticize the United States as he was when he had a passport."[94] This is an incredible statement. As Justice Brennan pointed out, by revoking Agee's passport the government inhibited his speech no less than his action, and Brennan scoffed at the majority's logic: "Under the Court's rationale, I would suppose that a forty-year prison sentence imposed upon a person who criticized the government's food stamp policy would represent only an 'inhibition of action.' After all, the individual would remain free to criticize the United States government, albeit from a jail cell."[95]

The chief justice's statement is incredible for another reason: It totally ignores the important relationship between speakers and their forums. A teacher fired for criticizing the government has lost her forum or her audience no less than Agee—however justifiably in his case—has lost direct access to the international community he seeks to influence. While the Court has traditionally granted the government considerably more leeway to restrict an individual or group's access to a particular forum than to restrict the content of their speech, until *Agee* the Court had never suggested that questions of access were simply irrelevant.

Freedom to travel is accorded even less favor than freedom of speech. The majority stated that "freedom to travel abroad . . . is subordinate to national security and foreign policy considerations; as such, it is subject to reasonable governmental regulations."[96] What does this mean? In *Zemel* v. *Rusk*, Chief Justice Warren asserted that restrictions on travel were justified only "by the weightiest considerations of national security."[97] The majority in *Agee* implied, however, that the Court will uphold any restrictions as long as they are "reasonable," and that it will grant the government utmost deference in making the determination.

In his dissent, Justice Brennan referred to *Agee* as "a prime example of the adage that 'bad facts make bad law.' "[98] The Court, no less than the average citizen, regarded Agee with antipathy and feared that unless restrained he could wreak further damage on the country's intelligence system. However, in its haste to punish this one individual, the Court jettisoned precedent, twisted history, and squandered some of its moral authority. The Court necessarily hears many cases involving unsavory defendants. Nonetheless, its stature rests on the fact that, unlike the "person on the street," the Court can overlook particular circumstances in order to fashion a law that is dispassionate and principled. Justice Brennan reiterated this point in his dissenting opinion:

> Philip Agee is hardly a model representative of our Nation. But just as the Constitution protects both popular and unpopular opinion, it likewise protects both popular and unpopular travelers. And it is important to remember that this applies not only to Philip Agee, whose activities could be perceived as harming the national security, but also to other citizens who may merely disagree with government policy and express their views.[99]

Agee's situation was unique, and the Court should have confined itself to the facts in his case. Before being hired, a CIA agent must sign a contract promising never to reveal classified information without the express written consent of the agency's director.[100] Judges have enforced this agreement through injunctions in a variety of contexts, and they have even fashioned a doctrine of contractual prior restraints. As the majority noted in *Kent* v. *Dulles,* the government routinely invalidates passports in order to prevent illegal activity,[101] and accordingly the Court could have enjoined Agee's CIA-related disclosures and then sustained the revocation of his passport as the only practical way to enforce this injunction.[102] Had the Court chosen to do this, rather than vest the president with broad power to revoke the passport of any resident whose actions could jeopardize national security or foreign relations, it would have succeeded in penalizing Philip Agee without simultaneously undermining the rights of the public at large.[103]

The right to travel is imperiled not only by the government policies that were upheld in *Zemel, Wald,* and *Agee,* but also by the machinations of zealous bureaucrats who equate patriotism with orthodoxy. Thomas Walker, a political scientist from Ohio, had personal experience with such bureaucrats.[104] In 1984, on returning from Nicaragua where he had gone to observe its elections, he was detained at the New Orleans airport by an agent from the Customs Bureau who inspected his luggage and scrutinized and photocopied his literature.[105] The agent then entered a notation alongside Walker's name in the bureau's computer, which two years later yielded this response: "Intelligence, subject in possession of literature pertaining to the election in Nicaragua—alleged."[106]

Edward Haase's experience was similar to Walker's.[107] A freelance journalist from Kansas City, Missouri, he too was stopped by customs officials on returning from Nicaragua in January 1985. The officials detained Haase, summoned an FBI agent to investigate the "possible seditious nature" of his materials, and photocopied his papers, diary, and personal address book.[108] Walker and Haase are two among hundreds of other Americans returning from countries in disfavor with the U.S. government who have been similarly detained, interrogated, subjected to verbal abuse, and occasionally manhandled. Some travelers have had their taxes audited, or their mail intercepted. Scholars and journalists still allowed to visit Cuba under TWEA guidelines have been subpoenaed to produce extensive documentation to prove that they were, in fact, engaged in permissible activity—not tourism.[109]

Supervisory officials claim legal authorization for such actions. They concede occasional errors in judgment, however, and the FBI admits that it has in the past interviewed scores of travelers on their return from Cuba or Nicaragua.[110] During trial and pretrial proceedings brought against the Customs Service, moreover, its agents have testified that they had, indeed, harassed travelers, although they claimed that their actions were well-intentioned.[111] One employee explained that it was her duty to be on the watch for "subversive actions," which she said included "anything against the Government, our Government. It can be threatening our laws, our ideas."[112] Another official explained that he was duty-bound to protect the country "from outside forces and outside influences."[113]

Errant agents are often encouraged not only by misplaced notions of patriotism, but also by legal and administrative guidelines that vest them with inordinate discretionary power. One provision of the TWEA, for instance, empowers border officials to search luggage for any evidence that travelers returning from Cuba have violated the act by spending hard currency,[114] while other statutes empower them to examine the personal effects of returning travelers in order to check for material that, according to federal law, is either subversive or obscene.[115] The Supreme Court has ruled, moreover, that customs officials can inspect luggage or personal effects without a warrant, on the theory that people crossing the border have no "expectation of privacy."[116]

In an effort to restrain its agents, the Customs Service in 1986 issued guidelines that cover such subjects as photocopying and individual searches, and which provide legal definitions for terms such as "sedition" and "treason."[117] According to the guidelines, agents may confiscate only material that they have probable cause to believe meets the legal definition of subversion;[118] they cannot seize mere "political propaganda," and "inspectors must refrain . . . in the presence of the owner from volunteering expressions and observations of disapproval or criticism of offensive materials."[119]

The travel restrictions upheld by the Supreme Court in *Zemel* v. *Rusk* and *Regan* v. *Wald* exempted journalists, so at least the public was not totally reliant upon the government for news about Cuba. In 1983, however, U.S. officials, in a historically unprecedented move, barred the press as well as the public from the site of an important military operation. On December 25, 1983, approximately 1,200 United States Marines, Army Rangers, and Navy Seal Commandos invaded the island of Grenada in order to protect it, the government explained, from "destabilizing" leftist forces.[120] The military, backed by the Reagan administration, imposed a total news blackout during the first three days of the siege. After three days reporters were granted access, although only to designated areas, and even then only in small "pool" groups under tight military escort. During the first crucial days of the invasion, reporters therefore had no choice but to rely on secondhand information, often from the military officers themselves.

Government censorship in military contexts is not uncommon: For over a century authorities have monitored telegraph and cable messages, mail, and even dispatches from the front lines. Until Grenada, however, the government had never denied the press access to combat zones, and at least since the Civil War, when on-site correspondents first appeared, there had never been a military operation at which the press was not present.[121] Reporters went along when the military landed in Normandy on D-Day, remained by its side throughout both World Wars, and ventured near the battlefront during the Korean and Vietnam wars. Reporters were there when U.S. troops invaded the Dominican Republic in 1965—an incursion roughly analogous to the storming of Grenada—and when the army attacked Cambodia in 1970. Their presence, moreover, rarely compromised military security. More than 2,000 members of the press were posted in Vietnam during the war, for instance, and although authorities pilloried them for disloyalty, only 6 among this number committed breeches serious enough to cost them their Defense Department accreditation.[122]

Subjecting the press to prepublication censorship, however serious, is radically different from denying it access altogether. Howard Simons, managing editor of the *Washington Post*, commented on this difference when he discussed the British invasion of the Falkland Islands in 1981.[123] He observed that journalists were permitted to accompany British soldiers on ships, and even to accompany them as they bombarded the island, although their dispatches were heavily censored at the time. As Simons noted, "If somebody had come to me and said, 'You can't report this until the operation is secure,' I would have said, 'Fine, [but] I want to be there. I want to see it with my own eyes, not the Pentagon's.' "[124]

Military authorities did not want reporters to see the invasion of Grenada "with their own eyes," however, because they are convinced that critical press coverage prevented the United States from winning the war in Vietnam. Former Secretary of State George Shultz admitted as much when he explained why journalists were banned from Grenada: "It seems as though the reporters are always against us. They're always seeking to report something that's going to screw things up."[125]

Of course, by influencing public opinion, the press affects as well as records historical events; in different ways, both the Vietnam War and the invasion of Grenada illustrate this point. In Vietnam the press enjoyed enormous mobility, and, as former U.N. correspondent Bernard Weinraub observed, as a consequence "reporters gleaned a sense of the war that would have been impossible had they been carefully escorted by military officials."[126] Press releases authorized by the government often bore little resemblance to dispatches sent from the front lines, and the discrepancies prompted many citizens to question, first, the candor of their government leaders, and, ultimately, the justification of the war itself.[127]

Grenada poses a sharp contrast to the policy in Vietnam. Barred from the island during the first days of the siege, reporters could neither verify nor dispute the news releases supplied by the government. Only later, when they finally gained access, did they realize that officials had made several critical misstatements. Stuart Taylor, a *New York Times* reporter, published an article two weeks after the invasion, for instance, in which he charged that Reagan administration officials had provided inaccurate accounts of the number of Cubans discovered on the island, the imminence of a Cuban takeover, and the magnitude of perils facing U.S. medical students studying in Grenada.[128] Taylor concluded that the Reagan administration, in fact, had no solid evidence to support its reasons for raiding the island.[129]

In an era in which the timeliness of news reporting is crucial, such a column as Taylor's, appearing two weeks after the event, could have little impact. The Reagan administration had already shaped the public's perception by monopolizing the media during the first pivotal days when its attention was riveted on Grenada. As reporters for *Newsweek* pointed out, viewers sitting in front of their television sets never saw any bloody footage of U.S. troops besieging the island. They saw only grateful students, evacuated from the St. George School of Medicine, falling on their knees to kiss the ground when their planes landed in the United States.[130]

The First Amendment was written, in large part, to prohibit the government from engaging in prepublication censorship—what the judiciary calls "prior restraint."[131] Individuals responsible for disseminating legally proscribed material may be punished after the fact, but government officials are rarely allowed to intervene before it is published because courts consider prior restraint a particularly dangerous expedient.

Once it is imposed, the public is denied access to information that may be constitutionally protected and of critical importance.

The news blackout imposed by military authorities in Grenada effectively constituted prior restraint. It is presumptively suspect, then, but not inevitably unconstitutional because the Supreme Court has indicated that even prior restraint is tolerable under extraordinary circumstances. In a landmark 1931 case entitled *Near* v. *Minnesota*,[132] Chief Justice Charles Hughes stated that "no one would question but that a government might prevent actual obstruction of its recruiting services or the publication of the sailing dates of transports or the number and location of troops."[133] His statement was only dictum, but it has become known as the Near Exception, and it resurfaced in another important case 40 years later.

In *New York Times* v. *United States*,[134] or the Pentagon Papers case, the Court refused to enjoin leading newspapers from publishing an Internal Defense Department study of the Vietnam War because, it said, the government's arguments were insufficiently compelling to overcome its historic reluctance to invoke prior restraint.[135] In his concurring opinion, however, Justice Potter Stewart conceded that the government would be justified in halting the publication of any information that would "surely result in direct, immediate and irreparable damage to our Nation or its people."[136] The legitimacy of the government's action, then, depends on whether it barred the press from Grenada in order to forestall "immediate and irreparable damage," or, as the evidence suggests, simply to avert public opposition.

Conclusion

When Lewis Zemel sued the Department of State for denying him permission to visit Cuba, he explained that he wanted to see that country in order "to satisfy [his] curiosity . . . and become a better informed citizen."[137] He lost his case, but not because his logic was faulty. Travel is, indeed, an important adjunct of citizenship, enabling individuals to see with their own eyes what is going on in Cuba, Nicaragua, Vietnam, or China, and thereby to evaluate their country's foreign policies on the basis of information that does not emanate exclusively from governmental or at least secondhand sources.[138]

Twenty-three years after *Kent*, however, and 16 years after *Zemel*, the Court seemed to have come almost full circle, suggesting that travel is not, after all, a right entitled to substantial constitutional protection, but merely a privilege, subject to revocation by the government. The Court first signaled its turnaround in *Haig* v. *Agee*, by implying that the government could revoke a passport whenever doing so would further some national security or foreign policy goal, and then confirmed this shift in

Regan v. *Wald,* by permitting the government to declare whole countries off-limits to U.S. travelers in order to further these same objectives.

In *Kent* and its progeny, the Supreme Court had stated that, because travel was a right "important to the well-being of an American citizen," it would "construe narrowly all delegated powers that curtail or dilute it."[139] By the time of *Agee* and *Wald,* however, this language was all but forgotten, and the Court was suggesting that it would sanction almost any restrictions on travel, even those, like the regulations at issue in *Wald,* that bear only the flimsiest relationship to any legitimate national objective. As one commentator observed, the Court's recent approach "reduces the status of a would-be traveler to that of an economic commodity, like cigars or sugars . . . the restrictions of whose movement is subject to the political whims of the administration in power."[140]

Notes

1. *Kent* v. *Dulles,* 357 U.S. 125–26 (1958).

2. Translation from W. McKechnie, *Magna Carta: A Commentary on the Great Charter of King John,* 2d ed. (Glasgow, 1914), *quoted in* Charles M. Whelan, "Passports and Freedom of Travel: The Conflict of a Right and a Privilege," 41 *The Georgetown Law Journal* 63, 66–67, n.12 (1952).

3. Robert Pear, "35 Nations Issue East-West Accord Assuring a Broad Range of Rights," *The New York Times,* Jan. 17, 1989, p. A–1.

4. *For discussion see* Louis Jaffe, "The Right to Travel: The Passport Problem," 35 *Foreign Affairs* 17, 25 (1956). *See also Shachtman* v. *Dulles,* 225 F. 2d 938, 941 (D.C. Cir. 1955) ("The right to travel, to go from place to place as the means of transportation permit, is a natural right subject to the rights of others and to reasonable regulation under law").

The right to travel has been recognized in almost every human rights covenant adopted by the international community. *See, for example,* "The Universal Declaration of Human Rights," G.A. Res. 217A (111), U.N. Doc. A/810, p. 71 (1948); "Conference on Security and Cooperation in Europe: Final Act," 37 *Department of State Bulletin* 323 (August 1, 1975), *reprinted in* Richard B. Lillich, ed., *International Human Rights Instruments: A Compilation of Treaties, Agreements, and Declarations of Special Interest to the United States* 470.1 (Buffalo, N.Y.: W. S. Hein, 1983).

5. William Blackstone, *Commentaries on the Laws of England* (Philadelphia: J. B. Lippincott & Co., 1876), p. 134, *cited in* Leonard Boudin, "The Constitutional Right to Travel," 56 *Columbia Law Review* 47, 48 (1956).

6. *Declaration of Independence* (1776), reprinted in the *Organic Laws of the United States of America,* 1 U.S.C. (1976), p. 32.

7. *For discussion see* Raymond C. James, "The Right to Travel Abroad," 42 *Fordham Law Review* 838 (1974); Boudin, "The Constitutional Right to Travel," p. 47; Thomas E. Laursen, "Constitutional Protection of Foreign Travel," 81 *Columbia Law Review* 902 (1981).

See also Kent v. *Dulles,* 357 U.S. 127, 129–30 (1958) (Fifth and First Amendments imply a freedom to travel); *Zemel* v. *Rusk*, 381 U.S. 1, 23–25 (1965) ("travel is at the periphery of the First Amendment"); *U.S.* v. *Guest*, 383 U.S. 745, 758 (1966) (the "freedom to travel . . . has long been recognized as a basic right under the Constitution").

8. *See The Passenger Cases*, 48 (7 How.) 282, 12 *Lawyers Edition* 702 (1849) ("For all the great purposes for which the Federal Government was formed, we are one people, with one country. We are all citizens of the United States and, as members of the same community, must have the right to pass and repass through every part of it without interruption, as freely as in our own States.")

Shapiro v. *Thompson*, 394 U.S. 618, 629 (1969) ("This Court long ago recognized that the nature of our Federal Union and our constitutional concepts of personal liberty unite to require that all citizens be free to travel throughout the length and breadth of our land uninhibited by statutes, rules, or regulations which unreasonably burden or restrict this movement.")

Crandall v. *Nevada*, 73 U.S. (6 Wall.) 35 (1867) (The Supreme Court invalidated a law that imposed a tax on everyone leaving the state by common carrier because the right to move freely throughout the Nation is a right of national citizenship.)

9. *Kent* v. *Dulles*, 357 U.S. 116 (1958).

10. 11 Stat. 60 (1856), *amended in* 1866 (14 Stat. 54), in 1875 (Rev. Stat. §4075), in 1902 (32 Stat. 386), and in 1926 (44 Stat. 657). It is now codified in 22 U.S.C. §211a (1952).

In its original form this act provided:

> that the Secretary of State shall be authorized to grant and issue passports to be granted, issued, and verified in foreign countries by such diplomatic or consular officers of the United States, and under such rules as the President shall designate and prescribe for and on behalf of the United States, and no other person shall grant, issue or verify any such passport; nor shall any passport be granted or issued to, or verified for, any other persons than citizens of the United States.

11 Stat. 60 (1856).

11. Act of July 3, 1926, 22 U.S.C. §211 (a).

12. Zechariah Chafee, *Three Human Rights in the Constitution of 1787* (Lawrence, Kansas: University of Kansas Press, 1956), p. 193.

13. Act of June 27, 1952, 8 U.S.C. §1185 (1982).

14. Subversives Activities Control Act of 1950, ch. 1024, §6, 64 Stat. 993. In 1968 the registration requirement for Communist organizations was repealed, Pub. L. No. 90–237, §5, 81 Stat. 766, and in 1973 Congress ceased funding the Subversives Activities Board. *See* 50 U.S.C. §785 (1976).

15. 22 C.F.R. §51.135–51.143, Aug. 28, 1952; U.S. Department of State, Press Release No. 686, Sept. 2, 1952. The 1952 regulations deny passports to three classes of people:

> (a) Persons who are members of the Communist Party or who have recently terminated such membership under such circumstances as to warrant the conclusion—not otherwise rebutted by the evidence—that they continue to act in furtherance of the interests and under the discipline of the Communist Party:
>
> (b) Persons, regardless of the formal state of their affiliations with the Communist Party, who engage in activities which support the Communist movement under such circumstances as to warrant the conclusion—not otherwise rebutted by the evidence—that they

have engaged in such activities as a result of direction, domination, or control exercised over them by the Communist movement;

(c) Persons, regardless of the formal state of their affiliation with the Communist Party, as to whom there is reason to believe, on the balance of all the evidence, that they are going abroad to engage in activities which will advance the Communist movement for the purpose, knowingly and wilfully of advancing that movement.

In 1966 the State Department withdrew its regulations authorizing the denial of passports to Communists. *See* 31 *Fed. Reg.* 13,540 (1966).

In 1952 Congress also passed the McCarran-Walter Immigration Act, one provision of which authorized the president at his discretion to proclaim the existence of a national emergency and thereupon to impose such restrictions on entry and exit as "the interests of the United States require." 8 U.S.C. §1185 (b) (1952).

16. *For discussion see* Boudin, "The Constitutional Right to Travel," pp. 70–75; Note, "Passport Refusals for Political Reasons: Constitutional Issues and Judicial Review," 61 *Yale Law Journal* 171 (Feb. 1952).

During this period the judiciary imposed few restraints on the secretary of state. *See, for example, Bauer* v. *Acheson,* 106 F. Supp. 445, 451–52 (D.D.C. 1952):

In the matter of passports the executive department of the government, acting through the Secretary of State, must necessarily be accorded wide discretion in determining when and where the protection of the United States may be extended to an American citizen traveling abroad, and that it should also have discretion to deny protection to persons whose activities abroad might be in conflict with its foreign policy. This court does not suggest that the Secretary of State is without authority to establish reasonable classifications of persons whose passports shall be revoked or not renewed.

17. Jaffe, "The Right to Travel," p. 24.

18. Ibid.

19. Chafee, *Three Human Rights,* p. 197.

20. Zechariah Chafee, "Book Review," 101 *University of Pennsylvania Law Review* 703, 705 (1953).

21. "U.S. Voids Passport of Savant Abroad," *The New York Times,* September 19, 1950, p. A–25; *see also* "Passport Refusals for Political Reasons," 61 *Yale Law Journal* 179 n.58 (February 1952).

22. Ibid., p. 176.

23. *See* Brief for Appellee, p. 20. *Robeson* v. *Acheson,* 198 F. 2d 985 (D.C. Cir. 1952).

24. *See Nathan* v. *Dulles,* Civil No. 12727, D.C. Cir., June 2, 1955.

25. Boudin, "The Constitutional Right to Travel," p. 178.

26. *Nathan* v. *Dulles,* 129 F. Supp. 951 (D.D.C. 1955), Exhibit A, Letter from Mrs. Ruth B. Shipley to Dr. Otto Nathan, March 25, 1953, *cited in* Boudin, "The Constitutional Right to Travel," pp. 65, 65 n.113.

27. "Passport Refusals for Political Reasons," p. 178.

28. *For discussion see* Chapter 1.

29. Passport Act of October 7, 1978, §707, 92 Stat. 992–93, *amending* 8 U.S.C. §1185; Travel Act of October 7, 1978, §124, 92 Stat. 971, *amending* 22 U.S.C. §211(a).

30. *Kent* v. *Dulles,* 357 U.S. 116 (1958).

31. Ibid. at 125–26.

32. Ibid. at 129.

33. Ibid. at 127–28. Walter Briehl, a physicist, was the plaintiff in a companion case. Briehl applied for a passport in order to attend conferences in Geneva and Istanbul. He had been accused of associating with several individuals suspected of espionage, however, and although these charges were vague and uncorroborated, they prompted the secretary of state to deny him a passport on the ground that he was "going abroad to engage in activities which will advance the Communist movement for the purpose, knowingly and willingly of advancing that movement." *Briehl* v. *Dulles*, 248 F. 2d 561, 564 (D.C. Cir. 1957). The Supreme Court concluded that the material facts in this case were indistinguishable from those in *Kent*, and reversed the lower court judgment that had upheld the secretary of state's actions. *See Kent* v. *Dulles*, 248 F. 2d 600 (D.C. Cir. 1957); *Briehl* v. *Dulles*, 248 F. 2d 561 (D.C. Cir. 1957).

34. 378 U.S. 500 (1964).

35. Subversive Activities Control Act of 1950, ch. 1024, §6, 64 Stat. 993.

36. 378 U.S. at 517.

37. Ibid at 514.

38. 381 U.S. 1 (1965).

39. Ibid. at 3–4.

40. Ibid. at 16.

41. Ibid. at 14, 16–17.

42. Ibid. at 14.

43. Ibid. 8. Plaintiffs in a related case, *MacEwan* v. *Rusk*, 228 F. Supp. 306 (E.D. Pa. 1964), fared no better than Louis Zemel. The judge in their case held that the Department of State's restrictions on travel to Cuba were authorized by statute and perfectly constitutional. According to the judge, although citizens have a right to travel, this right is subject to reasonable and appropriate regulation. Citizens may occasionally be prohibited from traveling to certain areas, for instance, lest they obstruct U.S. foreign policy or jeopardize their own safety. 228 F. Supp. at 308. Restricting travel under such circumstances is within a president's inherent power to conduct foreign policy. Ibid.

44. State Department regulations currently in force provide that area restrictions automatically expire after one year unless otherwise specified. 22 C.F.R. §51.72 (1971). For discussion of the constitutional problems posed by area-wide travel restrictions, *see* Notes, "National Security Interest and Civil Liberties," 85 *Harvard Law Review* 1130, 1141–48 (1972).

In *Zemel* the Supreme Court dealt with only one question: whether the secretary of state is authorized to issue passports with area restrictions. Left for another case were two related questions: whether an individual could travel to Cuba either without a passport or with a passport not validated for travel there. The Supreme Court answered these questions in a 1967 case, *United States* v. *Laub*, 385 U.S. 475, by holding that since the Immigration and Nationality Act required a passport only for entering or leaving the United States, individuals commit no criminal offense when they enter Cuba either without a passport or from a third country.

In another 1967 case, a district court also held that an individual was free to visit North Vietnam despite the fact that his passport was not validated for travel there. The court reasoned that the State Department could issue a passport with the condition that the bearer not bring it into a given country, but that it could not condition it on the bearer's pledge not to enter that country. *Lynd* v. *Rusk*, 389 F. 2d 940 (D.C. Cir. 1967).

To date individuals defying travel bans have not been punished. For instance, the government took no action after Attorney William Kunstler visited North Vietnam in October 1969 in order to talk with Xuan Oanh, a spokesman for the North Viet Nam delegation to the Paris peace talks. *See The New York Times*, Oct. 27, 1969, p. A–2.

45. Early in 1971, for instance, President Richard Nixon allowed a U.S. ping-pong team to visit China. This "ping pong diplomacy," as it came to be called, paved the way for improved relations between the United States and China after many years of hostility. *See* Fox Butterfield, "Though Unofficial, Change Is in the Air for U.S.-Hanoi Ties," *The New York Times*, Sept. 20, 1988, pp. A–1, A–8.

46. *See Zemel* v. *Rusk*, 381 U.S. at 14; *MacEwan* v. *Rusk*, 228 F. Supp. 306 (E.D. Pa. 1964). *For discussion see* Eugene Clark Lutz, "President Carter's Attempt to Halt Travel to Iran and the Constitutional Right to Travel," 9 *Syracuse Journal of Law and Commerce* 115 (Spring 1982).

47. Passport Act of October 7, 1978, §707, 92 Stat. 992–93, *amending* 8 U.S.C. §1185. Congress, in amending the Passport Act, stipulated that the executive can prohibit the use of passports for travel only to countries with which the United States is at war, where armed hostilities are in progress, or where there is danger to a visitor's health or safety. For instance, in 1981 the Department of State prohibited the use of passports for travel to Libya, and in 1987 for travel to Lebanon, on the ground that U.S. lives in these embattled regions would be imperiled. "Travel Restrictions," 12 *First Principles: National Security and Civil Liberties* (July 1986), p. 3. *See Senate Report*: "The freedom-of-travel principle is sufficiently important that it should be a matter of law and not dependent upon a particular Administration's policy." S. Rep. No. 842, 95th Cong., 2d Sess. 14 (1978), *cited in* Daniel A. Farber, "National Security, the Right to Travel, and the Court," *1981 Supreme Court Review* 263, 282 (1982).

Travel Act of October 7, 1978, §124, 92 Stat. 971, *amending* 22 U.S.C. §211a (omitting penalty for travel without a passport).

48. Trading with the Enemy Act of 1917, ch. 106, 40 Stat. 411 (1917) (codified as amended at 50 U.S.C. app. §§1–44 (1982).

49. Proclamation No. 2039, 31 C.F.R. 522 (1939), *reprinted in* 12 U.S.C. §95, *repealed* by Executive Order No. 11,825, 40 Fed. Reg. 1003 (1974).

50. S. Rep. No. 549, 93d Cong., 1st Sess. 17–46 (1973).

51. Proclamation No. 3447, 3 C.F.R. 26–27 (1962).

52. The Carter administration granted a general license "authorizing persons who visit Cuba to pay for their transportation and maintenance expenditures (meals, hotel bills, taxis, etc.) while in Cuba." 31 C.F.R. §515.560 (1977).

53. Revision of Trading with the Enemy Act, Markup before the House Committee on International Relations, 95th Cong., 1st Sess. at 7 (1977) (prepared statement of New York Representative Jonathan Bingham, Chairman of the House Subcommittee on International Economics, Policy and Trade).

54. Act of December 28, 1977, Pub. L. No. 95–223, §101(b), 91 Stat. 1625–26, *reprinted in* 50 U.S.C. app. §5(b) note (1982).

55. 50 U.S.C. §§1701(b), 1703 (1982).

56. Act of December 28, 1977, Pub. L. No. 95–223, §101(b), 91 Stat. 1625, *reprinted in* 50 U.S.C. app. §5(b) note (1982). Title 1 of Public Law 95–223 provides in part:

> Notwithstanding the amendment made by subsection (a), the authorities conferred upon the President by Section 5(b) of the Trading With the Enemy Act, which were being exercised with respect to a country on July 1, 1977, as a result of a national emergency declared by the President before such date, may continue to be exercised with respect to such country, except that, unless extended, the exercise of such authorities shall terminate (subject to the savings provisions of the second sentence of section 101(a) of the National Emergency Act) at the end of the two-year period beginning on the date of enactment of the National Emergencies Act. The President may extend the exercise of such authorities for one-year periods upon a determination for each such extension that the exercise of such authorities with respect to such country for another year is in the national interest of the United States.

57. 31 C.F.R. §515.560 (1982).

58. *Wald* v. *Regan*, No. 82–1690–T (D. Mass. July 22, 1982).

59. *Wald* v. *Regan*, 708 F. 2d 794, 795 (1st Cir. 1983). The district court had refused to grant a preliminary injunction against enforcement of the Department of State regulation. Its ruling was vacated and remanded by the First Circuit, however, with instructions to issue the injunction. 708 F. 2d at 795. According to the First Circuit, the travel restrictions that the Reagan administration reimposed were not properly formulated either under the provisions established by the IEEPA or under the grandfather clause exceptions. Ibid. The tribunal noted that "as a matter of common sense and common English" restricting commodity purchases and restricting travel purchases were sufficiently different that they could not count as exercises of the same authority. 708 F. 2d at 796–97. According to the court, the authorities that §5(b) of TWEA vested in the president and grandfathered by subsequent legislation "were frozen in place" on July 1, 1977, and thus could not be expanded beyond the prohibitions that actually had been in effect at that time. 708 F. 2d at 796.

The Eleventh Circuit Court of Appeals also invalidated the Treasury regulations on the ground that neither the amended TWEA nor IEEPA authorized travel bans to Cuba. *United States* v. *Frade*, 709 F. 2d 1387 (11th Cir. 1983).

60. Justice Harry Blackmun submitted a dissenting opinion, which Justices William Brennan, Thurgood Marshall, and Lewis Powell joined. Justice Powell also submitted a separate one-paragraph dissent.

61. 468 U.S. at 232.

62. Ibid. at 242.

63. Ibid. at 243.

64. *See* Note, "Right to Travel Abroad," 98 *Harvard Law Review* 184, 191 (1984).

65. *See Bullfrog Films, Inc.* v. *Wick*, 847 F. 2d 502 (9th Cir. 1988) ("as a result of our determination that appellants' content-based regulations infringe the First Amendment, appellants' burden in attempting to uphold its regulation is heavy. In order to justify its scheme . . . appellants must demonstrate that their regulations are 'necessary to serve a compelling state interest' and are 'narrowly

drawn to achieve that end' ") (citations omitted); *Shelton* v. *Tucker*, 364 U.S. 479, 488 (1960) ("even though the governmental purpose be legitimate and substantial, that purpose cannot be pursued by means that broadly stifle personal liberties when the end can be more easily achieved"); *see generally* Michael J. Perry, "Modern Equal Protection: A Conceptualization and Appraisal," 79 *Columbia Law Review* 1023, 1077–81 (1979).

66. Minimal scrutiny only requires that there be some rational relationship between the statutory classification and a legitimate governmental objective, and, as Chief Justice Earl Warren explained, judges applying this lenient standard will uphold even laws that result in some inequality "if any state of facts reasonably may be discovered to justify it." *McGowan* v. *Maryland*, 366 U.S. 420, 425–26 (1961). *See also Shapiro* v. *Thompson*, 394 U.S. 618, 658 (1969) (Harlan, J., dissenting); *Rapid Transit Corp.* v. *City of New York*, 303 U.S. 573, 578 (1938).

For discussion see Gerald Gunther, "Forward: In Search of Evolving Doctrine on a Changing Court: A Model for a Newer Equal Protection," 86 *Harvard Law Review* 1, 8 (1972).

67. Declaration of Hal Mayerson in *Regan* v. *Wald, cited in* Burt Neuborne and Steven R. Shapiro, "The Nylon Curtain: America's National Border and the Free Flow of Ideas," 26 *William and Mary Law Review* 719, 759 (1984–1985).

68. Ibid.

69. 453 U.S. at 283 n.2 (*quoting* appendix to Petition for Certiorari at 107a), *Haig* v. *Agee*, 453 U.S. 280 (1981).

70. *The New York Times*, July 5, 1980, p. A–1; *The New York Times*, Dec. 24, 1975, pp. A–1, A–10.

71. *Agee* v. *Muskie*, 629 F. 2d 80, 81 n.1 (D. C. Cir. 1980).

72. 22 C.F.R. §51.70 (b)(4) (1982). Between the revocation of Agee's passport and the time of his hearing before the Supreme Court, Secretary Vance had been replaced by Edmund Muskie, who in turn was replaced by Alexander Haig as Secretary of State.

73. *Agee* v. *Vance*, 629 F. Supp. 729 (D.D.C. 1980). The district court held that the regulation exceeded the authority granted the Secretary of State under the Passport Act, granted Agee summary judgment, and ordered that his passport be returned. According to District Judge Gerhard Gesell, the 1966 regulation was not authorized by express statutory language and certainly not by congressional acquiescence, since it had been used in the past on only one occasion (629 F. Supp. at 731), and in 1958 Congress had denied a presidential request for "the precise authority sought here." 629 F. Supp. at 732. Judge Gesell concluded that "implied authority is not gained in this fashion." Ibid.

Judge Gesell's decision was affirmed by the Court of Appeals for the District of Columbia, which held that under the Passport Act the secretary was required to show that the regulation was authorized by Congress either expressly or through approval of a "substantial and consistent" administrative practice. *Agee* v. *Muskie*, 629 F. 2d 80, 85 (D.C. Cir. 1980) (*citing Zemel* v. *Rusk*, 381 U.S. at 12). After reviewing the record of passport revocations for national security reasons, the court concluded that the secretary had failed to establish such a practice. 629 F. 2d at 86.

74. 453 U.S. 280 (1981).

75. Ibid. at 306. The court cites "specific presentations" to Congress in order

to establish that legislators were aware of the challenged practice. 453 U.S. at 299–301. However, as Daniel Farber observed, these presentations consisted of two Department of State reports explaining the 1956 regulation and a 1970 Senate Staff Report. Daniel Farber, "National Security, the Right to Travel, and the Court," *Supreme Court Review* 1981 (1982), p. 278. Farber pointed out, moreover, that none of these "specific presentations" provided any significant support for the Court's position. Ibid. The 1960 Staff Report, for instance, was presented to a committee without jurisdiction over the issuance of passports, and an earlier report, while made to an appropriate committee, in fact concluded that in other than wartime circumstances, passport restrictions must be specifically authorized by Congress. Ibid.

76. 453 U.S. at 306.

77. Ibid. In the years since *Kent* and *Aptheker*, the Court has drawn a sharp distinction between interstate and foreign travel: Whereas the former is "virtually absolute" (ibid.), the latter is "subordinate to national security and foreign policy considerations." Ibid. That foreign travel is entitled to considerably less constitutional protection than interstate travel was also indicated in *Califano* v. *Aznovorian* (439 U.S. 170, 176 [1978]), which involved a challenge to a Social Security Act amendment that eliminates disability benefits during periods when the recipient is out of the country for more than 30 days. In upholding the amendment, the Court noted that while the restrictions might have a "chilling effect" on recipients' freedom to travel, they were nevertheless reasonable given the problem the government would face in attempting to monitor recipients' needs while they were abroad. Ibid. at 177.

78. 453 U.S. at 308.

79. Ibid. at 309.

80. Ibid.

81. In addition to accusing the majority of "serious distortions and omissions" in its survey of the historical record (ibid. at 315–18), Justice Brennan maintained that the majority departed radically from the central holding in *Kent*, namely, that since "the Executive's authority to revoke passports touches on an area fraught with constitutional rights," the Court must "construe narrowly all delegated powers that curtail or dilute them." Ibid. at 318, *quoting Kent* v. *Dulles*, 357 U.S. at 129.

82. Farber, "National Security, the Right to Travel, and the Court," p. 278.

83. Ibid., pp. 274–77.

84. Ibid., p. 275.

85. Ibid., p. 284.

86. *For discussion see* ibid., p. 277.

87. For legislators' reactions, *see* ibid., p. 277, 277 n.92.

88. Ibid., pp. 278–82; *see* 104 *Congressional Record* 13046, 13062 (1958); H.R. Rep. No. 1151, 86th Cong., 1st Sess. 2 (1959) (remarks of President Dwight D. Eisenhower).

89. *See Roth* v. *U.S.* and *Alberts* v. *California*, 354 U.S. 476 (1957):

> There are certain well-defined and narrowly limited classes of speech, the prevention and punishment of which have never been thought to raise any Constitutional problem. *These include the lewd and obscene. [It] has been well observed that such utterances are no essential part*

of any exposition of ideas, and are of such slight social value as a step to truth that any benefit that may be derived from them is clearly outweighed by the social interest in order and morality.

354 U.S. at 485 (emphasis in original). *See also Miller* v. *California*, 413 U.S. 15 (1973).

90. *See Chaplinsky* v. *New Hampshire*, 315 U.S. 568, 571–72 (1942).

91. *New York Times* v. *U.S.* (The Pentagon Papers Case), 403 U.S. 713 (1971).

92. 453 U.S. 319 n.9 (Brennan, J., dissenting).

93. *Cited in* "Yankee Stay Home," 45 *Progressive* (Sept. 1981), p. 10.

94. 453 U.S. at 309.

95. Ibid. at 320 n.10. *For discussion see* Yale Kamisar, "The Agee Decision," *The New York Times*, July 28, 1981, p. A–15.

96. 453 U.S. at 306.

97. 381 U.S. at 16.

98. 453 U.S. at 319. Justice Byron White allegedly remarked during oral argument, moreover, that "if [the respondent] were anyone but Philip Agee he'd have no trouble winning his case." "I Don't Need a Passport," *The New York Times*, July 27, 1981, p. A–15.

99. 453 U.S. at 319.

100. *See Snepp* v. *U.S.*, 444 U.S. 507 (1980) (per curiam); *U.S.* v. *Marchetti*, 466 F. 2d 1309 (5th Cir.), *cert. denied*, 409 U.S. 1063 (1972).

101. 372 U.S. at 127–28.

102. This option was suggested by John E. Bolmer II in "The Public Forum Doctrine and *Haig* v. *Agee*," 10 *Hastings Constitutional Law Quarterly* 187, 209 (Fall 1982), and by Yale Kamisar, "The Agee Decision," *The New York Times*, p. A–15.

103. The Court's decision did little to stifle Philip Agee. Shortly after losing his case, he obtained a passport from Grenada and announced his intention to continue his crusade against the CIA. "Philip Agee's Grenadian Passport," *Newsweek*, Aug. 10, 1981, p. 15. He returned to this country in 1987, in part to promote his book, *On the Run* (Secaucus, N.J.: Lyle Stuart, 1987), in which he detailed his efforts to expose United States covert operations abroad. This book, significantly, was first submitted to the CIA's Prepublication Review Board in compliance with a 1980 injunction. *See* "In the News," 12 *First Principles* (July/August 1987), p. 7.

104. *See* Anthony Lewis, "When the Law Works," *The New York Times*, Sept. 15, 1986, p. A–15.

105. His literature included a book written in Spanish that was, ironically, an assassination manual that the CIA had prepared for the Nicaraguan Contras. Ibid.

106. Ibid.

107. *See Haase* v. *Webster*, 608 F. Supp. 1227, 1227–30 (1985); *Haase* v. *Webster*, 807 F. 2d 208, 210 (D.C. Cir. 1986).

108. 608 F. Supp. at 1229. Haase sued the FBI and the Customs Service, alleging that they had violated a number of his constitutional rights. *Haase* v. *Webster*, 608 F. Supp. 1227 (D.C. Cir. 1985). The government effectively admitted error and offered to destroy any material it had reproduced, to return to Haase all the papers it had seized, and to certify that these papers had not been further

copied or disseminated. The district court accordingly dismissed Haase's suit for declaratory relief.

The Court of Appeals reinstated the suit, however. *Haase* v. *Webster*, 807 F. 2d 209 (D.C. Cir. 1986). Haase had maintained that he was only one of many travelers who had been subjected to searches on returning from Nicaragua, and that such searches were part of an apparent government scheme to intimidate individuals who traveled to certain countries. The Circuit Court, considering this accusation credible, issued an order requiring the government to respond. 807 F. 2d at 216.

109. *See The New York Times*, Sept. 17, 1984, p. A–4; *The New York Times*, April 19, 1985, p. B–20; "Free Trade in Ideas: A Constitutional Imperative" (conference organized by the American Civil Liberties Union and the Fund for Free Expression, Washington, D.C., Sept. 17, 1984; published proceedings, pp. 125–26) (proceedings available from the American Civil Liberties Union, 122 Maryland Avenue, N. E., Washington, D.C., 20002).

110. According to Burt Neuborne and Steven Shapiro, while the FBI admits that it interviewed 100 such travelers upon their return, other sources contend that the number of people interrogated was far in excess of that number. "The Nylon Curtain," pp. 759–60.

111. Lewis, "When the Law Works," p. A–15.

112. Ibid.

113. Ibid.

114. 50 U.S.C. app. §16 (1982); 31 C.F.R. §515.560 (a)(1) (1977).

115. 19 U.S.C. §1305(a) (1982).

116. Within the United States itself, government authorities ordinarily need a warrant based on probable cause before they can search an individual. *See Wong Sun* v. *U.S.*, 371 U.S. 471 (1963). The Supreme Court has held, however, that customs agents require no warrant in order to search the luggage or effects of anyone crossing the U.S. border because, it reasons, under such circumstances individuals have no "reasonable expectation" of privacy. *U.S.* v. *Ramsey*, 431 U.S. 606 (1977).

117. "In the News," p. 14.

118. Ibid.

119. Ibid. Attorneys with the Center for Constitutional Rights, a public-interest law firm based in New York City, have defended several travelers who have been harassed by government officials on their return from Cuba or Nicaragua. They consider the mere existence of the guidelines an encouraging sign, but fear they will not be enforced. They point out, for instance, that only 14 days after the regulations were promulgated, an American citizen returning from Cuba was confronted by a hostile customs agent at the Newark Airport who seized a book from his luggage. Ibid., p. 14.

120. *See* Charles Kaiser, Lucy Howard, et al., "An Off-the-Record War," 102 *Newsweek*, Nov. 7, 1983, p. 52. The government explained that reporters were barred from Grenada for their own welfare—a rationale prompting widespread protest from journalists, who felt their very mission was being threatened by this unbidden solicitude. For instance, Richard Salant, president of the National News Council, sent a telegram to President Reagan declaring that reporters "are ready once again to risk their lives just as our troops are doing." Ibid.

Journalists greeted with equal skepticism the government's second rationale, which the *New York Times* dubbed the "I'm just a civilian ploy," in reference to the explanation offered by Defense Secretary Caspar Weinberger when he was asked why reporters were excluded from Grenada. The secretary responded that since military commanders wanted all media representatives barred during the offensive, civilian leaders "wouldn't even dream of overriding their decision." Ibid.

121. *See* Howard B. Homonoff, "The First Amendment and National Security: The Constitutionality of Press Censorship and Access Denial in Military Operations," 17 *New York University Journal of International Law and Policy* 369, 372–83 (Winter 1985).

122. Ibid., p. 379.

123. Kaiser, Howard, et al., p. 52.

124. Ibid. *See also* "Secrecy and the Public's Need to Know," 18 *Center* (May/June 1985), pp. 15–22 (round-table discussion).

125. *Quoted in* Walter Karp, "Liberty under Siege: The Reagan Administration's Taste for Autocracy," 271 *Harper's* (Nov. 1985), p. 63.

126. "U.S. Press Curbs: The Unanswered Questions," *The New York Times*, Oct. 29, 1983, p. A–1.

127. *See* Anthony Lewis, "What Was He Hiding?" *The New York Times*, Oct. 31, 1983, p. A–10. Neil Sheehan tells how David Halberstam, as a *New York Times* correspondent not yet vested with an international reputation, started writing dispatches from Vietnam suggesting that U.S. troops were in fact losing key battles, and that the Viet Cong had considerably more men and was winning considerably more victories than Americans had been led to believe. Neil Sheehan, "In Vietnam, the Birth of the Credibility Gap," *The New York Times*, Oct. 1, 1988, p. A–27. Halberstam's reports differed markedly from those emanating from official Washington sources.

In August 1963, the Diem regime in North Vietnam staged a series of mass arrests, and, as Sheehan pointed out, both the U.S. embassy in Saigon and the Central Intelligence Agency issued an "administration" version of these arrests that differed in almost every detail from Halberstam's account. Ibid. The State Department released the official version in Washington, D.C., and, after an acrimonious internal debate, the *New York Times* finally decided to print both this version and Halberstam's story. Both were run side-by-side on the front page under the same headline, with a statement below the headline explaining that the conflict reflected "the confused situation in South Vietnam." Ibid. Three days later the Department of State was compelled to admit that the official version had been wrong and that, in its essence, Halberstam's account had been correct. Ibid.

Sheehan has written a Pulitzer Prize–winning book about the myriad "misstatements" government officials made throughout the Vietnam War. Neil Sheehan, *A Bright Shining Lie: John Paul Vann and America in Vietnam* (New York: Random House, 1988). *See also* Fred Friendly, "Reporting the News in a Communiqué War," *The New York Times*, Oct. 26, 1983, p. A–23.

128. Stuart Taylor, "In Wake of Invasion, Much Official Misinformation by U.S. Comes to Light," *The New York Times*, Nov. 6, 1983, p. A–20.

129. Ibid.

130. After the Grenadian invasion, the Pentagon established a Media-Military Relations panel, headed by retired Major General Winant Sidle, to establish guidelines for the press in future military operations. *See* Howard B. Homonoff, "The First Amendment and National Security: The Constitutionality of Press Censorship and Access Denial in Military Operations," 17 *New York University Journal of International Law and Policy* (Winter 1985), p. 403. The commission's Statement of Principle asserts that "it is essential that the United States media cover United States military operations to the maximum degree possible consistent with mission security and the safety of United States forces." Ibid. The Sidle Commission also made a number of recommendations, which included the establishment of a press pool under allowable circumstances, an accreditation system for correspondents, and a system that would encourage the media to comply voluntarily with security guidelines. Ibid.

131. Thomas Emerson explained the concerns that gave rise to the "prior restraint" doctrine:

> A system of prior restraints is in many ways more inhibiting than a system of subsequent punishment. It is likely to bring under government scrutiny a far wider range of expression; it shuts off communication before it takes place; suppression by a stroke of the pen is more likely to be applied than suppression through a criminal process; the procedures do not require attention to the safeguards of the criminal process; the system allows less opportunity for public appraisal and criticism; the dynamics of the system drive toward excesses, as the history of all censorship shows.

The System of Freedom of Expression (New York: Random House, 1970), p. 506.

132. 283 U.S. 697 (1931).

133. Ibid. at 716.

134. 403 U.S. 713 (1971).

135. Ibid. at 714.

136. Ibid. at 730. The *Near* and *New York Times* cases establish that under extraordinary circumstances the government may prevent the publication of certain information, but they are not directly applicable to Grenada-like situations in which the media was denied access to the information in the first place. Only recently have courts started handling "access" cases of this sort.

Richmond Newspapers v. *Virginia*, 448 U.S. 555 (1980) was the first major case involving a question of access—specifically, the constitutionality of a court order denying the press and the public access to a murder trial. The Supreme Court invalidated the order on First Amendment grounds, and Chief Justice Warren Burger, speaking for the plurality, asserted that "the explicit, guaranteed right to speak and to publish . . . would lose much of its meaning if access to observe the trial could, as it was here, be foreclosed arbitrarily." 448 U.S. at 576–77. He pointed out that the enumerated First Amendment freedoms have a "common core purpose of assuring freedom of communication on matters relating to the functioning of government" (ibid. at 575), and hence that the press requires a general right of access in order to function well in a democracy. The Chief Justice noted in conclusion, however, that the press has no general "right of access" to any place it chooses; rather, using history as a guide, this right is restricted to those places traditionally opened to the public. Ibid. at 577.

In *Globe Newspapers* v. *Superior Court*, 457 U.S. 596 (1982), the Supreme Court nullified a Massachusetts statute that prohibited the public and press from attending any trial involving sexual assaults on minors. Justice William Brennan, speaking for the majority, explained that press access to criminal trials is imperative not only because this country has a history of open trials, but also because the presence of the press hones the fact-finding process, provides a check on the judiciary, and encourages public respect for judicial procedures by promoting the appearance of fairness. Ibid. at 605–6.

Justice Brennan's logic in *Globe*, Chief Justice Burger's logic in *Richmond*, and indeed the Court's logic in both the *Near* and Pentagon Papers cases, is transferable to the military context: The press historically has had access to theaters of war, and its presence would assuredly render civilian leaders more accountable, military leaders more professional, and the public at large less skeptical and hence more supportive of the policies being waged in its name.

137. *Zemel* v. *Rusk*, 381 U.S. at 3–4.

138. The Court in *Kent* v. *Dulles* quoted Zechariah Chafee, who stresses the importance of direct access to information:

> Foreign correspondents and lecturers on public affairs need first-hand information. Scientists and scholars gain greatly from consultations with colleagues in other countries. Students equip themselves for more fruitful careers in the United States by instruction in foreign universities. Then there are reasons close to the core of personal life—marriage, reuniting families, spending hours with old friends. Finally, travel abroad enables American citizens to understand that people like themselves live in Europe and helps them to be well-informed on public issues. *An American who has crossed the ocean is not obliged to form his opinions about our foreign policy merely from what he is told by officials of our government or by a few correspondents of American newspapers.* Moreover, his views on domestic questions are enriched by seeing how foreigners are trying to solve similar problems. In many different ways contact with other countries contributes to sounder decisions at home.

Three Human Rights, pp. 195–196, *quoted in Kent* v. *Dulles*, 357 U.S. at 126–27 (italics supplied).

139. 357 U.S. at 129.

140. Note, "The Right to Travel Abroad," 98 *Harvard Law Review* 184, 194 (1984). *Agee* and *Wald* are disturbing not only for their impact on travel, but also because the Court in these cases inflates the presidency at the expense of Congress. The architects of the U.S. Constitution, fearing above all the evils of concentrated power, designed with meticulous forethought a system in which governmental power would be divided into three coequal branches of government, the ambitions of each countering the ambitions of the others. In an important 1952 case, Justice Robert Jackson reemphasized the importance of this carefully balanced system when he warned that the Court could sustain presidential action that contravened the express or implied will of Congress "only by disabling the Congress." *Youngstown Sheet and Tube Co.* v. *Sawyer*, 343 U.S. 579, 635 (1952).

In the late 1970s Congress, still reeling from Watergate, adopted several measures designed to reassert its own authority over foreign affairs and reduce the president's discretionary powers. Among these measures it amended both the Passport and Travel Acts in order to restrict those occasions in which the executive could impede a citizen's right to travel. Shortly afterwards, however, the Court, in *Agee* and *Wald*, reinvested the executive with almost as much authority to circumscribe travel as it had enjoyed in its pre-*Kent* heyday. In so doing, the Court acted as if Congress had not spoken, as if Justice Jackson's admonition had outlived its relevance, and as if the right to travel itself was an insignificant and expendable one.

3

What's in a Word: The Foreign Agents Registration Act and Political Propaganda

> "When I use a word," Humpty Dumpty said in a rather scornful tone, "it means just what I choose it to mean—neither more nor less." "The question is," said Alice, "whether you *can* make words mean so many different things." "The question is," said Humpty Dumpty, "which is to be master—that's all."[1]
>
> Lewis Carroll

A statute intended to cast a "spotlight of pitiless publicity"[2] on Nazi and fascist propaganda has become, over time, a vehicle for labeling and stigmatizing foreign films. This statute, the Foreign Agents Registration Act (FARA),[3] was enacted on the recommendation of the House un-American Activities Committee, which claimed to have discovered that hundreds of agents in the United States, acting at the behest of foreign interests, were disseminating "Nazi and other subversive propaganda."[4] The bulk of this propaganda was produced abroad, but either because its source was not revealed, or because it bore false U.S. credentials, it escaped the scrutiny its foreign origin might have invited.

Congress, accordingly, passed an elaborate disclosure statute intended to "protect the national defense, internal security, and foreign relations of the United States."[5] The FARA, with its accompanying regulations, requires any agent serving foreign principals who engages in political activities to register with the Internal Security Division of the Department of Justice (DOJ).[6] The act applies to all agents operating in the United States, regardless of the country they represent.

A foreign principal is defined basically as any government, party, corporation, or individual outside the United States who is not a citizen or domiciliary of the United States.[7] An agent, in turn, is anyone engaging in political activities in the United States who acts "directly or indirectly" at the request of, or "in the interests of," a foreign principal.[8] For instance, Billy Carter, the brother of former President Jimmy Carter, was compelled to register as an agent of the government of Libya after it was disclosed that he had been paid $22,000 to perform various favors in its behalf.[9]

An amendment to FARA in 1942 requires foreign agents to place on file with the DOJ two copies of any material considered "political propaganda." The statutory definition of political propaganda is long and convoluted, but essentially includes any communication intended to influence the American public about the foreign relations of the United States or another country, as well as material that promotes "racial, political or religious disorder, civil riot, or other conflict involving the use of force or violence."[10] Agents must place a conspicuous label on any film, record, or publication that meets this definition,[11] and although the prescribed label does not include the word propaganda, the fact that the government has thus designated the material is a matter of public record.[12] Agents must also comply with a host of other cumbersome registration and reporting requirements.[13]

During the 1950s and 1960s, the Post Office and Customs Bureau coupled FARA's broad definition of political propaganda with the Espionage Act of 1917, using the combined authority of these statutes to confiscate and destroy massive amounts of material sent from foreign, and particularly Eastern-bloc, countries.[14] The material ranged from Lenin's *The State and the Revolution* to *Chess for Beginners*.[15] In recent years, however, FARA has served primarily to monitor the lobbying activity of foreign principals.

Since the DOJ employs only one full-time evaluator, it depends primarily on the agents themselves to determine whether their material constitutes political propaganda.[16] Of the material that is reviewed by the department's meager staff, roughly 40 percent is thus classified.[17] According to a still-relevant General Accounting Office study, however, this is only the "tip of the iceberg," since few agents even report to the DOJ, and fewer still report adequately.[18]

Why do so few agents comply? It is because FARA is associated with subversive activity, a 1977 Senate Staff Report concluded, and as a result this "has stigmatized the registration process," making voluntary observance difficult to achieve.[19] Mere compliance, the study noted, made the registrants feel they were "making admissions with criminal or subversive overtones."[20]

The judiciary certainly has done nothing to discourage compliance, having since 1943 defeated challenges to FARA's general constitutionality,[21] to its registration and disclosure requirements,[22] and even to its selective enforcement.[23] The Supreme Court sanctioned its registration procedures, for instance, on the ground that they promoted national security by "identifying agents of foreign principals who might engage in subversive action or in spreading foreign propaganda,"[24] and a federal circuit court held in 1981 that even if individuals were selectively prosecuted under FARA, this was constitutionally permissible since Congress clearly intended the attorney general to operate according to "considerations of foreign policy and national security."[25]

By 1983 FARA's only major provision not yet contested in court was arguably its most controversial—the one requiring advocacy material to be labeled "political propaganda." In March of that year, however, this section was challenged in two separate lawsuits filed almost simultaneously.[26] Both suits arose after the National Film Board of Canada's (NFBC) New York office, its registered agent, submitted to the Investigative Unit of the DOJ a list of 62 new films it intended to distribute in the United States.[27] In January of 1983, the unit, after screening five of the submissions, notified the board that three of them constituted "political propaganda." All were short docudramas. One film, *If You Love This Planet*, won an Academy Award in 1982 for its discussion of the dangers of nuclear war. The other two films, *Acid from Heaven* and *Acid Rain: Requiem or Recovery*, explore the environmental effects of industrial pollution. All three were clearly labeled as Canadian.[28]

Barry Keene, a California state senator, brought one suit. He wanted to stimulate debate among his constituents by showing them the Canadian films, but he hesitated because a Gallup Poll he had commissioned indicated that both his political career and his reputation in the community would be seriously harmed if he sponsored films labeled political propaganda by the United States government.[29] During his trial the results of this poll were corroborated by expert witnesses. Keene consequently claimed that Section 1(j) of FARA, under the terms of which the Canadian films were labeled political propaganda, deprived him of his rights under the First Amendment.

The second case was initiated by Mitchell Block, the U.S. distributor of *If You Love This Planet*, two environmental groups, and the New York Library Association.[30] They either wanted to distribute the films or had already done so, and feared that showing anything officially branded as political propaganda would jeopardize both their profits and their reputations.

In both cases the government argued that political propaganda was defined in FARA as a neutral term of art.[31] Any pejorative connotations were merely the result of the public's "subjective misunderstanding," for which it was not responsible. The government also maintained that potential exhibitors could avoid any perceived stigma either by electing not to show the documentaries in the first place or by simply removing the labels before screening them.[32]

Barry Keene's case was presided over by Federal District Judge Raul Ramirez, who issued an opinion in September 1985 enjoining the government from enforcing "any portion of FARA which incorporated the term 'political propaganda' as a term of art."[33] As FARA's legislative history makes "abundantly clear," he ruled, Congress intended to denigrate the material so labeled and thereby to suppress or restrict constitutionally protected speech.[34]

Mitchell Block and his co-plaintiffs did not fare so well: Their suit was dismissed on its merits when it reached the Circuit Court for the District of Columbia, which concluded that the term political propaganda as defined by FARA was not pejorative.[35] Judge (now Supreme Court Justice) Antonin Scalia wrote the opinion, and he explained that even if the label were pejorative, its use would not be unconstitutional because the government is entitled to participate in the marketplace of ideas, and even to criticize the thoughts and expressions of private parties.[36]

The Supreme Court granted *certiorari* only in Barry Keene's case, and in May 1987 it handed down an opinion that was unanimous on only one point: The state senator had standing to sue.[37] Justice John Paul Stevens, speaking for the majority, explained that while simply alleging a "chilling effect" on one's First Amendment rights is not in itself a sufficient basis for standing, Keene had produced uncontroverted evidence that sponsoring films designated political propaganda would harm both his reputation and his prospects for reelection.[38]

When Justice Stevens turned to the merits of the case, he spoke for a Court that was now sharply divided.[39] The application of FARA was sufficient to confer standing, he said, but it fell "far short" of constituting censorship.[40] FARA merely provides that certain material must be classified as political propaganda, and the details of their dissemination must be duly reported. Under the terms of the act exhibitors remain perfectly free to sponsor whatever productions they choose, and they can combat any resulting bias simply by explaining "that the films had not been officially censured by the DOJ."[41] Above all, FARA does not impede free speech because, as the government had argued, it defines political propaganda in a neutral way.

Although in popular parlance the term propaganda connotes "slanted, misleading speech that doesn't merit serious attention," Justice Stevens explained, the term may also refer to any advocacy materials, including those "that are completely accurate and merit the closest attention and highest respect."[42] Indeed, standard reference works use the term in this sense.

The government had exhorted the Court to remember that since it does not sit "as some sort of ultimate committee of lexicographical revision to ensure the linguistic purity of statutory language . . . it should [not] set aside congressional enactments based upon no more than the often transient 'connotations' that a phrase may have in the public's mind."[43] Justice Stevens agreed, and concluded this section of his opinion by declaring that the Court would assess the constitutionality of the term political propaganda in light of its neutral definition.[44] Defined in this manner, the term does not burden speech. Justice Stevens went further, however, asserting that the term actually enhances First Amendment values by providing "additional disclosures that would better enable the public to evaluate the import of the propaganda."[45]

According to the Supreme Court, then, political propaganda is a neutral phrase, a legislative term of art, intended neither to denigrate the material nor stigmatize its distributors. The Court agreed with the government that it should not assume the public would ignore the statutory definition in favor of a "visceral negative connotation."[46]

Is propaganda in fact a neutral word? The term originated as an ecclesiastical reference to a body of Roman Catholic Cardinals, the Congregation for the Propagation of the Faith, which was vested with the obligation of disseminating church doctrine.[47] The expression gradually assumed a secular political meaning, however, and in 1962 two lexicographers, John Whitton and Arthur Larson, wrote that "the word 'propaganda' . . . has gradually come to acquire a tainted and unpleasant connotation. It suggests that someone is trying to put one over on us."[48] Edwin Neuman, head of the Usage Panel of the American Heritage Dictionary, agrees: "Whatever its origin, propaganda has become a 'dirty word.' . . . [W]hen something is labeled propaganda, it should be looked at closely and with suspicion. Indeed, calling something 'propaganda' amounts, for all practical purposes, to saying that it's not worthy considering, that it's to be dismissed."[49]

Justice Harry Blackmun, who spoke for the dissenters in *Keene* v. *Meese*, had argued that even if the statutory definition of political propaganda is neutral, "it is the common understanding of the government's action that determines the effect on discourses protected by the First Amendment," and "it simply strains credulity for the court to assert that 'propaganda' is a neutral classification."[50] His words echo those of Judge Ramirez, who had stated in his district court opinion that a word's popular connotations could not simply be dismissed:

> Even Congress must ultimately respect the limits of the English language. . . . This Court therefore harbors some doubt about the power of Congress to select a term which has widely understood negative connotations and designate it as a term of art theoretically having no negative connotations. It may be beyond the power of Congress to determine, for example, that all materials addressing public policy issues and originating from foreign sources shall hereinafter be called "poison" or "obscenity." There are words which cannot be stripped [of] their nuance.[51]

Political propaganda is, in fact, an expression laden with negative implications, and the Court is at best naive to assume that people "in the streets" will construe it in its neutral, statutory sense. Indeed, the Court granted standing to Barry Keene in the first place precisely because it recognized the professional risks he would incur by exhibiting films officially labeled political propaganda. Curiously, though, it then denied him relief on the ground that his injury would result not from the government's action but from the public's misperception.

Even if members of the public regard political propaganda as a pejorative term, however, does it matter? Although the First Amendment was drafted primarily to protect private expression from governmental suppression, *Meese* v. *Keene* raises an important question: Does it also protect the government's speech? If the DOJ chooses to stigmatize *Acid from Heaven,* is that its constitutional right?

Only Judge Scalia, writing for the appellate court in *Block* v. *Meese,* addressed this issue directly. Even if the term political propaganda did convey official disapproval of the material thus labeled, he maintained, the government is entitled to express its opinions, to espouse its own ideological positions, and to criticize those views with which it disagrees.[52] In fact, he said, the government's political speech is as much entitled as private political speech to full First Amendment protection: "The short of the matter is that control of government expression (which would always seem to fall in the category of political expression, the most protected form of speech), is no more practicable, no more appealing, than control of political expression by anyone else."[53] As he put it, it makes no sense to permit the government "to make war on Hitler's Germany, but not to denounce Nazism."[54] The government may not regulate the marketplace of ideas, he concluded, but it may be an active participant.[55]

The majority in *Keene* referred to Scalia's opinion only in a footnote, but in defending FARA it implicitly endorsed his thesis.[56] It maintained that FARA's disclosure requirements serve to expand the information available to the public, and it suggested that since almost any governmental contributions to the intellectual arena serve the same function, these contributions are almost invariably salutary.[57] The Court, in fact, went so far as to chastise the lower tribunal for its "paternalistic strategy of protecting the public from information"[58] by prohibiting the government from using the term political propaganda, and it quoted from a 1943 opinion in which Justice Hugo Black had defended FARA's registration requirements precisely because they serve to enlighten the citizenry:

> [The Act] rests on the fundamental constitutional principle that our people, adequately informed, may be trusted to distinguish between true and false, [and that] this bill is intended to label information of foreign origin so that hearers and readers may not be deceived by the belief that the information comes from a disinterested source. Such legislation implements rather than detracts from the prized freedoms guaranteed in the First Amendment.[59]

The Court's argument has much appeal: Since the U.S. Constitution grants freedom of speech to hatemongers of every stripe, surely the government is entitled to counter their venom, and moral suasion may be the only practical tool at its disposal.[60] Indeed, even the most ardent civil libertarians agree that the government is not only entitled, but even obligated, to assume a strong educational and ethical position on important civic matters. The real issue in *Keene* is not whether the government can express its own opinions—as of course it can—but the extent to which it can disparage other opinions with which it disagrees.

The government has such phenomenal resources, and its word is regarded as authoritative by so many people, that its voice will almost always command more respect than that of any rival. By labeling someone a Communist, for instance, it can sully that person's reputation in a way no private party could.[61] In a society dedicated to free inquiry, this power necessarily carries with it a corresponding responsibility for restraint.

By saying the government enjoys the same First Amendment rights as any individual, Judge Scalia downplayed the need for such restraint. His argument, left unqualified, suggests that the government can ridicule a person's religious or political views, for instance, the same way a street corner preacher can do.[62] Having asserted elsewhere in *Block* v. *Meese* that the government may not regulate the "marketplace of ideas,"[63] moreover, Judge Scalia later contradicted that statement by deriding as "unworkable" and "undesirable" any efforts to discourage it from "expressing its approval or disapproval of ideas."[64] He thus implied that the government may do more than enter a debate, that it may effectively dominate the debate by disparaging the views and perhaps even the character of fellow contestants.

Clearly the government goes beyond mere participation once it begins to overwhelm, stigmatize, or otherwise inhibit the expression of contending points of view, and at this stage its actions become constitutionally suspect. According to traditional First Amendment principles, in fact, the government can burden private political speech only to further an important state interest, and dominate—rather than merely burden—this speech only to further a compelling concern.[65] The point at which the government's action becomes either burdensome or domineering depends upon the circumstances: In one context, its voice, however clamorous, may still be only one of many, or one countered by another voice of roughly equal magnitude, such as that of the defense industry or the tobacco lobby;[66] in another context, it might be in a position to shout down all dissenters.[67]

By labeling the three Canadian films political propaganda the government did not dominate the debate. It neither suppressed nor expurgated the films, and even its negative characterization did not prevent one of them from receiving an Academy Award. The government did burden constitutionally protected speech, however, because the operation of FARA casts a chill over the First Amendment rights of anyone involved in the production, distribution—indeed, even the viewing—of films labeled political propaganda. In *Keene* the majority found nothing objectionable in this labeling since it did not amount to censorship. This conclusion represents a sharp break with tradition, however, because for at least half a century the Court has invalidated scores of assorted laws on the theory that "constitutional violations may arise from the deterrent, or 'chilling' effect of government regulations that fall short of a direct prohibition against the exercise of First Amendment rights."[68]

The Court has accordingly struck down many taxes, licensing and zoning requirements, and parade and publication permits that impose even moderate, indirect, and nondiscriminatory restraints on political expression.[69] Why these restraints are constitutionally troublesome was explained by the Court in *Lamont* v. *Postmaster General*, a 1962 case that should have governed the disposition of *Meese* v. *Keene*.[70] At issue in *Lamont* was the legitimacy of a 1962 postal statute that defined political propaganda in the same way the term is defined in FARA.[71] The statute authorized the postmaster general to detain all foreign mail containing such propaganda and to notify the addressees that it would not be delivered unless they explicitly requested it. The Post Office was required to keep a list of everyone making such requests.

The Supreme Court overturned this statute, reasoning that because it required the addressees to undertake an affirmative obligation to receive their mail, it would almost certainly have "a deterrent effect," especially on those in sensitive positions:

Their livelihood may be dependent on a security clearance. Public officials, like schoolteachers who have no tenure, might think they would invite disaster if they read what the Federal Government says contains the seeds of treason. Apart from them, any addressee is likely to feel some inhibition in sending for literature which federal officials have condemned as "Communist political propaganda."[72]

State Senator Barry Keene is a stouthearted fellow, accustomed to the rough-and-tumble of political life; yet, like the public officials referred to in *Lamont*, he was reluctant to be identified with material stigmatized by the government. Mitchell Block, the New York agent for the NFBC, was similarly reluctant to risk public censure. He could exercise his First Amendment rights, moreover, only by assuming the same kind of "affirmative obligations" that the Court found objectionable in *Lamont*.

FARA's Section 614(b) requires agents associated with any film designated as political propaganda to equip this film with a label that specifically states that they have registered with the DOJ, and that "registration does not indicate approval of the contents by the U.S. government."[73] Agents are required to report "full information as to the places, times, and extent of such [dissemination],"[74] and to include the names of every organization and theater that uses or screens material designated as political propaganda, together with the dates of these screenings and the estimated attendance at each. Section 614(b) requires them, finally, to list the names and addresses of individuals and organizations who receive 100 or more copies of the propaganda material, and it obliges the DOJ to keep these lists on permanent file.[75]

In 1983 a congressional subcommittee held a hearing to review FARA's implementation,[76] and its chairman, California Representative Don Edwards, observed that if he were a "timid distributor," he would not even accept a film designated as political propaganda if he knew that by doing so his "name was going to go to the Justice Department and be put on some list."[77] A "timid distributor" might balk for yet another reason: Since the Justice Department bestows its censure on only a handful of films, the public might view with particular suspicion anyone associated with these few aberrations.

Only 3 of the 62 films submitted by the NFBC in 1982 were classified as political propaganda,[78] and according to Joseph Clarkson, head of the DOJ's Internal Security Division, "only ten or so out of [700] films are routinely overtly checked by the Department."[79] Why are so few singled out? How are these few selected for review? It is done on the basis of their titles: Clarkson explained during the Subcommittee's hearing that his section reviews films with "suggestive titles"[80] (prompting the committee's counsel to rejoin that if the distributors of a film on the nuclear weapons freeze movement could use an innocuous title, such as *How to Bake a Cake*, it might escape inspection).[81]

Susan Shaffer, an attorney representing the American Civil Liberties Union at the hearing, pointed out that potential viewers, no less than distributors, might avoid any film categorized as political propaganda, especially viewers who did not live in a "sophisticated town" such as Washington, D.C., where controversial films are common fare.[82] She might have added that during periods when public paranoia runs high, like the 1950s, even people in sophisticated cities might distance themselves from anything that bears an official taint.

Sponsors and potential viewers must contend with yet another worry: What does the government intend to do with the lists it stores at the DOJ? It has at its fingertips the names of distributors and individual and group exhibitors throughout the country who show films dealing with politically provocative themes. According to the majority in *Keene*, the government maintains such lists only to provide the public with "additional disclosures," but this is an incredible statement: In the past, the judiciary has rarely tolerated any governmental policy that strips anonymity from individuals engaged in a constitutionally protected yet sensitive activity.[83]

FARA operates in a variety of ways, then, to discourage individuals from exercising their constitutional rights.[84] This conclusion does not end the inquiry, however, since the government may burden speech, and even smother it outright, in order to further compelling or at least important state interests, provided only that these interests cannot be advanced in less drastic ways.

According to government officials, because FARA requires political propaganda to be appropriately labeled, it serves an important governmental interest by enlightening the public. The officials undercut the logic of this assertion, however, by reminding the Court that exhibitors are perfectly free to remove these labels at any time—spurring Justice Blackmun to conclude in his dissenting opinion that the government has advanced no argument, compelling or otherwise, to justify "even the slightest burden on protected speech."[85]

If FARA were redrafted, however, it could become a legitimate and even beneficial statute.[86] Simply requiring foreign agents to reveal the source of their material, without compelling them to supply additional unnecessary and insinuating information, would serve the function of a disclosure statement, and as the Court pointed out in *Keene*, such statements "better enable the public to evaluate the impact of the propaganda."[87] Why, then, shouldn't disclosure statements accompany all advocacy material, regardless of its source? If the objective is public enlightenment, why should only material of foreign origin be singled out?

Is foreign-based material inherently suspect? Is it presumptively less trustworthy than domestic expression?[88] Throughout its opinion in *Meese* v. *Keene*, the Court suggested that it is. It pointed out, for instance, that when the DOJ designates Canadian films on acid rain as political propaganda, exhibitors can "combat any bias [stemming from the labels] . . . simply by explaining that Canada's interest in the subject does not necessarily undermine the integrity or the persuasiveness of its advocacy."[89] By making this statement, the Court accepts as legitimate the requirement that a Canadian film espousing one view on acid rain must bear an admonitory label, while a domestic production advocating another point of view—perhaps even the administration's—need not. Neither is the Court troubled by the fact that anyone exhibiting the Canadian films must undertake a personal campaign to "combat any bias" and to comply with onerous administrative requirements in addition, while the sponsors of domestic productions face no such obligations.

In a 1943 opinion upholding FARA's registration requirements, Justice Hugo Black suggested that FARA was "intended to label information of foreign origin so that hearers and readers may not be deceived by the belief that the information comes from a disinterested source."[90] His statement is disturbing but perhaps understandable, since it reflects a wartime xenophobia from which few were immune. That the Supreme Court should quote it approvingly and reaffirm its logic some 34 years later in *Meese* v. *Keene* is less understandable, however, and is considerably more disturbing.

Conclusion

During the 1983 congressional hearing held to assess the impact of FARA, Pennsylvania Representative George Gekas asked an important question: Without FARA, how could the government apprise the public of its disapproval of certain material, such as a film from South Africa glorifying apartheid?[91]

One answer is that the government has plenty of ways to communicate its opinions. When U.S. producers released the film *Missing*, for instance, administration officials were dismayed by what they considered its serious misrepresentation of U.S. policy in Chile, and they fought back by issuing press releases, writing op-ed articles, appearing on talk shows, and even assisting former employees in filing a lawsuit.[92] As long as these countermeasures do not dominate the debate, they are preferable to the system prescribed by FARA under which unidentified bureaucrats are authorized to single out and stigmatize certain foreign films, saddling their promoters with such inhibitive reporting requirements that, in contrast to well-financed domestic productions like *Missing*, many are effectively prevented from even competing in the intellectual arena.

Another answer for Representative Gekas is that Americans are virtually inundated with domestically produced television programs, movies, and radio broadcasts that espouse points of view from the bizarre to the banal, from the far left to the far right, and yet somehow most manage to retain their ideological moorings. That, of course, is the philosophy underlying the First Amendment: Americans are capable of shifting through this material, and of judging for themselves what is and what is not worthwhile, without a paternalistic nudge from Uncle Sam.[93]

Notes

1. Lewis Carroll, *The Annotated Alice: Alice's Adventures in Wonderland and Through the Looking Glass,* ed. Martin Gardner (New York: C. N. Potter, 1960), p. 269, *cited in Keene* v. *Smith,* 569 F. Supp. 1513, 1522 (E.D. Cal. 1983), *sub nom. Keene* v. *Meese,* 619 F. Supp. 1111 (E.D. Cal. 1985).

2. The House of Representatives issued a report on the act of 1938 in which it stated that "the spotlight of pitiless publicity will serve as a deterrent to the spread of pernicious propaganda." H. R. Rep. No. 1381, 75th Cong., 1st Sess. 2 (1937).

Members of Congress maintained that it was necessary to monitor "subversive activities by the nationals of foreign governments," "propaganda agents," and "secret spies" who "work to strike at the very things we cherish and which are the very fundamentals of our government." *See* 79 *Congressional Record* 2, 668 (1935) (Statement of New York Representative Samuel Dickstein); H.R. Rep. No. 423, 73d Cong., 2d Sess., 78 *Congressional Record* 11, 169 (1944). *See also* H.R. Res. 198, 73d Cong., 2d Sess., 78 *Congressional Record* 13 (1944).

3. Act of June 8, 1938, ch. 327, 52 Stat. 631; *present citing* 22 U.S.C. §§611–21 (1982 and Supp. 11 1982).

4. In 1935 this committee issued a report in which it stated that "during the past two years this country has been flooded with propaganda material." *Investigation of Nazi and Other Propaganda,* H.R. Rep. No. 153, 74th Cong., 1st Sess. 2 (1935) (quoting Committee Chairman, Massachusetts Representative John W. McCormack). The Nazi Party itself was responsible for "tons of propaganda literature" being slipped into the United States as part of its "strenuous efforts . . . to enlist" Americans of German descent. H.R. Rep. No. 153, p. 3. The committee also noted that propaganda was being disseminated by the Third International in Moscow, using the American Communist Party as its conduit. H.R. Rep. No. 153, p. 13.

5. When FARA was substantially amended in 1942, its drafters attached an introductory statement explaining that it was intended

> to protect the national defense, internal security, and foreign relations of the United States by requiring public disclosure by persons engaging in propaganda activities and other activities . . . for or on behalf of . . . foreign principals so that the government and the people of the United States may . . . appraise their statements and actions in the light of their associations and activities.

Pub. L. No. 532, 56 Stat. 248–49 (1942). 77th Cong., 2d Sess. (1942).

6. *Canadian Films and the Foreign Agents Registration Act: Oversight Hearing before the Subcommittee on Civil and Constitutional Rights of the House Judiciary Committee,* 98th Cong., 1st Sess. 7 (1983) (hereinafter cited as *Canadian Films Hearing*).

D. Lowell Jensen, assistant attorney general of the DOJ's Criminal Division, explained that the reviewer's job "necessarily involves some discretion and expertise, primarily a sensitivity to the leading political themes of the day... [but] [r]eview of the films is strictly limited to whether they meet the statutory criteria. The reviewer is not permitted to speculate about the motive or bias of the author; the standard is set forth in the definition. The test, in two words, is political advocacy." Ibid.

7. 22 U.S.C. §611 (1982 and Supp. 11 1982).

8. Ibid. (c)(1). Exemptions from FARA are granted for "*bona fide* religious, scholastic, academic or scientific pursuits or of the fine arts." Ibid. §613 (e)(1982); and for individuals engaged in private, nonpolitical activities that further a foreign principal's *bona fide* trade and commerce. Ibid. (d).

9. Although he initially refused to register as a foreign agent, Billy Carter was ultimately compelled to do so after it was revealed that he had accepted $220,000 from the Libyan government for various services he had performed on its behalf. William Safire, "Igor and Billy," *The New York Times*, June 26, 1980, p. A–19.

10. "Political propaganda" is defined in §1 (j) to include:

> any oral, visual, graphic, written, pictorial, or other communication or expression... which is reasonably adapted to, or which the person disseminating the same believes will, or which he intends to, prevail upon, indoctrinate, convert, induce, or in any other way influence a recipient or any section of the public within the United States with reference to the political or public interests, policies, or relations of a government of a foreign country or a foreign political party or with reference to the foreign policies of the United States or promote in the United States racial, religious, or social dissensions.

22 U.S.C. §611 (j) (1) (1982).

11. The standard identification statement reads:

> This material is prepared, edited, issued, or circulated by [name and address of registrant] which is registered with the Department of Justice, Washington, D.C., under the Foreign Agents Registration Act as an agent of [name and address of foreign principal]. Dissemination reports on this film are filed with the Department of Justice where the required registration statement is available for public inspection. Registration does not indicate approval of the contents of this material by the United States Government.

Ibid. §614 (b) (1982).

12. As representatives from the American Civil Liberties Union explained to members of the subcommittee investigating FARA, however, "because [the act] was intended to and does generate publicity of its activities in labeling propaganda, the 'propaganda' classification of labeled material is likely to be known to viewers and readers despite the absence of the word 'propaganda' on the label itself." Statement of Susan W. Shaffer, staff counsel, ACLU Project on the National Security, and Heathcote W. Wales, professor, Georgetown University Law Center, on behalf of the ACLU, Subcommittee Hearing, p. 68.

13. Agents must also submit to the Justice Department the "name of station,

organization, or theater using" the agent's film, the "date or dates" shown, and the "estimated attendance." *See* Form OBD–69 (now CRM–159), Joint Appendix at 17. *Meese* v. *Keene*, 107 S. Ct. 1862 (1987).

FARA's accompanying regulations also require an agent who transmits a film containing "political propaganda" to submit "either a film strip showing the label required by §4(b) of the Act or an affidavit certifying that the required label has been made a part of the film." 28 C.F.R. §5.400 (c) (1987). Another regulation requires that the names and addresses of "any station, organization or theater" exhibiting a propaganda film be disclosed on Form OBD–69. 28 C.F.R. §5.401.

Anyone who violates FARA is subject to a fine up to $10,000 and/or a five-year prison sentence. 22 U.S.C. §618 (1982).

14. Federal Espionage Act of 1917, ch. 30, 40 Stat. 217 (codified as amended at 18 U.S.C.A. §§793–98, 2388 [West 1976 and Supp. 1987]).

15. *See* Note, "Government Exclusion of Foreign Political Propaganda," 68 *Harvard Law Review* 1393–94 (1955); Murray L. Schwartz and James C. N. Paul, "Foreign Communist Propaganda in the Mails: A Report on Some Problems of Federal Censorship," 107 *University of Pennsylvania Law Review* 621, 633 (1959).

16. Ava Marion Plakins, "Heat Not Light: The Foreign Agents Registration Act After *Meese* v. *Keene*," 11 *Fordham International Law Journal* 184, 186 (Fall 1987).

17. "Justices Classified 11 Foreign Films as Propaganda," *The Washington Post*, June 22, 1983, p. A–21.

18. United States General Accounting Office, *Improvements Needed in the Administration of Foreign Agent Registration*, Enclosure 1, 1–6 (1980).

19. American Law Division, Cong'l Research Service, 95th Cong., 1st Sess., *The Foreign Agents Registration Act* 14 (Senate Foreign Relations Comm. Print 1977).

20. Ibid.

21. *United States* v. *Peace Information Center*, 97 F. Supp. 155 (D.D.C. 1951).

22. *Viereck* v. *United States*, 318 U.S. 236 (1943). *See Attorney General* v. *Irish Northern Aid Committee*, 346 F. Supp. 1384 (S.D.N.Y.), *affirmed* 465 F. 2d 1405 (2nd Cir.), *cert. denied*, 409 U.S. 1080 (1972). The Court held in this case that a U.S.-based organization that supports the objectives of a foreign political power, even one that is not a country's official government, like the Irish Republican Army, and that sends money to this power rather than receiving money from it, must nevertheless register as a foreign agent if it is controlled or directed by it in any way. Such a power, moreover, can be compelled to disclose the names of Americans who are members or contributors.

23. *Attorney General* v. *Irish Northern Aid Committee*, 530 F. Supp. 241 (S.D.N.Y. 1981), *affirmed*, 668 F. 2d 159 (2d Cir. 1982); *Attorney General* v. *The Irish People, Inc.*, 502 F. Supp. 63 (D.D.C. 1980), *reversed*, 684 F. 2d 928 (D.C. Cir. 1982), *certiorari denied*, 459 U.S. 1172 (1983). *The Irish People* Circuit Court stated that "it is clear that Congress intended to allow the Attorney General to be motivated in part by foreign policy, international political, and national security considerations [in enforcing FARA]. . . . A showing that the Attorney General acted in such a way is not a showing of improper motive at all." *Irish People*, 684 F. 2d at 934.

Judge Patricia Wald, in her concurrence, said that she could not agree that

FARA enforcement may permissibly be focused on one side (i.e., the side currently supported by the Administration) of foreign policy controversies that may be the subject of debate among Americans. . . . In this context . . . issues of constitutionally improper motivation surface disturbingly. . . . [S]ome unevenness was built into [FARA]. . . . But that unevenness may not permissibly be expanded through prosecutorial discretion to discredit views currently in disfavor while withholding the "spotlight of pitiless publicity" from views our government . . . prefer[s] be presented to the American public in a more palatable form.

684 F 2d at 956 (emphasis eliminated).

24. *Viereck* v. *United States*, 318 U.S. 236, 251 (1943) (Black, J., dissenting on other grounds).

25. *Attorney General* v. *The Irish People, Inc.*, 684 F. 2d at 934.

26. *Block* v. *Smith*, 583 F. Supp. 1288 (D.C. Cir. 1984); *Block* v. *Meese*, 793 F. 2d 1303 (D.C. Cir. 1986); *Keene* v. *Smith*, 569 F. Supp. 1513 (E.D. Cal. 1985).

When William French Smith resigned as attorney general, he was succeeded by Edwin Meese, whose name appears as the appellant when the case goes beyond the district court level. The other defendant was Joseph E. Clarkson, Chief of the Registration Unit of the Department of Justice.

27. The National Film Board of Canada's New York Office has been its registered agent since 1947, and in this capacity it periodically provides the Department of Justice with a list of the film titles it intends to distribute, *Plaintiffs' Memorandum of Points and Authorities in Support of their Motion for Summary Judgment and in Opposition to Defendants' Motion to Dismiss or, in the Alternative, for Summary Judgment*, at 4, *Block* v. *Smith*, 583 F. Supp. 1283 (D.C. Cir. 1984). (Hereinafter cited as *Block Plaintiffs' Memo*.)

28. Mary McGrory, a columnist with the *Washington Post*, said in reference to *Acid Rain: Requiem or Recovery*: "A more tactful, neutral, inoffensive presentation of a fearful problem that is being visited on one country (theirs) by another country (ours) cannot be imagined." Anne Dorfman, "Neutral Propaganda: Three Films 'Made in Canada' and the Foreign Agents Registration Act," 7 *Comm/ent Law Journal* 435, 436–37 n.13 (1985) (quoting McGrory, "Justice Department's Boos Make Film Subjects Boffo Box Office," *Washington Post*, March 1, 1983, p. A–3).

If You Love This Planet featured Dr. Helen Caldicott, an authority on the environmental and human effects of nuclear war. (The documentary includes a scene from a 1940s movie entitled *Jap Zero* in which Ronald Reagan is featured as an avid "Jap Hunting" aviator who asks, "How soon do I get a chance to knock one of them down?" McGrory, "Justice Department's Boos," p. A–3.)

29. *Keene* v. *Smith*, 569 F. Supp. at 1515. According to this survey, which a leading pollster designed and the Gallup Organization administered, the public had an "overwhelmingly negative" reaction to a politician who showed foreign films that had been classified as "political propaganda" by the Department of Justice. Brief for Appellee at 30. *See also Meese* v. *Keene*, 107 S. Ct. 1862, 1867–68 n.7.

30. *Block* v. *Meese*, 793 F. 2d 1303, 1308 (D.C. Cir. 1986).

31. *Defendants' Memorandum of Points and Authorities in Opposition to Plaintiffs' Motion for Summary Judgment and in Reply to Opposition to Motion to Dismiss or, in*

the Alternative, for Summary Judgment at 2, *Block* v. *Smith,* 583 F. Supp. 1288 (D.D.C. 1984). (Herein cited as *Block Defendants' Memo.*)

32. *See Block* v. *Smith,* 583 F. Supp. at 1291; *Block* v. *Meese,* 793 F. 2d at 1307 n.1; *Keene* v. *Smith,* 569 F. Supp. at 1519 and n.2.

According to Federal District Judge Raul Ramirez, "since the chief importance of the labeling requirement is obviously to inform viewers of the origin of the film, it is frankly surprising to learn that exhibitors of material covered by the Act may, with impunity, frustrate Congressional intent." 569 F. Supp. at 1519 n.2. "No reasonable reader of the statute and regulations could have imagined that the recipient of the material was free to remove the label." Ibid.

As Judge Ramirez points out, the government's claim is supported neither by the language of FARA nor by the statute's implementing legislation. *See* 22 U.S.C. §§611–18 (1982); 28 C.F.R. §§5.400–402 (1983).

33. 619 Supp. at 1128. On September 7, 1983, the United States District Court for the Eastern District of California had granted Keene's motion for a preliminary injunction, 569 F. Supp 1513, and on September 12, 1985, it granted his request for summary judgment and a permanent injunction. 619 F. Supp. 1111 (E.D. Cal. 1985).

34. Ibid at 1125.

35. *Block* v. *Meese,* 793 F. 2d 1303 (D.C. Cir. 1986), *certiorari denied* 106 S. Ct. 3335 (1986), after the Supreme Court had noted probable jurisdiction in *Meese* v. *Keene,* 106 S. Ct. 1632 (1986).

36. 793 F. 2d at 1310–14.

37. *Meese* v. *Keene,* 107 S. Ct. 1862 (1987).

38. Ibid. at 1867–68.

39. Ibid. at 1867. Justice William Rehnquist and Justices Byron White, Lewis Powell, and Sandra Day O'Connor joined Justice John Paul Stevens's opinion. Justice Harry Blackmun wrote an opinion dissenting in part, in which Justices William Brennan and Thurgood Marshall joined. Justice Antonin Scalia did not participate in the consideration or decision of the case.

40. Ibid. at 1873. In an effort to demonstrate that the act does not suppress speech, the Court cited several foreign films that had been released in the United States notwithstanding the fact that they had been labeled "political propaganda": *Berlin Means Business and More* (Berlin Economic Development Corporation); *Hong Kong Style* (Government of Hong Kong); *A Conversation with Golda Meir* (Consulate General of Israel); and *Ballad of a Soldier* (Sovexportfilm). Ibid. at 1872 n.17. Many of these films, the Court pointed out, were made by this country's allies and promoted policies presumably favored by the U.S. government. Ibid.

41. Ibid. at 1871.

42. Ibid. at 1869.

43. *Block Defendants' Memo,* p. 2.

44. 107 S. Ct. at 1870. The Court's willingness to examine the term "political propaganda" without reference to its common understanding represents a departure from its traditional practice of examining laws and administrative policies in terms of their *effects* as well as merely their language. *See, for example, F.E.C.* v. *Mass. Citizens for Life,* 107 S. Ct. 616, 626 (1986) (plurality opinion) ("the fact

that the statute's practical effect may be to discourage protected speech is sufficient to characterize [it] as an infringement on First Amendment activities").

45. 107 S. Ct. at 1870–71.

46. *Block Defendants' Memo*, p. 17n.

47. VIII *The Oxford English Dictionary*, ed. Sir James Augustus Henry Murray (Oxford: Clarendon, 1933), p. 1466.

48. John Boardman Whitton and Arthur Larson, *Propaganda, Towards Disarmament in a War of Words* (Dobbs Ferry, NY: Oceana Publications, 1963), p. 9.

49. *Block Plaintiffs' Memo*, pp. 27–28, 28n.

50. 107 S. Ct. at 1874.

51. 569 F. Supp. at 1522.

52. 793 F. 2d at 1310–14.

53. Ibid. at 1314.

54. Ibid. at 1313.

55. Ibid.

56. 107 S. Ct. at 1873 n.18.

57. Ibid. at 1870–71.

58. Ibid. at 1871–72.

59. *Viereck* v. *U.S.*, 318 U.S. at 251 (Black, J., dissenting on other grounds).

60. *See, for example, Collin* v. *Smith*, 578 F. 2d 1197 (7th Cir. 1978) (ordinances designed to prohibit Nazi demonstrations violate First Amendment), *cert. denied*, 439 U.S. 916 (1978); *Village of Skokie* v. *National Socialist Party of America*, 69 Ill. 2d 605, 373 N.E. 2d 21 (1978) (Nazis have right to demonstrate and display swastika).

61. *See Joint Anti-Fascist Refugee Committee* v. *McGrath*, 341 U.S. 123 (1951). The Court held that plaintiff organizations, which claimed that they had been arbitrarily classified as "Communists" by the U.S. attorney general, stated a claim for which relief could be granted. In concurring opinions, four justices indicated that they based their decisions in part on the public stigma that the official designation created. 341 U.S. at 139 (plurality opinion of Burton, J.); ibid. at 142 (Black, J., concurring); ibid at 160–61 (Frankfurter, J., concurring); ibid. at 175 (Douglas, J., concurring).

62. *See Thornhill* v. *Alabama*, 310 U.S. 88, 104–5 (1940) (when the government officially disparages other points of view it can "interfere with the development of that 'informed and educated public opinion' which is essential for national and social decision making").

63. 793 F. 2d at 1313.

64. Ibid. at 1313, 1314.

65. Legislation and administrative policy that restrict "fundamental rights," such as political expression, will ordinarily be sustained only if it furthers interests that are not only important, but also compelling. As the Supreme Court noted in a 1943 case:

> The right of a state to regulate, for example, a public utility may well include . . . power to impose all of the restrictions which a legislature may have a "rational basis" for adopting. But freedom of speech and of press, of assembly, and of worship may not be infringed on such slender grounds. They are susceptible of restriction only to prevent grave and immediate danger to interests which the state may lawfully protect.

West Virginia Board of Education v. *Barnette,* 319 U.S. 624, 639 (1943).

The Supreme Court has held, moreover, that even legislation that serves compelling governmental interests can be no broader than necessary to achieve these interests. *See, for example, N.A.A.C.P.* v. *Button,* 371 U.S. 415, 438 (1963): "Broad prophylactic rules in the area of free expression are suspect. Precision of regulation must be the touchstone in an area so closely touching our most precious freedoms." *See also Lamont* v. *Postmaster General,* 381 U.S. 301, 310 (1965) ("in the area of First Amendment freedoms, government has the duty to confine itself to the least intrusive regulations which are adequate for the purpose") (Brennan, J., concurring); *United States* v. *O'Brien,* 391 U.S. 367, 377 (1968) (government regulation of political speech is justified only "if it furthers an important or substantial governmental interest; if the governmental interest is unrelated to the suppression of free expression; and if the incidental restriction on alleged First Amendment freedoms is no greater than is essential to the furtherance of that interest").

66. "Leading Cases," 101 *Harvard Law Review,* 119, 218–19 (1987). This article provides an excellent discussion of the importance of "context" in determining the extent to which "government speech" is constitutionally permissible.

67. For a thorough and provocative discussion of the constitutional dimensions of "government speech," *see* Steven Shiffrin, "Government Speech," 27 *U.C.L.A. Law Review* 565 (1980).

Legal commentators and members of the judiciary agree that the government has an affirmative obligation to participate in public debate. Joseph Tussman maintains, for instance, that a polity's very survival depends on the government's ability to recruit new members, focus attention on its problems, provide a "fruitful life of communication," and "cultivate the knowledge and wisdom it needs." *Government and the Mind* (New York: Oxford University Press, 1977), p. 14. He also notes that a government must nurture the democratic character, since individuals do not spontaneously adopt the values necessary to sustain a liberal republic. Ibid., pp. 13–14.

See also Richard Delgado, "The Language of the Arms Race: Should the People Limit Government Speech?" 64 *Boston University Law Review* 961, 989 (1984): ("Much that government wishes to say is harmless or is necessary for effective government functioning. For example, government needs to educate, to promote industry and commerce, and to marshal support for its policies"); *P.A.M. News Corp.* v. *Butz,* 514 F. 2d 272, 277 (D.C. Cir. 1975) (By disseminating information the government "furthers a cornerstone of the First Amendment—the maximum distribution of information in the marketplace").

As Mark Yudof points out, however, "[t]he power to teach, inform, and lead is also the power to indoctrinate, distort judgment, and perpetuate the current regime," and technological advances, he continues, have vastly enhanced the government's ability to accomplish these negative objectives. *When Government Speaks: Politics, Law, and Government Expression in America* (Berkeley: University of California Press, 1983), pp. 10–14, 42. ["In a democratic polity," Yudof writes, "it's one thing to employ mass communication to *implement* decisions that in some loose sense represent the majority will; quite another to attempt to fashion a majority will through uncontrolled indoctrination activities." *When Government Speaks,* p. 15 (emphasis in original)].

At what point, then, does the government's participation in the intellectual arena become domination? At what point does it cease to educate and begin to indoctrinate? According to Steven Shiffrin, this point arises only when it has eliminated so many competing ideas that it has effectively monopolized the debate. "Government Speech," pp. 568–69.

Thomas Emerson observed that domination takes place not only when the government stifles other points of view, but also when its criticism "arouses hostility in the community against certain opinions and thereby brings private economic or social pressure to bear against those who espouse the unpopular position." *System of Freedom of Expression* (New York: Random House, 1970), pp. 699–700, *quoted in* Brief of the American Civil Liberties Union, et al., *Amici Curiae*, in support of Appellee at 20 n.14, *Meese* v. *Keene*, 107 S. Ct. 1862 (1987).

See also Yudof: "Government has an affirmative obligation to promote individual choice and autonomy by expanding the individual's knowledge . . . yet it should be constrained from programming the citizen to make preconceived choices." *When Government Speaks*, p. 15. "Preconceived choices," he explains, "are choices compelled by indoctrinated value systems and not choices that emerge as the result of considered judgments "arrived at by a process of evaluation of the efficacy of both the particular choice and the value systems which generate various decisions." Ibid.

State courts have at least implicitly addressed the problem of government domination in a number of cases in which public officials have attempted to use tax dollars to influence the outcome of issues before the electorate. They usually have held that expenditures for such purposes impede the democratic process. *See, for example, Citizens to Protect Public Funds* v. *Board of Education*, 13 N.J. 172, 98 A. 2d 673 (1953) (a school board had implied authority to use public funds to inform voters about a bond proposal but not to urge them to vote a particular way); *Stern* v. *Kramarsky*, 84 Misc. 2d 447, 375 N.Y.S. 2d 235 (1975) (no statutory language authorized a state commission to support a proposed equal rights amendment to the state constitution for which voter approval was required); *but see Miller* v. *California Commission on the Status of Women*, 151 Cal. App. 3d 693, 198 Cal. Rptr. 877 (1984). The court held in this case that the government is entitled to advocate a position on an issue not before the electorate "provided it does not drown out private communication." In determining at what point the government threatened to "drown out" other voices, the court continued, several variables should be considered, including the amount of resources it expended, and its method of communication. 151 Cal. App. 3d at 702, 198 Cal. Rptr. at 883.

For discussion see David Haberman, "Governmental Speech in the Democratic Process," 65 *Washington University Law Quarterly* 209, 212 (1987).

68. *For discussion see* Ava Marion Plakins, "Heat Not Light: The Foreign Agents Registration Act after *Meese* v. *Keene*," 11 *Fordham International Law Journal* 184 (Fall 1987).

69. In *Thomas* v. *Collins*, for instance, the Supreme Court struck down a Texas law that required anyone who addressed a union rally to obtain a state union organizer's card. Even though anyone who sought a card was automatically granted one, the Court held that only an imminent danger to the public interest

could justify even "minimal" restrictions on speech because "it is from petty tyrannies that large ones take root and grow." 323 U.S. 516, 543 (1945).

The Court struck down another law in 1963 that authorized a state commission to designate certain books sold to the public as "morally objectionable" because even these "informal sanctions" "may sufficiently inhibit the circulation of publications to warrant injunctive relief." *Bantum Books* v. *Sullivan*, 372 U.S. 58, 67 (1963).

See also Murdock v. *Pa.*, 319 U.S. 105 (1943) (a city ordinance that requires Jehovah's Witnesses to have a license if they distribute literature and solicit donations door-to-door violates the First Amendment); *Lovell* v. *City of Griffin*, 303 U.S. 444 (1938) (a city ordinance is unconstitutional on its face that requires anyone distributing literature to secure a license); *Minneapolis Star and Tribune* v. *Minnesota Commissioner of Revenue*, 460 U.S. 575 (1983) (taxes on newspapers violate the First Amendment right to freedom of the press); *F.E.C.* v. *Mass. Citizens for Life, Inc.*, 107 S. Ct. 616, 626 (1986) (plurality opinion) ("The fact that the statute's practical effect may be to discourage protected speech is sufficient to characterize [it] as an infringement of First Amendment activities"); *Miami Herald Publishing Co.* v. *Tornillo*, 418 U.S. 241, 257 (1974) (A Florida "right-of-reply" statute is unconstitutional because "political and electoral coverage would be blunted or reduced").

70. 381 U.S. 301 (1965).

71. 381 U.S. at 302–7. The Postal Service and Federal Employees Salary Act of 1962 provided in part:

> Mail matter, except sealed letters, which originates . . . in a foreign country and which is determined by the Secretary of the Treasury . . . to be "Communist political propaganda," shall be detained by the Postmaster General upon its arrival for delivery in the United States . . . and the addressee shall be notified that such matter has been received and will be delivered upon the addressee's request.

§305, 76 Stat. 840 (1962) (codified at 39 U.S.C. §4008 (b) (Supp. 4 1962).

72. 381 U.S. at 307.

73. 22 U.S.C. §614 (b) (1982).

74. Ibid. §614 (a).

75. Ibid. §616 (a).

76. United States Congress, Committee on the Judiciary, *Canadian Films and the Foreign Agents Registration Act*, Oversight Hearing Before the Subcommittee on Civil and Constitutional Rights of the Committee on the Judiciary, 98th Cong., 1st Sess., March 18, 1983 (hereinafter cited as *Subcommittee on Constitutional Rights Hearing*).

77. Ibid., p. 46.

78. Ibid., p. 49.

79. Ibid.

80. Ibid., p. 48.

81. Ibid., p. 49, *quoting* Catherine A. Leroy, counsel for the subcommittee.

82. Ibid., p. 55.

83. In 1950 the Supreme Court nullified a Los Angeles ordinance that prohibited the dissemination of any handbill that failed to disclose the names and addresses of everyone who produced and distributed the bills. Justice Hugo

Black, who wrote the majority opinion in this case, explained why anonymity is often crucial:

Anonymous pamphlets, leaflets, brochures and even books have played an important role in the progress of mankind. Persecuted groups and sects from time to time throughout history have been able to criticize oppressive practices and laws either anonymously or not at all. The obnoxious press licensing law in England, which was also enforced on the Colonies, was due in part to the knowledge that exposure of the names of printers, writers and distributors would lessen the circulation of literature critical of the government. . . . Before the Revolutionary War colonial patriots frequently had to conceal their authorship of distribution of literature that easily could have brought down on them prosecutions by English-controlled courts. Along about that time the Letters of Junius were written and the identity of their author is unknown to this day. Even the Federalist Papers, written in favor of the adoption of the Constitution, were published under fictitious names. It is plain that anonymity has sometimes been assumed for the most constructive purposes.

Talley v. *California*, 362 U.S. 60, 64–65 (1960). (This is the same Justice Black who earlier had praised FARA's disclosure requirements because they helped "hearers and readers . . . not be deceived by the belief that the information comes from a disinterested source." *Viereck* v. *United States*, 318 U.S. at 251.)

Many organizations that want to show films designated as "political propaganda" merit anonymity because, like the "colonial patriots" to whom Justice Black refers, without it they also fear persecution. Groups affiliated with the Nuclear Freeze Movement, for instance, had reason to fear government sanctions because, as California Representative Don Edwards explained during the subcommittee hearing, "the Administration has been very political [sic] of [this Movement]. The President has said there were KGB connections with the Movement and the FBI jumped in and said, Yes, the President is correct. . . . So you can understand the political implications of it." *Subcommittee on Constitutional Rights Hearing*, p. 46.

The Supreme Court has tolerated disclosure laws only when the resulting benefit to the public is substantial. *See, for example*, *Buckley* v. *Valeo*, 424 U.S. 1 (1976) (campaign finance laws requiring the public disclosure of the names of individuals contributing to political campaigns are legitimate because they are necessary to protect the integrity of the election process); *United States* v. *Harriss*, 347 U.S. 612 (1954) (the Federal Regulation of Lobbying Act's disclosure requirements are permissible because they are necessary to prevent the corruption of the legislative process).

84. FARA defines crucial terms like "foreign agent," "foreign principal," and "political propaganda" in language that is both exceedingly broad and vague, and according to the American Civil Liberties Union this is yet another reason why the act offends the First Amendment. *Subcommittee on Constitutional Rights Hearing*, p. 63.

FARA defines a "foreign agent," for instance, as anyone engaging in political activities in the United States who acts "directly or indirectly" at the request of, or "in the interests of," a foreign principal. Susan Shaffer, testifying on behalf of the American Civil Liberties Union at the 1983 subcommittee hearing, pointed out that the definition was so vague that it could embrace even private individuals who receive foreign correspondence: "Thus a person who, upon receipt of a letter from a friend or relative who is a United States citizen domiciled in

Israel, speaks to neighbors about conditions in Israel, could be deemed an agent of a foreign principal." Ibid., p. 63.

An environmental group could also be considered a foreign agent, Shaffer continued, if it wishes to show without charge the NFBC's acid rain films, regardless of whether it had any concerns for Canadian interests. Ibid. "Indeed," she concluded, "any domestic speaker intending to persuade others to a particular point of view on a political issue who can be shown to have been influenced in his views by a foreign speaker or information source, is eligible to the regulatory sweep of FARA." Ibid.

The plaintiffs in *Block* v. *Meese* made the same point: "An agent is at sea in determining whether his speech 'influenced' public opinion in the United States regarding 'the public interests' of his principal or whether the DOJ might think so." 793 F. 2d at 1314, *citing* Brief for Appellant at 56.

Officials at the DOJ are no less "at sea." In a 1963 case Justice Brennan observed that a vague and overbroad statute is objectionable because it is capable of "sweeping and improper application" [*N.A.A.C.P.* v. *Buttons*, 371 U.S. 415, 433 (1963)], and these officials must administer just such a statute. They must determine, for instance, whether a U.S. citizen is acting "at the request of" or "in the interests of" a foreign principal, and they must somehow be able to distinguish between situations in which Americans, acting according to their own political convictions, incidentally benefit foreign interests, and situations in which they are acting primarily at the behest of these interests. Moreover, agents making what California Congressman Don Edwards calls these "Godlike determinations" (*Subcommittee on Constitutional Rights Hearing*, p. 47) operate unchecked by judicial review, specific statutory standards, formal agency guidelines, or even an elementary "how to" manual. Ibid.

Federal courts have never faulted FARA for its loose terminology, which is surprising because they ordinarily invalidate any vague or overbroad statute that impinges on fundamental rights. The judiciary traditionally has considered a law impermissibly vague if "men of common intelligence must guess at its meaning," [Hynes v. *Mayor of Oradell*, 425 U.S. 610, 620 (1976), *quoting Connally* v. *General Contractors Co.*, 269 U.S. 385, 391 (1926)], and it has usually invalidated criminal statutes, moreover, if they lack sufficient objective criteria to prevent those charged with their enforcement from engaging in "standardless sweeps . . . to pursue their personal predilections." *Kolander* v. *Lawson*, 461 U.S. 352, 353–54 (1983).

Courts consider a law impermissibly broad, on the other hand, if it penalizes activity that is constitutionally protected in addition to activity which authorities may properly curtail or prevent. *See Broadrick* v. *Oklahoma*, 413 U.S. 601 (1973).

85. *Meese* v. *Keene*, 107 S. Ct. at 1878. Deputy Attorney General Edward C. Schmults informed a House subcommittee in 1982 that the DOJ was prepared to replace "political propaganda" with "a more neutral term" like "political advocacy" or "information." Thus, even the agency entrusted with FARA's enforcement believes no compelling interest is served by requiring certain material to be designated as "political propaganda." Letter from Schmults to Robert W. Kastenmeier, chairman, Subcommittee on Courts, Civil Liberties, and the Administration of Justice, of the House Committee on the Judiciary, August 8,

1983. Appellee's Motion to Affirm, *Meese* v. *Keene*, 107 S. Ct. 1862 (1987) at Appendix A.

86. For several years a coalition of public interest groups, coordinated by the American Civil Liberties Union and the New York City–based Fund for Free Expression, has been urging Congress to reform FARA. Although members of the coalition want those sections of the act retained that relate to the lobbying of Congress and government agencies by representatives of foreign interests, they have been urging legislators to eliminate those other provisions that require certain material to be labeled "political propaganda" and that impose intrusive disclosure requirements. *See* Leslie Harris, "Bills Introduced to Amend Requirements of the Foreign Agents Registration Act," 12 *First Principles* (July-August 1987), p. 7.

The coalition found a good ally in Representative Robert Kastenmeier, chairman of the Subcommittee on Courts, Civil Liberties and the Administration of Justice, who introduced legislation both in 1983 and 1985 to effect the changes it recommended. *See* H.R. 1969, 98th Cong., 1st Sess. (1983); H.R. 3957, 99th Cong., 1st Sess. (1985).

In the last few years the coalition has worked in particular with Representatives Barney Frank and Howard Berman in the House, and Paul Simon (Ill.) in the Senate, who have also cosponsored legislation to substitute "advocacy material" for "political propaganda," and to eliminate most of FARA's reporting requirements. H.R. 3827, 99th Cong., 1st Sess. (1985); S. 1268, 100th Cong., 1st Sess. (1987); H.R. 1967, 100th Cong., 1st Sess. (1987).

87. 107 S. Ct. at 1870–71.

88. That *Meese* v. *Keene* was written by Justice Stevens is perplexing since only one year earlier he had submitted a dissenting opinion in which he had urged his colleagues to invalidate a Puerto Rican law on the ground that it impermissibly discriminated between domestic and foreign-based media. *Posades de Puerto Rico Associates* v. *Tourism Co. of Puerto Rico*, 106 S. Ct. 2968, 2972 n.9 (1986).

Franklyn Haiman questions the logic as well as the propriety of an act that requires only those who represent foreign interests to disclose their identities:

> Why [does] the advocacy of legitimate foreign interests, be they economic or political, need to have its sponsorship identified when it comes from persons taking their direction from a foreign power and not when it comes from others who spontaneously promote the very same goals. If the rationale is that foreign governments are advantaged competitors in the market-place of ideas because of the financial resources they have at their disposal, then disclosure should not be required of those who are *unpaid* agents of foreign interests and it *should* be required of the many wealthy proponents of domestic causes. If the rationale is that the First Amendment doesn't apply to foreign participation in American public discourse, then why have we not prohibited it altogether rather than merely requiring its disclosure?
>
> The answer to this last question, I presume, is that we have confidence in the ability of our citizens to evaluate the communication to which they may be exposed by foreign powers, just as they must pass judgment on the merits of domestic persuasion. If that is so, it seems a contradictory lack of trust to insist upon the imposition of a special label which tells them to beware of advocacy which is inspired from abroad.

Speech and Law in a Free Society (Chicago: University of Chicago Press, 1981), pp. 366–67 (emphasis in original). *See also* Stephen R. Barnett, "United States Regulations of Transborder Speech," 9 *Comm/ent* 635, 664–66 (Summer 1987).

89. 107 S. Ct. at 1871.

90. *Viereck* v. *United States,* 318 U.S. at 251 (Black, J., dissenting on other grounds), *quoted* at 107 S. Ct. at 1871 n.15.

91. *Subcommittee on Constitutional Rights Hearing,* pp. 51, 75.

92. Information about the government's response to the film *Missing* was provided by Susan Shaffer, staff counsel, American Civil Liberties Union, *Subcommittee on Constitutional Rights Hearing,* p. 75.

93. In *Meese* v. *Keene* the majority accused Judge Ramirez of "paternalistic behavior" because he enjoined the DOJ from designating certain material as "political propaganda." 107 U.S. at 1871–72. It is the government itself that displays "paternalism," however, by insisting on the label in the first place. Judge Patricia Wald made this point in *Attorney General* v. *Irish People,* a case in which the Washington, D.C., Circuit Court upheld FARA's registration requirements: "I resist the notion that the power of persuasion may be used selectively to manage the information put before the American people in debates over foreign policy." 684 F. 2d 928, 956 (concurring opinion).

When the government becomes a "big brother," attempting in heavy-handed ways to mold public perception, it becomes what Mark Yudof calls a "preceptor state." *When Government Speaks,* p. 51. The framers wrote the First Amendment, however, to prevent the emergence of just such a state. As Justice Robert Jackson noted, "the very purpose of the First Amendment is to foreclose public authority from assuming a guardianship of the public mind through regulating the press, speech, and religion. In this field everyone must be his own watchman for truth, because the forefathers did not trust any government to separate the true from the false for us." *Thomas* v. *Collins,* 323 U.S. 516, 545 (1945) (concurring opinion).

See also West Virginia Board of Education v. *Barnette,* 319 U.S. 624, 642 (1943) ("If there is any fixed star in our constitutional constellation, it is that no official, high or petty, can prescribe what shall be orthodox in politics, nationalism, religion, or other matters of opinion").

4

Censored Screens: Why Some Films Are Not Certified for Export

> [The First Amendment] presupposes that right conclusions are more likely to be gathered out of a multitude of tongues, than through any kind of authoritative selecting. To many this is, and always will be, folly; but we have staked upon it our all.
>
> Judge Learned Hand

Imported films may be labeled political propaganda and their distributors may be forced to shoulder burdensome administrative requirements.[1] Domestic productions destined for export often fare no better: officials at the United States Information Agency (USIA), implementing the so-called Beirut Agreement, have frequently denied these films the trade concessions they need to compete in the export market.

In order to encourage "the free flow of ideas" and promote "the mutual understanding of people," the United States and 20 other countries adopted measures to facilitate the international dissemination of audiovisual materials.[2] These measures were codified in the Beirut Agreement, which was signed on September 13, 1949, at the third meeting of UNESCO (United Nations Educational, Scientific, and Cultural Organization) held in Beirut, Lebanon.[3] The agreement entered into force in 1954, although the U.S. Senate did not ratify it until 1960,[4] and it did not become part of domestic law until Congress passed, and President Lyndon B. Johnson signed, a resolution in 1966 giving it effect.[5]

The Beirut Agreement is designed to promote the international circulation of films, recordings, slides, and other audiovisual material that are both educational in nature and, in contrast to blockbuster motion pictures or best-selling books, unlikely to enjoy any commercial success. Under the terms of the agreement, material deemed eligible by both sending and receiving countries is accordingly granted an exemption from import duties, taxes, and licensing requirements. Individuals seeking this privileged treatment for audiovisual materials must apply for a certificate of "educational, scientific or cultural character" from an agency designated by the exporting country. The certificate is then submitted to the receiving country, which gives it "due consideration," but ultimately decides for itself whether to grant concessions.[6] Without these certificates, anyone distributing educational or documentary film faces import and licensing fees that are frequently prohibitive.[7]

In determining whether to certify a film or other material, agencies are guided by criteria set forth in the Beirut Agreement. Article One, for instance, specifies that films

> shall be deemed of an educational, scientific or cultural character when their primary purpose or effect is to instruct or inform through the development of a subject or aspect of a subject or when their content is such as to maintain, increase, or diffuse knowledge, and augment international understanding and good will.[8]

The agreement also requires films to be "representative, authentic, and accurate."[9]

Article Five of the agreement, significantly, grants receiving states the right "to censor material in accordance with their own laws" or as they deem necessary for "reasons of public security or order."[10] This concession, coupled with the provision granting receiving states final authority to decide for themselves which material to accommodate, was welcomed by many of the U.S. legislators who ultimately supported the agreement.[11] As Arkansas Congressman Wilbur Mills pointed out at the time, the Beirut Agreement "does not require us to bring in a single film from Yugoslavia that is Communistic in nature."[12]

The USIA, which provides information about the United States to people throughout the world (chiefly through the Voice of America), was assigned the additional task of implementing the Beirut Agreement. It has established extensive procedures for determining whether to "authenticate" material certified by other countries, and whether, in turn, to "certify" domestic material and thereby qualify it for duty-free status.[13]

In order to obtain certification in the United States, those holding "basic rights" to a film must provide the USIA with both a copy of the film and an application form in which its contents are summarized.[14] After reviewing this application USIA's chief attestation officer and his staff usually consult with a group of advisers who comprise the Interdepartmental Committee on Visual and Auditory Materials for Distribution Abroad.[15] Among those sitting on this formidably titled committee are representatives of the executive departments headed by cabinet secretaries, the postal service, the Congressional Budget Office, the National Aeronautic and Space Administration, and the Library of Congress. In addition, USIA officers consult other experts, often from the private sector, before determining whether a given film merits certification.[16]

Congress hoped that the Beirut Agreement would stimulate the international circulation of U.S. documentaries, and under USIA's tutelage it has done just that: The documentary film industry has grown into a billion-dollar-a-year enterprise, and the roughly 5,000 U.S. productions that receive Certificates of International Educational Character from the USIA each year represent more films than are exported by all other countries combined.[17]

Despite its successful record, however, the USIA is nevertheless criticized by filmmakers and civil libertarians because while it rejects only some 25 to 30 productions a year, it often does so on the basis of regulations that are unnecessary, highly restrictive, or ideologically biased.[18] Of the 72 nations that are currently parties to the Beirut Agreement, only the United States and Canada have found it necessary to supplement its criteria.[19] The supplemental regulations adopted by the USIA, moreover, were contemplated neither by Congress when it gave domestic effect to the Beirut Agreement, nor by President Johnson when he empowered the agency to administer its certification process.[20]

By virtue of its self-imposed regulations, the USIA refuses to certify films that are intended to "amuse or entertain,"[21] or that deal with current events, such as newsreels or newscasts.[22] It will not certify materials "which by special pleading" attempt generally "to influence opinion, conviction or policy,"[23] that "espouse a cause,"[24] or, conversely, that discredit "economic, religious, or political views or practices."[25] USIA rejects anything that is not "balanced and truthful," that may "lend itself to misinterpretation or misrepresentation of the United States or other countries, their people or institutions," or that is "likely to be misunderstood or misinterpreted by foreign audiences lacking adequate American points of reference."[26]

John Mendenhall, the chief attestation officer of the United States, defends these regulations on the grounds that they serve to eliminate controversial films that other countries might reject.[27] These regulations, however, distort the certification process, which was intended to provide a means by which participating countries could attest to the educational, noncommercial nature of a film, not a means by which they could pass judgment on its content. Armed with its many regulations, however, the USIA does, in fact, pass judgment, refusing to validate not only categories of films that are clearly not "educational" within the Beirut Agreement's definition of the term—those involving promotional advertising or heavy-handed religious proselytizing, for instance—but also that deal with politically sensitive issues in ways the agency finds objectionable.[28]

In 1979 the USIA refused to certify *The Killing Ground*, a nationally syndicated ABC News documentary focusing on the problem of toxic waste disposal. Having received two Emmys and a bevy of international awards,[29] *The Killing Ground* is considered a classic by social historians because it brought national attention for the first time to a festering environmental crisis.[30] The USIA denied *The Killing Ground* a certificate, however, after consulting experts at the Environmental Protection Agency, who claimed in their evaluation report that the documentary was "mainly of historical interest" because the United States has "made great progress in managing hazardous waste."[31] Further, "the tone of [the film] would mislead a foreign audience into believing that the American public needed arousing to the dangers of hazardous wastes" when "this is no longer the case."[32]

Soldier Girls, a vérité documentary that follows a platoon of female army recruits through basic training, won first prize at the United States Film Festival, a British Academy Award, and the Prix Italia.[33] *Soldier Girls*, however, was denied certification because it contained sections that "may lend themselves to be misunderstood or misinterpreted," according to USIA officials.[34] They had been influenced, in turn, by army consultants who noted in their evaluation that the documentary "focuses on aberrations in the basic training process and was obviously filmed and edited more for artistic and dramatic effect than to present an accurate, balanced representation of basic training."[35] (The army subsequently forbade its overseas libraries to distribute the film.)

The USIA also denied certification to *In Our Own Backyard*, a 1981 documentary dealing with health hazards created by uranium mining and milling operations. In this case the agency has sought out officials at the Department of Energy, who claimed the film was generally "emotional rather than technical," its primary purpose or effect being "less to instruct or inform in an educational sense than to present a special point of view."[36] *Save the Planet*, which focused on the dangers of nuclear weapons, was denied a certificate, also on the Department of Energy's recommendation, because it "resurrected the traditional U.S. guilt of the bombings of Hiroshima and Nagasaki."[37]

A fifth film denied certification, *The Last Resort*, recounts a campaign launched by area citizens against a nuclear plant at Seabrook, New Hampshire. The Review Board, affirming USIA's verdict, explained that while *The Last Resort* was balanced, it might lead foreign audiences to conclude "that our system of laws was ineffective or unfair or that civil disobedience is not only a 'last resort,' but may well be 'the only resort.' "[38] Similarly, *Resurgence: The Movement for Equality v. the Ku Klux Klan* was penalized because it "could too easily be construed as typical of the United States as a whole,"[39] and *Campaign '80* was denied tax concessions because it "could lead to misunderstanding of the United States and [its] political institutions by foreign audiences."[40]

Not all documentaries that explore contentious issues are denied certification, however. *The Secret Agent*, which discusses the effect of Agent Orange, a defoliant used by the United States during the Vietnam War, was deemed by the Review Board to present "a difficult, even emotional, subject in a responsible and balanced manner." Furthermore, the film showed the American system "at its best."[41] *To Catch a Cloud: A Thoughtful Look at Acid Rain*, produced by the Edison Electrical Institute, also received favorable treatment, as did *Radiation . . . Naturally*, which takes the position that uranium and atomic energy are fundamentally safe.[42]

The producers of *In Our Own Backyard*, *Save the Planet*, and five other films denied certification by the USIA eventually sought redress in court.[43] They received full support from Federal District Court Judge A. Wallace Tashima, who struck down three of the agency's "interpretive regulations" on the grounds that they violated either the First Amendment or the due process clause of the Fifth Amendment and ordered the agency to draft new criteria with which to reconsider the plaintiffs' films.[44] Judge Tashima emphasized the important role that free speech plays in a democratic society, and he concluded his opinion by vesting the First Amendment with unprecedented reach: "In the absence of some overriding interest such as national security," he said, "the First Amendment protects communication with foreign audiences to the same extent as communication within our Border."[45]

This district court ruling was unanimously affirmed by the United States Court of Appeals for the Ninth Circuit on May 17, 1988.[46] Judge Cecil Poole, who wrote the opinion in this case, *Bullfrog Films* v. *Wick*, first examined the three USIA regulations under challenge: the one requiring eligible films to be "balanced and truthful"; the one disqualifying films that either criticize or espouse any political, religious, or economic views; and the one denying certification to any film which, "by special pleading," seeks to influence opinion or policy. These regulations, Judge Poole said, "are so ambiguous that they provide U.S.I.A. officials with a virtual license to engage in censorship."[47] They restrict the free exchange of ideas, which is central to the educational process, and by penalizing films that express opinions on controversial public issues, they curtail "public debate in the area most privileged by the First Amendment."[48]

The government conceded that the regulations might, in fact, discourage the expression of opinion, but defended them on the ground that they were applied evenhandedly to any film that expressed a point of view, regardless of its partisan orientation. The Circuit Court was not convinced, noting, for instance, that the agency had denied certification to *In Our Own Backyard* because it expressed a "point of view" on the subject of nuclear power, while it granted certification to *Radiation . . . Naturally*, which also presented a point of view, albeit a very different one. "Arguably," said Judge Poole, "*In Our Own Backyard* was denied certification because its viewpoint was one with which the U.S.I.A. and the Department of Energy could not agree."[49] Moreover, by refusing to certify any films that "espouse a cause," "attack a particular persuasion," or "lend [themselves] to misinterpretation or misrepresentation of the United States or other countries[,] . . . the regulations seem to disapprove materials that criticize and approve those that accept the prevailing state of affairs on a given topic."[50]

The challenged regulations also violate the due process clause of the Fifth Amendment because they are not fundamentally fair—that is, comprehensible to the average person, and specific enough to discourage biased application.[51] On the contrary, the Ninth Circuit concluded, they are written in "mystifying language," and applied in an "arbitrary and discriminatory manner."[52] By what standard, the court asked, "does the U.S.I.A. determine whether material lends itself to misinterpretation or misrepresentation of the United States or other countries, their people or institutions?" How does it determine whether material ". . . augment[s] international understanding or good will," or whether it is "representative," "authentic," and "accurate"?[53]

USIA's regulations, then, were judged invalid for several reasons: They are ambiguous, couched in language that is vague and subjective, and "to the extent that they are susceptible to interpretation at all," the circuit court concluded, "they appear to preclude virtually anything that someone would consider either educational or a documentary."[54]

Even before the Ninth Circuit had invalidated the old regulations, however, the USIA had new ones in place. They went into effect in December 1987, and provided that no film dealing with a controversial topic would be certified unless it discussed this topic in a "primarily factual manner" and covered "a wide range of opinions."[55] Certain politically sensitive films, moreover, would hereafter be characterized as propaganda.[56] Although USIA officials would still certify these films, independent producers pointed out that most receiving states would presumably balk at the prospect of granting trade privileges to productions officially categorized as propaganda.[57]

The original plaintiffs in *Bullfrog* again went to court, this time challenging these new regulations, under which one of their films had been classified as propaganda and four others denied certification altogether.[58] They claimed the revamped regulations were as constitutionally offensive as their antecedents. USIA's attorneys countered with an argument first propounded a year earlier by Judge Antonin Scalia in *Block* v. *Meese*:[59] The government is as entitled as the plaintiffs to exercise "its freedom of speech in a manner authorized by the interim agreements," and accordingly to withhold its endorsement from any film it considers misguided or unbalanced.[60]

Judge Tashima again sided with the filmmakers.[61] On May 13, 1988, he enjoined the USIA from enforcing its new regulations, and he ordered it to certify the contested films immediately and to draft yet a third set of regulations that would not discriminate on the basis of content.[62] Whether his ruling will be sustained on appeal is questionable, however, because it is arguably inconsistent with the Supreme Court's holding in *Meese* v. *Keene*.[63] In that 1987 case the Court held that under the Foreign Agents Registration Act, the Department of Justice could legitimately classify certain films as political propaganda as long as the statutory definition of this term was nonpejorative.

On appeal, the High Court might also be more sympathetic than either the district or the circuit courts were to another argument raised by the government and paraphrased by the Ninth Circuit in *Bullfrog Films*:

> When United States citizens direct their speech to foreign audiences, the government may regulate such speech on the basis of content; further[,] . . . the traditional standard for determining if a law is unconstitutionally vague should be relaxed when foreign audiences are involved, since the government must be permitted to fashion foreign-affairs related regulations in a broad manner.[64]

This same reasoning was advanced by the solicitor general in *Haig* v. *Agee*[65] when he implored the Supreme Court to remember that "the freedom of speech that we enjoy domestically may be different from that we can exercise in [the context of foreign affairs]."[66] In *Agee*, as in many other cases, the Court has ratified the solicitor general's thesis, assigning the government's asserted foreign policy interests considerably more weight than the First Amendment rights of the individual.

As a consequence, the Supreme Court is likely to disagree strenuously with what the Ninth Circuit termed Judge Tashima's "well-reasoned conclusions."[67] The judge had declared in *Bullfrog Films* v. *Wick* that "in the absence of some overriding governmental interest such as national security, the First Amendment protects communication with foreign audiences to the same extent as communication within our Border."[68] He pointed out, for instance, that the government could not constitutionally prohibit an American political science professor from expressing his or her opinions at an international symposium in Paris on the theory that foreign members of the audience are not participants in this country's political process.[69] Judge Tashima conceded that under some circumstances the government could restrict speech addressed to foreigners, but he emphasized that these circumstances must be narrowly conceived:

> It is clear that there is no "sliding scale" of First Amendment protection under which the degree of scrutiny fluctuates in accordance with the degree to which the regulation touches on foreign affairs. Rather, the only permissible non-neutral inquiry into the content of speech is whether the statements adversely affect foreign policy interests to such a degree that the speech is completely unprotected. As *Haig* v. *Agee* itself indicates, the clearest example of the kind of compelling government interest that would lead to such a result is where the speech poses a clear and direct threat to national security.[70]

Judge Tashima thus extended the First Amendment well beyond its conventional scope because the Supreme Court has traditionally held that the rights it guarantees are generally enforceable only within territory governed by United States law.[71] The government maintained in *Bullfrog Films* that "the world is not a 'First Amendment Forum,' " and the Court has invariably concurred with this thesis.[72] Judge Tashima and the Ninth Circuit apparently would not agree; at the least they might counter that in today's interdependent world, such a statement is no longer axiomatic.

Conclusion

The film *From the Ashes: Nicaragua Today* was denied certification under USIA's original regulations after reviewers concluded that it was "non-educational" because it suggested that "in the U.S.-Nicaraguan relationship since 1979 the United States has been the aggressor."[73] In 1987 USIA adopted new regulations, under which this same film became the first domestic production to be officially labeled propaganda. However, this label was not to be its sole distinction: *From the Ashes,* produced in 1981 and originally shown on public television, was also singled out for a public thrashing by William H. Bennett, then chairman of the National Endowment for the Humanities. Bennett, who excoriated the film for its "unabashed socialist-realism propaganda," was particularly incensed that it had received some government financing.[74]

Although the abuse it sustained was exceptional, this treatment of *From the Ashes* nevertheless serves to illustrate the difficulties that can confront anyone in the United States who either imports or exports independent documentaries. Ironically, by disquieting and even infuriating its audience, *From the Ashes* also fulfills the very function that such documentaries are intended to serve. Erik Barnaouw, a distinguished broadcast historian, explained this function:

[an independent documentary] . . . is not intent upon reassuring people. The little child who surprised and horrified everyone by saying "the emperor has no clothes on"—that little child grew up to be a documentarist. She or he is still going around noticing things, puzzling about them and getting others to notice.[75]

Because the independent documentary explores unpopular or controversial topics, Barnaouw concluded, it has a definite social role: "Clearly, it operates at the cutting edge. It is the very essence of participatory democracy."[76]

Good documentaries, then, can challenge a society and even contribute to its rejuvenation, and it is unfortunate that public officials in the United States have collectively discouraged their production. John O'Connor, a film critic for the *New York Times*, observed that "the Reagan Administration hasn't been very hospitable to the independent documentary, especially those with political ramifications," but with equal justification he could also have indicted preceding administrations and members of Congress.[77]

It was Congress, after all, that passed and now refuses to amend the Foreign Agents Registration Act, one provision of which authorizes the Department of Justice to designate as "political propaganda" any foreign film that is intended to "influence a recipient" on any issue "involving United States policies."[78] Congress, commendably, did pass a resolution in 1966 giving domestic effect to the Beirut Agreement, but since then it has watched in silence while the USIA has systematically subverted the spirit of this agreement by denying indispensable trade concessions to any documentary intended for export that attempts, essentially, to influence opinion. What this means is that any film capable of surviving economically either as an import or an export must eschew the very qualities that, according to Erik Barnaouw, characterize independent documentaries at their best: It must neither tackle controversial issues nor offend established powers, and, above all, it must focus on what is right rather than what is wrong with the United States.

Notes

1. The Foreign Agents Registration Act, 22 U.S.C. §611–21 (1982 and Supp. 11 1982); *for discussion see* Chapter 3.

2. Agreement, preamble, 17 U.S.T. 1578, 1580; *see also* UNESCO Preparatory Commission Report, Chapter 111, *Mass Communication*, UNESCO §c/2, p. 6, *UNESCO Documents* 1945–1946.

3. Agreement for Facilitating the International Circulation of Visual and Au-

ditory Materials of an Educational, Scientific, and Cultural Character, *opened for signature* July 15, 1949, 17 U.S.T. 1578, T.I.A.S. No. 6116, 197 U.N.T.S. 3 (*entered into force for the United States* Jan. 12, 1967).

4. 106 *Congressional Record*, 11, 192 (1960).

5. H.R.J. Res. 688, 89th Cong., 2d Sess., 112 *Congressional Record*, 22, 218 (1966).

6. Beirut Agreement, art. 4, 17 U.S.T., pp. 1582–84.

7. Some import duties on documentary films run as high as $50,000 per print, often equal to the cost of the film itself. Nancy S. Robinson, "Silenced Screens: The Role of the United States Information Agency in Denying Export Certificates to American Films," 17 *New York University Journal of International Law and Politics* 77–78 (1978).

8. Beirut Agreement, art. 4, §2 and art. 1.

9. Ibid., §1 (b).

10. Ibid., art. 5.

11. Ibid., art. 4.

12. Sharon Esakoff, "USIA Censorship of Educational Films for Distribution Abroad," 3 *Cardozo Arts and Entertainment Law Journal* 403, 408 (1984).

13. Executive Order No. 11, 311, 22 C.F.R. §636 (1984), *reprinted in* 19 U.S.C. 2051 (1980); *for discussion see* Robinson, "Silenced Screens," p. 77.

14. 22 C.F.R. §502.3 (a), (g)(1), (3).

15. Ibid., §502.4 (a).

16. Comments of John Mendenhall, *cited in* Joel Brinkley, "In Focus: The U.S. Movie Reviewer," *The New York Times*, March 19, 1984, p. B–8 (hereinafter cited as comments of John Mendenhall).

Decisions made by the USIA officers are reviewed by the chief attestation officer, whose negative decision may, in turn, be appealed to a Review Board, and ultimately to the Director of the USIA.

17. Howard Rosenberg, "For Our Eyes Only," *American Film* (July-August 1983), p. 40.

18. Comments of John Mendenhall, p. B–8.

19. Bill McAllister, "U.S.I.A. Labels U.S. Film 'Propaganda,' " *The Washington Post*, Jan. 17, 1988, p. A–23.

20. *See* H.R.J. Res. 688, 89th Cong., 2d Sess., 112 *Congressional Record* 22, 218–19 (1966).

21. 22 C.R.F. §502.6 (b)(1) (1984).

22. Ibid. (b)(2).

23. Ibid. (b)(3) (1984).

24. Ibid.

25. Ibid. (b)(5).

26. Ibid.

27. Comments of John Mendenhall.

28. 22 C.F.R. §502.6 (b)(4).

29. Floyd Abrams, "The New Effort to Control Information," *The New York Times*, Sept. 25, 1983, Section 6, p. 24 (Magazine).

30. Rosenberg, "For Our Eyes Only," p. 43.

31. Letter from John Mendenhall to American Broadcasting Co., Inc. (Dec. 13, 1982), *cited in* Esakoff, "U.S.I.A. Censorship," p. 411 n.73.

32. Internal memorandum, Reporters Committee for Freedom of the Press, based on interview with USIA attestation assistant Sally Lawrence (August 9, 1983), *cited in* Esakoff, "U.S.I.A. Censorship," p. 412, n.76. (Hereinafter cited as Reporters Committee Memo).

Ironically, soon after the Environmental Protection Agency had termed the film "dated," a congressional investigation of the agency's own toxic waste program revealed that it had allowed chemical companies to review and selectively "edit" its official reports. Stuart Taylor, "EPA Inquiries Center on Four Issues," *The New York Times*, March 13, 1983, p. A-36.

33. Burt Neuborne and Steven R. Shapiro, "The Nylon Curtain: America's National Border and the Free Flow of Ideas," 26 *William and Mary Law Review* 719, 742 (1984–1985).

34. Rosenberg, "For Our Eyes Only," p. 42.

35. Reporters Committee Memo, *cited in* Esakoff, "U.S.I.A. Censorship," p. 412.

36. Rosenberg, "For Our Eyes Only," p. 40.

37. David Cole, "Letter to the Editor," *The New York Times*, Aug. 21, 1988, p. H-9.

38. Letter from Review Board to Green Mountain Post Films (March 29, 1984), *cited in* Esakoff, "U.S.I.A. Censorship," p. 413. The director of the USIA overturned this decision on July 12, 1984. Ibid.

39. Neuborne and Shapiro, "Nylon Curtain," p. 742.

40. Ibid.

41. Letter from Review Board to Green Mountain Post Films (March 29, 1984), *cited in* Esakoff, "U.S.I.A. Censorship," p. 413.

42. The USIA also certified *The Family: God's Pattern for Living*, produced by the Moody Institute of Science, which calls for the return of traditional moral values. *See* "Fade-Out: Censor," 246 *The Nation* (June 11, 1988), p. 812.

43. The other films were briefly summarized by the appellees:

> *Ecocide: A Strategy of War* documents the environmental impact of U.S. military tactics in Vietnam; *From the Ashes... Nicaragua Today* traces the historical roots of the 1979 Nicaraguan Revolution; *Whatever Happened to Childhood?* addresses the changing reality facing children growing up in modern-day urban America, principally through first-hand interviews and statistical evidence: *Peace: A Conscious Choice* attempts to teach its viewers about the first step toward peace in a Cold War society, by suggesting that the United States and the Soviet Union are inextricably related, and that their relationship has implications for world peace; *The Secret Agent* examines the use and effects of dioxin, a toxic ingredient in Agent Orange, through archival footage and interviews.

Aples.' Brief, pp. 6–11, *Bullfrog Films, Inc.* v. *Wick*, 847 F. 2d 502, 505 (9th Cir. 1988).

44. *Bullfrog Films, Inc.* v. *Wick*, 646 F. Supp. 492, 507–8 (D.C. Cal. 1986).

45. 646 F. Supp. at 502.

46. 847 F. 2d 502 (9th Cir. 1986).

47. 847 F. 2d at 514.

48. 847 F. 2d at 511. *See N.A.A.C.P.* v. *Claiborne Hardware Co.*, 458 U.S. 886, 913 (1982) (" 'expression on public issues' has always rested on the highest rung of the hierarchy of First Amendment values"); *Police Department* v. *Moseley*, 408 U.S. 92, 95–96 (1972) ("Government may not grant the use of a forum to people whose views it finds acceptable, but deny use to those wishing to express less favored or more controversial views").

The government makes a valuable government benefit—certification—dependent on a film's content, moreover, and its producers are therefore confronted with a Hobson's choice: They may either exercise their First Amendment rights and forego their opportunity to receive the trade concessions that certification provides, or curb their expression and receive these concessions. "The imposition of this sort of dilemma," Judge Cecil Poole explained:

> patently transgresses the well-established principle that government may not condition the conferral of a benefit on the relinquishment of a constitutional right: For at least a quarter-century, this Court has made clear that even though a person has no "right" to a valuable governmental benefit . . . [i]t may not deny a benefit to a person on a basis that infringes his constitutionally protected interests—especially his interest in freedom of speech.

47 F. 2d at 511, *quoting Perry* v. *Sindermann*, 408 U.S. 593, 597 (1972).

49. 847 F. 2d at 509–10 n.11.

50. Ibid.

51. Ibid. at 513–14.

52. Ibid. at 513.

53. Ibid. The USIA also withholds certification from any film that is not "balanced and truthful." As Judge Poole pointed out, however, such editorial oversight violates the First Amendment because it forces the government to discriminate on the basis of content. Ibid. at 510.

The USIA goes so far as to penalize films not only because certain views are apparently missing, but also because, in its judgment, certain other views are insufficiently developed. Ibid. Judge Poole faulted the agency for this practice as well: "The First Amendment does not allow the government to require independent filmmakers to present all views on a subject, or indeed any view contrary to the filmmaker's own." Ibid.

See Miami Herald Publishing Co. v. *Tornillo*, 418 U.S. 241 (1974) (A Florida statute is unconstitutional that required newspapers in the state to present "balanced campaign coverage" by publishing letters written by the candidates in response to unfavorable editorial coverage.)

54. 847 F. 2d at 513–14. To illustrate the "constitutional infirmity" of USIA's regulations, Judge Poole compared them to those at issue in *Big Mama Rag* v. *United States*, 631 F. 2d 1030 (D.C. Cir. 1980). Big Mama, a nonprofit feminist organization denied tax-exempt status by the Internal Review Service, claimed a regulation defining "educational institutions" was impermissibly vague. The relevant part of the regulation provided:

> An organization may be educational even though it advocates a particular position or viewpoint so long as it presents a *sufficiently full and fair exposition of the pertinent facts* as to permit an individual or the public to form an independent opinion or conclusion. On the other hand, an organization is not educational if its principal function is the mere presentation of unsupported opinion.

847 F. 2d at 514, *quoting* 631 F. 2d at 1034 (emphasis in original). The court held the regulation unconstitutionally vague. 631 F. 2d at 1035–39.

See also Beckerman v. *City of Tupelo,* 664 F. 2d 502, 557 (5th Cir. 1981) (A municipal ordinance that authorized the police chief to deny a parade permit where "conduct of the parade will probably cause injury to persons or property or provoke disorderly conduct or create a disturbance" is "unconstitutionally vague since it contains no instructions directing the Chief in the formulation of his opinion").

55. "Propaganda as Educational and Cultural Material; World-Wide Free Flow [Export-Import] of Audio-Visual Materials." *Federal Register,* Nov. 16, 1987, pp. 43753–757 (correction 12/11 *F.R.*, p. 47029); *see* Bill McAllister, "USIA Labels U.S. Film 'Propaganda,' " *The Washington Post,* January 17, 1988, p. A–23.

56. Ibid. *See also* "USIA Revises Stand on Documentary Films," *The Los Angeles Times,* Jan. 20, 1988, Section 6.

57. "U.S. Rules on Documentaries Challenged," *The New York Times,* Jan. 6, 1988, p. C–13.

58. Ibid.

59. 793 F. 2d 1303, 1310–14 (D.C. Cir. 1986); *for discussion see* Chapter 3.

60. Richard C. Stearns, *quoted in* "U.S. Rules on Documentaries Challenged," *The New York Times,* Jan. 6, 1988, p. C–13.

61. Matt Lait, "USIA Loses Film Appeal," *The Washington Post,* May 19, 1988, p. C–4.

62. Ibid.

63. 107 S. Ct. 1862 (1987); *for discussion see* Chapter 3.

64. 646 F. Supp. at 503 (*paraphrasing* Defts.' Supp. Memo, p. 4). The judiciary will ordinarily uphold laws and administrative regulations that impinge on fundamental rights like "political expression" only when these laws and regulations satisfy the very demanding "strict scrutiny" test, according to which they must be "necessary to serve a compelling state interest" and be "narrowly drawn to achieve that end." *Perry Education Association* v. *Perry Local Educators' Association,* 460 U.S. 37, 45 (1983) *quoted at* 847 F. 2d at 511.

In *Bullfrog Films,* however, the government urged the court to use a "deferential," rather than a strict standard because decisions made by the USIA implicate "the delicate area of foreign relations." Appellants Br., p. 32, 847 F. 2d at 511. Judge Poole agreed with the district court, however, that the protection afforded by the First Amendment is not diminished "when the expression is directed abroad." 847 F. 2d at 511.

Judge Poole referred to a recent case in which the Supreme Court rejected the solictor general's request to use a deferential standard in assessing the constitutionality of government regulations forbidding protestors to display placards critical of foreign countries outside these countries' embassies. Even the government's claim that it was obligated under international law to safeguard the "dignity" of diplomats and foreign embassies could not persuade the Court to relax its standard. 847 F. 2d at 512, *citing Boos* v. *Barry,* 108 S. Ct. 1157, 1165 (1988).

The judge is incorrect to suggest, however, that the Court ordinarily subjects government policy affecting foreign relations to strict scrutiny. On the contrary, when foreign relations are even tangentially affected it almost invariably applies an extremely deferential standard, even when the government's actions curtail the exercise of First Amendment rights. *For discussion see* Chapters 2 and 3.

65. 453 U.S. 280, 319 n.9 (Brennan, J., dissenting). *For discussion see* Chapter 2.

66. Ibid.

67. 847 F. 2d at 509 n.9.

68. 646 F. Supp. at 502.

69. Ibid. at 507.

70. Ibid. at 504.

71. *For discussion see* Introduction and Chapter 1.

72. 646 F. Supp. at 503 n.16.

73. Neuborne and Shapiro, "Nylon Curtain," p. 742.

74. John J. O'Connor, "Is the Documentary Making a Comeback?" *The New York Times*, June 26, 1988, p. H–27.

75. *Quoted in* ibid.

76. Ibid.

77. Ibid.

78. 22 U.S.C. §611 (j) (1982 and Supp. 11 1982); *for discussion see* Chapter 3.

5

The Secrecy Habit Is Hard to Kick: The Export Control Laws and Scientific Exchange

A popular government, without popular information or the means of acquiring it, is but a prologue to a farce or a tragedy; or perhaps both. Knowledge will forever govern ignorance. And a people who mean to be their own governors, must arm themselves with the power knowledge gives."[1]

James Madison

Recognizing that knowledge is power, the United States government in the 1980s launched an all-out campaign to prevent the transfer of strategically important information to foreign adversaries. The Ronald Reagan and George Bush administrations have waged this campaign not, as might be expected, with statutes designed to curb espionage and treason, but with the so-called Export Control Laws that were originally enacted to restrict the transmission of tangible items, particularly military hardware, to Eastern-bloc countries. The transmutation of these laws began after the Defense Science Board Task Force concluded in 1976 that U.S. security now depended less on stockpiles of armaments or massive troop buildups than on the acquisition and preservation of scientific knowledge.[2] "Thoughts and ideas" were now the key weapons, the task force reasoned, and it made no sense for the United States to restrict the export of military hardware without also restricting the export of the technological know-how that had created and now serviced this hardware.[3]

Shortly after the task force announced its conclusions, several prominent government officials began charging that foreign nationals were "stealing us blind." Admiral Bobby Inman, then deputy director of the CIA, accused foreign intelligence officers of "collecting all types of information in the United States,"[4] while Frank Carlucci, then deputy secretary of defense, reproached the Soviet Union for undertaking an "orchestrated effort" to gather military technology in this country.[5] Carlucci's accusation was bolstered by a government report that claimed that the Soviet Union was sending hundreds of spies to the United States each year "outfitted" as journalists, diplomats, and trade representatives.[6]

Admiral Inman, Secretary Carlucci, and their cohorts in the defense and intelligence communities have since assumed an active role in shaping "information export policy." They have received staunch support from the Department of Commerce and from many leading industrialists, who consider technological superiority indispensable to U.S. economic as well as military competitiveness.[7] Together these parties have encouraged the adoption of policies designed to prevent hostile nations from acquiring so-called "critical military technologies."

These officials were not the first, of course, to recognize the vital link between scientific knowledge and national defense. In the years immediately preceding World War II, President Franklin Roosevelt instituted the first security-related classification system, citing as authority a 1938 statute restricting public access to military installations, equipment, and "information relative thereto."[8] During both the "hot" and protracted cold wars that followed, scientists also complied with an assortment of voluntary and mandatory restraints that were designed, for instance, to prevent the Germans from learning about the Manhattan Project, or, later, the Soviets from acquiring nuclear, computer, or laser technology.[9]

These early restrictions were different from their present-day counterparts, however, because they applied primarily to classified information having immediate military utility. More recent regulations, by contrast, also govern information that is unclassified, that may bear only a tangential relationship to military technology, and that may be the fruit of individual, as opposed to government-sponsored, research.[10] These new, wide-ranging controls are justified on the theory that in the computer age, no information is harmless. Administration officials worry that saboteurs may be able to extract and piece together vital scientific and technical data from the massive amounts of unrelated material now accessible by computers.[11] To illustrate their fears, they often refer to journalist Howard Morland, who in 1979 wrote an article explaining how to construct an atom bomb. Morland had amassed his data exclusively from unclassified information unearthed in a variety of scientific journals available to the public.[12]

President Ronald Reagan articulated these fears in a 1984 directive in which he compared information to a mosaic; isolated data, harmless in themselves, he asserted, "can reveal highly classified and other sensitive information when taken in the aggregate."[13] He therefore declared that the government "shall encourage, advise and, where appropriate, assist the private sector" in protecting "sensitive non-government information, the loss of which would adversely affect national security."[14] The government has since acted to fulfill this pledge, adopting numerous policies designed to safeguard both publicly and privately generated data. As former Defense Secretary Caspar Weinberger pointed out, it has made "technology transfer control" a "key element of national security policy."[15]

Such potentially dangerous information transfer may be effected not just by conspirators who raid computer data bases or bribe navy engineers, but also, as the Department of Defense concluded in a 1980 report, by the entire tradition of scientific openness.[16] In 1982 Admiral Inman told participants at a Washington, D.C., symposium that unless scientists acted voluntarily to control the "hemorrhage" of sensitive research information to countries hostile to the United States, there would follow a "tidal wave" of legislation designed to curb the publication of such information. "Congress," he warned, "is ready to resolve the conflict between academic freedom and national security in favor of the latter."[17]

Even before Admiral Inman made his remarks, the government adopted a number of policies in favor of national security. In fact, since the later 1970s, universities—traditional bastions of academic independence—have often been told where their members may lecture, what they may publish, and even whom they may teach. Several factors have contributed to this phenomenon, including the fact that many influential people like Admiral Inman blame the university research community whenever adversaries of the United States acquire classified information. They persist in this view despite the conclusions of the Corson Report, published in 1982 under the auspices of the National Academy of Science, which found that while Soviet-bloc countries were indeed stealing massive amounts of military technology from the West, the academic community "accounted for only a minor part of this technological hemorrhage."[18]

A new, increasingly intimate relationship between the government and the university community has also contributed to the erosion of the latter's independence. Whereas administrators and individual faculty members were once loath to allow or undertake any research that might compromise academic freedom, the increasing availability of substantial federal grants, at least for earmarked projects, has encouraged many individuals to abandon such compunctions.[19] Finally, from the day it took office, the Reagan administration insisted on a strict interpretation of the export control laws, and the constant monitoring thus required is a third major reason why government officials and university scientists now find themselves in an uncomfortable embrace.

Those who wrote the original export control statutes might be surprised to learn that laws enacted to restrict the shipment of strategic commodities to the Soviet Union are now being used to censor academic papers delivered to photo-optical conferences. By authorizing federal administrators to regulate the export of "technical data," these statutes now constitute the principal means by which the government limits the access of foreigners and citizens alike to unclassified information.

The government relies in particular on two statutes that, unlike other export control laws, are framed in language loose enough to permit even peacetime restrictions on intangible items. One is the Arms Export Control Act of 1976,[20] and the other is the Export Administration Act of 1979.[21] Both affect the dissemination of basic and applied research by requiring scientists to obtain a license before "exporting" technical data. Information is considered exported whenever it is communicated overseas by "oral, visual, or documentary means," including "visits abroad by American citizens"; whenever individuals apply "personal knowledge or technical expertise" acquired in the United States to "situations abroad"; or even when it is communicated within the United States itself by anyone who intends it to be transmitted out of the country.[22]

"Technical data," in turn, is defined as information of any kind—even data that results entirely from privately, as opposed to governmentally funded, research—that can be used, or adopted for use, in the "design, production, manufacture, utilization or reconstruction" of any article or material that appears on one of two lists.[23] The first, the Commodity Control List,[24] is maintained by the Department of Commerce, and the second, the Munitions List,[25] is kept by the departments of State and Defense. Technical data associated with any items on these lists requires an export license unless this data is already in the public domain. Securing such a license is a complicated and bewildering process, but without it individuals face substantial fines or a stiff prison sentence.[26]

The Department of Commerce implements the Arms Export Control Act through the so-called International Traffic in Arms Regulations (ITAR), which govern the transmission of any commodities and "technical data" having "military utility."[27] Military utility is an expansive concept, encompassing not only information that obviously relates to warfare, but also that touches even tangentially on arms and munitions, that "advances the state of the art," that "establishes a new art in an area of significant military applicability, . . . or that through adaptation can serve a military purpose."[28] Semiconductors, for instance, play a vital role in missile guidance systems, so any information associated with their production or use becomes "technical data" under ITAR.

The other principal statute used to regulate the transmission—or "export"—of scientific information is the Export Administration Act, adopted in 1979 and significantly amended in 1985,[29] which the Department of Commerce implements through the Export Administration Regulations.[30] This act applies to "dual-use" technologies—those capable of both military and civilian application—in contrast to the Arms Export Control Act, which, in theory if not in practice, affects only material having an exclusively military utility.

The Department of Defense maintains a "militarily critical technologies" list (the MCTL), which specifies the materials, equipment, and know-how that "would make a significant contribution to the military potential" of an adversary.[31] The MCTL is not itself a control list, but rather a guidebook intended to assist both the Department of State and the Department of Commerce, on the one hand, and members of the research community, on the other, in determining whether specific technology or data requires a license under the export control statutes before it can be transferred out of the country.[32]

In its unabridged form, the MCTL provides researchers with little assistance, however, since it is considered too sensitive for public disclosure. Even if it were accessible, its usefulness would be limited because it is larger than the Manhattan Yellow Pages and growing by the day. An unclassified version of the MCTL is also available, but it, too, is tome-like—some 212 single-spaced pages—and only slightly more helpful than its classified counterpart since, as one Department of Defense official observed, it is "really a list of modern technology."[33]

A third statute, the Atomic Energy Act, also imposes broad restraints on the dissemination of information, but it has elicited less criticism from members of the scientific community than the other major export control statutes because they know from the outset that any research they undertake on atomic energy will be subject to government restrictions.[34] The Atomic Energy Act obliges the Nuclear Regulatory Commission and the Department of Energy to promote "that free exchange of ideas and criticism [about atomic energy] which is essential to scientific and industrial progress and public understanding."[35] The act allows the agencies little room to maneuver, however, because it forbids the dissemination of "restricted data," which means virtually any data concerning the design, construction, utilization, or effects of nuclear energy.[36] Read literally, the definition of restricted data would prohibit a social studies teacher from discussing the impact of the 1979 reactor crisis at Three Mile Island.[37]

The export laws thus pose difficulties for anyone expected either to implement or to comply with them. They impose on four departments—

State, Defense, Commerce, and Energy—distinct legislative mandates, each setting forth different standards for classification and licensing. Because the export laws are vague and sweeping, officials in these departments have almost carte blanche authority to censor information that is not classified and over which the government has no proprietary interest. Researchers, for their part, are never sure whether their data requires preclearance, or even whether in delivering a lecture or teaching a class they may run afoul of these dragnet statutes.

International conferences play a valuable role in the scientific community, at their best providing intellectual "free-for-alls" in which participants can profit mutually from the exchange of information. In the name of national security, however, and under the mandate of the export control laws, government officials have recently imposed restrictions both on who can attend and on what can be said at these conferences.

The Defense Department claims the right to preclear or even cancel papers scheduled for delivery before international audiences. In addition to the Arms Export Control Act, it relies for its authority on the Defense Authorization Act of 1984, which empowers the Secretary of Defense to withhold from disclosure under the Freedom of Information Act (FOIA) any information that cannot be disseminated under the export control acts.[38] The department reasons that if it can bar the release of information under the FOIA to prevent its exportation, it can likewise ban its release at conferences attended by foreigners.[39]

The Department of Commerce also imposes restrictions on academic conferences, and was, in fact, the first federal agency to do so. On February 11, 1980, shortly after the Soviet Union reinvigorated the Cold War by invading Afghanistan, Senator Henry Jackson assailed the Commerce Department for its failure to vigorously enforce the recently enacted Export Administration Act.[40] The department, smarting from this public rebuke, sprang into action; its first target was the hapless American Vacuum Society.

The society had arranged an International Bubble Memory Conference for late February 1980 in Santa Barbara, California.[41] Five days before this meeting was to begin, however, the Department of Commerce informed its organizers that they could not hold the conference without first securing an export license.[42] Although none of the papers scheduled for delivery contained classified information, some apparently dealt with "sensitive" material covered by the Export Administration Regulations. Because the deadline for securing a license had long since passed, however, Commerce officials proposed a compromise: The organizers could hold their conference as planned provided they would exclude participants from unfriendly countries and secure pledges from all those in attendance not to divulge any information acquired at the conference to individuals from these countries.[43]

The conference organizers hesitated, since scientists from China and the Eastern-bloc nations were already en route, but another last-minute phone call resolved their uncertainty: The Department of Commerce informed John Vossen, president of the Vacuum Society, that he would be heavily fined and perhaps even imprisoned if the society did not accede to its terms.[44] The society thereupon acceded, preparing "letters of assurance" which representatives from "friendly" nations were required to sign, and allowing the FBI to station agents at the conference doors to bar anyone from China, Hungary, Poland, or the Soviet Union.

The Vacuum Society is only one of many organizations that have agreed, however reluctantly, to the government's terms. Another is the Society of Photo-Optical Instrumentation Engineers[45] (SPIES—an unfortunate acronym that one commentator suggests may have contributed to its woes).[46] SPIES had scheduled a conference for August 1982 in San Diego, California, but the Pentagon concluded that several of the papers intended for delivery there might violate the export control laws. As a consequence, when some 2,700 scientists arrived from all over the world, they learned for the first time that more than 150 papers had been cancelled, including many that dealt with nonmilitary research.[47]

SPIES held another conference three years later, and again its organizers were forced to cancel several papers, to secure nondisclosure agreements from participants, and to bar specified foreigners from attending what the Department of Defense called "export control sessions."[48] This conference accomplished some unintended good, however, by prompting the presidents of 12 scientific and engineering societies to write a letter in September 1985 to Defense Secretary Caspar Weinberger, announcing that thereafter they would neither sponsor nor participate in "closed or restricted access technical sessions."[49]

Most scientific and engineering societies have shied away from so bold a stance, however, and they continue to face difficult demands. For instance, they must provide the Commerce and Defense departments with copies of any presentations scheduled for delivery at their forthcoming conferences, source lists for any information contained in these presentations, and declarations stating whether this information is proprietary or public in nature.[50] Participants in such conferences, however, often speak without a prepared text, or with a text whose final pages were typed just minutes before its delivery, and they often have no idea whether their data is proprietary or public. These conferences are often most stimulating, moreover, after the formal program has concluded and informal exchanges have begun, the content of which can rarely be anticipated.[51]

The export laws consequently serve to induce self-censorship. Knowing that they face anything from a slap on the wrist to a stint behind bars if they inadvertently violate these laws, many prospective organizers play it safe. Either they refuse to schedule any papers that fall within the vast gray area where an export license may be required, or they follow the lead of the prestigious Ceramics Society, whose leaders distributed the following announcement before its January 1984 meeting: "This Conference is open to United States citizens only. You must prove citizenship in order to be admitted."[52]

Foreign scientists denied permission to attend academic conferences may also be denied the right to accept appointments at U.S. universities unless they first agree to abide by several government-imposed restrictions on their freedom of movement. A Hungarian specialist in electronic circuitry refused an appointment offered by Cornell University, for instance, because the Department of Commerce insisted that as a condition of his visa he receive no prepublication copies of research papers.[53] In another case, Stanford University cancelled the visit of a Russian expert in robotics because the Department of State had imposed what the university considered unreasonable and insulting conditions on his visit.[54]

Exchange students attending classes or performing research in the United States are as much affected by the export laws as their older compatriots. The Department of State first signaled its intention to monitor these students in 1981 when it sent a letter to every university in the country warning that the teaching of even some unclassified subjects to students from China constitutes an "export" requiring an appropriate license.[55] University professors also received letters admonishing them not to teach certain classes such as advanced computer design or microelectronics without first determining whether they needed a license. Instructors teaching computer science and satellite technology at Stanford University were ordered to deny their Chinese students access to certain unclassified data,[56] and their colleagues at other institutions were instructed to inform the Department of State whenever exchange students visited industrial or research facilities, conducted "specific experiments" on campus, or used any of several itemized "instruments or specialized equipment."[57]

Many universities have accepted these government restrictions. In June 1984, for instance, the University of California at Los Angeles went so far as to advertise a course on Metal Matrix Composites, which involved unclassified technical data appearing on an export control list, as restricted to "United States Citizens only."[58] Other universities have acquiesced only grudgingly, and several individual professors and academic institutions have refused outright to comply.[59] Harvard University, for instance, would not honor the Department of State's request for information about certain graduate students on the grounds that such an inquiry constituted "an interference into matters at the very heart of the academic enterprise."[60]

Treating foreign students equitably makes sense for reasons that are pragmatic as well as principled. Because university research in the United States is heavily dependent on these students (by 1980 they comprised fully one third of those doing postdoctoral work in science and engineering), restricting their access to necessary data or technical facilities significantly reduces the amount of research performed in U.S. educational institutions.[61] Moreover, since these same students eventually constitute about 40 percent of all the Ph.D.s employed by scientific and technological enterprises in the United States,[62] Robert Park is correct in observing that "the work force we are keeping ignorant is to a large extent our own."[63]

Before 1980 most university researchers would have been appalled at the prospect of government bureaucrats determining to whom and under what conditions their work could be disseminated. They were accustomed to restraint only on those rare occasions when they contracted with the government to perform classified projects, usually during wartime. Since 1980, however, these researchers have both contributed to and been victimized by a new phenomenon: prepublication censorship.[64] Taking the form of governmentally imposed restrictions on the right to publish, patent, copyright, or otherwise disseminate data, this censorship results both from the expanded use of the export control laws and from researchers' increased willingness to accept federal funds even with the attendant conditions.

The policy of NASA (National Aeronautics and Space Administration) is illustrative. Since 1984 the agency has required those whom it funds "not to establish claim to copyright, publish, or to release to others computer software first produced in performance of this contract without prior written permission of the contracting officer."[65] Many other contracts also contain clauses stipulating that a government agency has the right either to intervene directly—to provide "technical assistance"—or to change unilaterally and without notice the scope or even the content of the research.[66]

The National Institute of Health, the Environmental Protection Agency, and the Food and Drug Administration are among the many federal agencies that now routinely insert such clauses in any contract they sign—even when the assigned work involves unclassified research in social policy. The National Institute of Health, for instance, required a prepublication contract for a study entitled "International Comparison of Health Science Policies,"[67] prompting one critic to suggest that federal overseers require review clauses only incidentally to ensure compliance with the export laws, and primarily to monitor the content of the research.[68]

Even university researchers who spurn any direct involvement with the government are subject to the export control laws, and accordingly must submit unclassified as well as classified data for prepublication review if it concerns any subject that is considered sensitive. The National Security Agency has designated as sensitive the entire field of cryptology, for instance, and anyone in the United States who does research in this area must now submit this work to the agency for preclearance.[69] Information concerning nuclear energy or electronic data bases—the latter comprising a crucial part of the computerized information center at every major public and private institution in the country—is increasingly considered "born classified," and, as such, inherently subject to government control.[70]

As a matter of principle, many universities have prohibited their research staffs from performing classified work or accepting any other limits on their academic independence.[71] However, other institutions, including even such distinguished ones as the Massachusetts Institute of Technology, Carnegie-Mellon, Stanford, and Brown, permit their staffs to accept contracts not only from the government but from private industry as well, regardless of the accompanying restraints.[72]

Members of the university research community are not the only people affected by the export laws, as was underscored by an FBI announcement on May 18, 1988, that in order to prevent the unlawful transmission of information covered by these laws, the bureau would "pursue any contact between a Soviet national and an American citizen, regardless of where the contact occurs or the profession of the person contacted."[73] Among those "contacted" have been scores of librarians.

The FBI's May 18 announcement was included in a report accusing the Soviet Intelligence Service of having conducted a massive, 30-year effort to exploit the specialized and technical libraries of the United States.[74] In response, the bureau explained, it had launched the so-called "Library Awareness Program." James H. Geer, assistant director of the Bureau's Intelligence Division, explained that agents serving the program "seek to inform selected librarians that they and their libraries are, or have been, significant targets for Soviet intelligence activities and recruitment."[75]

Geer offered a hypothetical example of a situation in which library monitoring could be useful: Suppose a Soviet official who is listed as an agricultural attaché frequently sits at a library devouring information on technical, nonagricultural subjects. Such an individual "operating outside the scope of his assigned duties" is clearly not an agricultural attaché but a KGB agent.[76] The FBI has accordingly asked librarians to be "on the lookout" for anyone who might be working for Soviet intelligence, to note the books and journals they read, and to observe whether they seemed to be recruiting agents for counterintelligence.[77] They are being asked, in short, to serve as government informants—a role at odds with their ethical traditions, and perhaps even the law, since 38 states have policies safeguarding the confidentiality of library patrons.[78]

Librarians have been galvanized by the Library Awareness Program as by few other issues. In October 1987 the American Library Association's (ALA) Office for Intellectual Freedom released an Extraordinary Memorandum in which it protested "this attempted infringement on the right to receive information protected by the First Amendment,"[79] and in June 1988 individuals representing the ALA and other library associations requested a hearing before the House Judiciary Subcommittee on Civil and Constitutional Rights in order to voice their opposition to the program.[80] California Representative Don Edwards, the subcommittee's chairman and himself a former FBI agent, wondered how librarians could know who might be working undercover: They "can only act based on whether the person has a Russian or European-sounding name," he conjectured, and "such determinations could be very subjective and might be dangerously over-inclusive."[81] Edwards expressed appreciation for "the awesome responsibilities" facing the FBI in foreign counterintelligence,[82] but concluded that this program had been neither authorized by Congress nor properly implemented by the bureau itself, and that what little useful data it unearthed was vastly outweighed by the confusion and ill will it engendered.[83]

Acceding to pressure both from librarians and from the House subcommittee, the FBI announced on November 1, 1988, that it had imposed strict limits on the Library Awareness Program.[84] According to the bureau's director, William S. Sessions, the program would thereafter be confined to the New York City area and it would rely exclusively on librarians' voluntary compliance.[85] These concessions do not satisfy the ALA, however, which continues to maintain that none of its members can properly facilitate the dissemination of information while simultaneously conducting surveillance.[86]

Traditional First Amendment doctrine is rooted in the theory that, apart from a few judicially recognized exceptions, almost any speech contributes to the marketplace of ideas. Even erroneous or misguided ideas often facilitate the search for "truth," if only by forcing people to examine and clarify their own cherished notions.[87] As a consequence, federal courts have ordinarily allowed the government to restrict constitutionally protected expression in only two narrow circumstances: It can classify information within its control to safeguard national security,[88] and it can suppress information not within its control if nothing short of suppression will prevent an "imminent and overwhelming danger."[89]

Such standard First Amendment analysis may be adequate for dealing with ordinary expression—information and ideas that encourage good citizenship, self-fulfillment, or the search for truth—but has it any relevance to scientific and technological communication? Does it provide the judiciary with any guidance in determining, for instance, whether U.S. professors should be allowed to discuss laser technology with their Soviet colleagues?

According to one point of view, technological data is different in kind from the types of information the First Amendment was designed to protect. In the first place, because its acquisition can dramatically bolster an adversary's economic position, it resembles a commodity more than it resembles traditional forms of information or ideas.[90] Perceived as such, technical data should be equally subject to regulation as are vats of oil or bales of wheat.[91] In the second place, because modern technological information—in sharp contrast to ordinary speech—is capable of creating instruments of mass destruction, a country assumes untenable risks in awaiting a "clear and present danger" before suppressing it.[92]

Even those who maintain that technical data merits First Amendment protection as much as ordinary speech must acknowledge the force of these arguments and agree that a country has the right to withhold information that could be of direct military use to its enemies. Problems arise only in determining the propriety of government censorship in more ambiguous situations, where the competing claims of national security and the First Amendment are of comparable weight.

Should the government be allowed to suppress information that may benefit an enemy if the benefit will occur only in an indirect, incremental, or long-term sense? Should it be able to prevent the dissemination of sensitive data on microelectronics or supercomputers, for instance, on grounds that its acquisition could enhance an adversary's research facilities, its industrial plants, or even its understanding of U.S. defensive strategies? Should the United States sequester information concerning business administration on the theory that if the Soviets learn how to run their factories more efficiently, they could channel the resulting profits into weapons production?[93]

A judge who appreciates the imperatives of free expression must attempt to distinguish situations that pose "immediate and substantial dangers" from those that pose only distant or hypothetical ones. However, in order to make this distinction, which is difficult in itself, he or she is first obliged to answer a series of equally difficult antecedent questions: Is the information the government seeks to suppress available to the receiving nation from another source? Does the receiving nation have the resources necessary to exploit the information? Are there alternatives to outright suppression? Finally, and most important, is national security ultimately better served when information is censored in a given situation or when it is disclosed?

In 1979 a case arose that required for its proper disposition an answer to all these questions. *United States* v. *Progressive*[94] involved an article entitled "The H Bomb Secret: How We Got It, Why We're Telling It."[95] The editors of *Progressive* magazine, with whom Howard Morland had contracted to write the article, intended to publish the piece in their April 1979 issue.

Morland, a freelance journalist with little scientific training, set out to learn all he could about the construction of a bomb, using the methods available to any resourceful reporter. Relying exclusively on unclassified information, he went to libraries and read journals, physics texts, encyclopedias, and government reprints. By arrangement with the Department of Energy, he also visited nuclear production facilities.[96] Erwin Knoll, the editor of *Progressive*, pointed out that scientists subsequently confirmed what he had suspected all along, that a competent physicist could learn in a week what Morland had spent months trying to piece together.[97]

The article, as District Judge Robert Warren later conceded, was no "do-it-yourself bomb kit," but rather little more than a layperson's description of the principles involved in a nuclear explosion.[98] Still, the Department of Energy panicked: Given a copy of Morland's work by one of the scientists who had agreed to review it for accuracy, the department warned *Progressive*'s editors that unless they squelched the article immediately, they would end up in court.[99] The editors refused to squelch it and geared for action. When they eventually appeared in court they were well prepared but scarcely anxious, assuming that under applicable precedent they would win their case. Applicable precedent consisted of a series of opinions beginning with *Near* v. *Minnesota*[100] in 1931 and including *New York Times* v. *United States*[101] in 1972—the celebrated Pentagon Papers case—in which the Supreme Court reaffirmed its antagonism to prior restraint.

Prior restraint, that is, official action prohibiting the publication of some form of communication, is considered so serious a remedy, so clearly subject to abuse, and so inimical to basic First Amendment values, that prior to *United States* v. *Progressive* no federal court in recent history had sanctioned its use. Courts have never explicitly outlawed prior restraint, but they have made its imposition extremely difficult to justify.[102] In cases like *Near* and the Pentagon Papers, for instance, they have refused to allow the government to censor information without first proving that its publication would "surely and inevitably" result "directly and immediately" in "grave and irreparable harm."[103] In establishing the certainty of harm, moreover, the government must present evidence, not speculation; as the Supreme Court noted in the Pentagon Papers case, proof that publication "could," "might," or "may" cause the requisite harm is insufficient.[104]

Government officials never alleged that publication of Morland's article would lead "directly and immediately" to "grave and irreparable harm." Rather, they rested their case almost entirely on the claim that Morland's article contained Restricted Data, the dissemination of which is prohibited by the Atomic Energy Act. Restricted Data is an expansive concept, defined in one provision of the Atomic Energy Act as any information concerning the "design, manufacture, or utilization of atomic weapons."[105] According to the government, it includes even unclassified information in the public domain if, like the material in Morland's article, it can be drawn together, synthesized, and collated in such a way as to present substantial harm to the country.[106] In fact, Restricted Data includes any information at all pertaining to nuclear energy, even that which is "born in the minds of private individuals," because, as the government explained in the *Progressive* case, such information is "born classified," or "restricted at birth."[107]

On March 26, 1979, Judge Warren enjoined *Progressive* from printing Morland's article.[108] He based his decision primarily upon the provisions of the Atomic Energy Act prohibiting the dissemination of Restricted Data, but he explained that even without statutory authority the government could suppress communication that could result in serious harm, and Morland's article incontestably could "provide sufficient information to allow a medium-sized nation to move faster in developing a hydrogen weapon."[109] "It could provide a ticket to by-pass blind alleys," the judge continued, and "it could accelerate the membership of a candidate nation in the thermonuclear club."[110]

Although such distant and hypothetical fears would not satisfy the standard established in the Pentagon Papers case, Judge Warren considered this precedent inapplicable anyway. In that case the government had argued that publication of classified information dealing with U.S. involvement in the Vietnam War would grievously harm the national security, but the Supreme Court was not convinced that information primarily of historical interest could wreak such havoc.[111] The present facts were altogether different, Judge Warren reasoned: Here the government, far from challenging historical documents, was seeking to restrain the publication of "information dealing with the most destructive weapon in the history of mankind, information of sufficient destructive potential to nullify the right to free speech and to endanger the right to life itself."[112] The link between Morland's article and such catastrophic potential was never established, yet Judge Warren concluded that its publication "could pave the way for the thermonuclear annihilation of us all."[113]

The significant and troubling case of *United States* v. *Progressive* ended not with a bang but with a thud. Three days after the Seventh Circuit Court of Appeals heard oral arguments in the case and attorneys for *Progressive* implored it to squash Judge Warren's injunction, the case became moot. On September 16, 1979, a small Wisconsin newspaper called the *Madison Press Connection* published a letter written by Charles Hansen, a California computer programmer, which contained essentially the same information as the Morland article.[114] The next morning, with 8,000 copies of the paper in circulation, the government announced that it would ask the appellate court to dismiss its case against *Progressive*.[115]

After the publication of Hansen's letter, observers noted that the government had won the battle in district court only to lose the war. However, maybe the government won the war, after all: *Progressive* never published Morland's article, and neither the appellate nor the Supreme Court was ever able to circumscribe Judge Warren's ruling or even to clarify his fuzzy and alarmist thinking. For more than a decade his ruling has thus stood unchallenged—a reminder to scientists, journalists, and other concerned citizens of the risks involved in the mere discussion of what Judge Warren termed "the most destructive weapon in the history of mankind."[116]

Conclusion

Export control laws originally enacted to prohibit the transfer of militarily useful commodities to hostile countries have gradually become vehicles by which U.S. citizens, no less than foreign nationals, are denied access to crucial information. Government officials who wrought this transformation often had the best of intentions: Convinced that technological leaks were benefiting U.S. adversaries and jeopardizing its own security, they attempted to "plug" these leaks by imposing censorship on the scientific community, using the export laws as authority. Many distinguished scientists, academicians, and industrialists, while not minimizing the damage technological leaks can inflict, nevertheless consider the government's response impractical and self-defeating. In an interdependent world with multiple access points, it is not possible to prevent foreigners from acquiring unclassified information without diminishing the very freedom by which U.S. science has developed and flourished.

In 1982 the National Academy of Science concluded that "national security is best served by a policy that stresses scientific and technological accomplishment rather than curbs on the free flow of information."[117] Many liberals would agree with its assessment, but so would such rock-ribbed conservatives as Edward Teller, one of the fathers of the atomic bomb:

> For a couple of Centuries the discoveries of science have generally been shared without respect to international boundaries. New discoveries in one country have been the building blocks for further advancement in another. In contrast,

when each country works in secrecy, these vital benefits of sharing are lost as isolated laboratories must struggle for breakthroughs that may have already been achieved in another place. The effect of secrecy on our defense is particularly questionable because openness is a deeply rooted academic tradition: many of the best American scientists do not lend their talents to secret defense-oriented research.[118]

Teller concluded that in the last third of the twentieth century, "the United States has lost its position in all military fields, most specifically in those where we practice secrecy."[119] He indicts in particular those officials who use the export laws to discourage innovation, debate, and creativity. The Center for Strategic Studies at Georgetown University in Washington, D.C., which shares Teller's conservative philosophy, released a report in 1985 in which it, too, indicted the U.S. system of export controls for "no longer adequately serv[ing] United States security or economic interests."[120]

The export laws have abetted the two archenemies of scientific progress: secrecy and censorship. Rarely the lone eccentrics depicted in stereotypes, scientists are much more likely to thrive in an atmosphere enriched by cross-fertilization, in which colleagues throughout the world may examine, duplicate, validate, build upon, and contribute to one another's work. Technological marvels, from medicine to munitions, are increasingly the result of international collaboration. Walter Gilbert, a Harvard professor, insists that he could not have won his Nobel prize without inspiration from a molecular biologist from the Soviet Union;[121] similarly, a U.S. optical firm, Bausch-Lomb, could not be manufacturing soft contact lenses if a team of Czechoslovakian chemists had not first developed the technology.[122]

The export control laws are thus the political equivalent of shooting oneself in the foot. Besides denying U.S. scientists the fruits of international collaboration, they deny U.S. entrepreneurs the opportunity to compete with other countries on an equal basis for the lucrative Eastern-bloc market. Moreover, since Asian and Western European countries show little inclination to adopt the rigorous U.S. system of information controls, the U.S. export laws have the perverse effect of penalizing the country's own citizens while still not appreciably blocking Soviet access to advanced science and technology.[123]

The Soviet Union itself bears witness to the dangers of a closed society. In a book entitled *Science in Chains*, a former Soviet science writer named Mark Popovsky maintains that secrecy is the minor product of the hundreds of Soviet research and development institutes. It may be called the life blood of Soviet science."[124] He explains that debate and open inquiry have traditionally been considered tantamount to treason in his society, and scores of observers in addition to Popovsky have documented the sterility that results. The American Physical Society noted, for instance, that Soviet progress in such fields as solid state electronics and biology have been set back for years because its officials have restricted communication,[125] and Robert Park points out, more specifically, that Soviet biology lags far behind that in the West in large part because its leaders insisted for decades on supporting the discredited theories of Lysenko: "It is hard to believe that these decisions could have long persisted in an atmosphere of free discussion," Park says,[126] and he concludes that "at times the United States seems intent on emulating their failed system by a careless application of the export control laws."[127]

Of course, some information must be kept confidential. Officials have the right to restrict data subject to security clearance, government contract controls, and proprietary or trade secret limitations—although even here overzealous bureaucrats tend to censor far more than is necessary to serve any legitimate state interest. When restrictions extend to scholarly exchanges, scientific inquiry, and basic research that is publicly available and privately generated, however, U.S. long-term interests are poorly served.

In the name of secrecy, U.S. citizens are poorly served, as well, which is precisely why *Progressive* wanted to publish Morland's article. The article, "The H Bomb Secret: How We Got It, Why We're Telling It," provided no blueprint for terrorists, but rather, as its editors explained, presented a challenge "to the mythology of secrecy":

> It was our feeling . . . that the Government had invoked secrecy for thirty years to keep America from questioning the new arms race. . . . Was such secrecy justified? Was information being withheld that might help people make informed judgments on such crucial questions as environmental risks, public health and safety threats, nuclear proliferation, the staggering costs of the nuclear build-up?[128]

John Buell, associate editor of *Progressive,* pointed out that if the government can perpetuate the illusion that national security can be protected only so long as any information about H bombs is kept secret, it can intimidate critics, stifle debate,and deflect any challenge to the economic and political policies that serve to create and mass-produce these bombs:

> The effect of the secrecy mystique—the notion that there are vital decisions which only a select few can and must make—is to keep out of the public domain information that is indispensable to the formation of intelligent public policy: weapons builders have argued for years, for example, against a comprehensive nuclear test ban treaty on grounds that continued underground testing is essential to "national security." But they have never explained why, insisting that the information is "classified." Morland's article explains the reasons for testing,

so that citizens can assess the validity of the weapons builders' claims. Any potential builder of bombs has this information, but the myth of secrecy and expertise fosters a passive or fatalistic attitude among citizens who might otherwise confront the government with troublesome questions.[129]

The twentieth century's most distinguished scientist would agree with Buell. Before his death, Albert Einstein observed that "there is no secret and no defense [against an atomic holocaust]; there is no possibility of control except through the aroused understanding and insistence of the peoples of the world."[130]

Notes

1. Gaillard Hunt, ed., *The Writings of James Madison*, vol. 9 (New York: G. B. Putnam and Sons, 1910), p. 103.

2. United States Department of Defense, Office of the Director of Defense Research and Engineering, Report of the Defense Science Board Task Force on Export of U.S. Technology: *An Analysis of Export Control of U.S. Technology—A DoD Perspective* (Washington, D.C.: U.S. Govt. Printing Office, 1976) (hereinafter cited as *DoD Report*). *For discussion see* Donald N. Langenberg, "Secret Knowledge and Open Inquiry," 23 *Society* (July-August 1986), p. 9.

3. *DoD Report*. *See also* Christina M. Ramirez, "The Balance of Interests between National Security Controls and First Amendment Interests in Academic Freedom," 13 *Journal of College and University Law* 179, 181 (Fall 1986).

4. United States Congress. *Impact of National Security Considerations on Science and Technology*: Hearing before the Subcommittees on Science, Research and Technology and Investigations and Oversight of the House Committee on Science and Technology, 97th Cong., 2d Sess. 6–7 (1982).

5. W. D. Carey and F. Carlucci, "Scientific Exchange and U.S. National Security," 215 *Science* (1982), p. 139. *See also* Floyd Abrams, "The New Effort to Control Information," *The New York Times*, Sept. 15, 1983, Section F (Magazine), p. 22.

6. "Soviet Acquisition of Militarily Significant Western Technology: An Update" (Washington, D.C.: Central Intelligence Agency Report, September 1985), *cited in* Sumner Benson, "Overcoming Complacency," 23 *Society* (July-August 1986), p. 14.

7. Rosemary Chalk, "Continuing Debate over Science and Secrecy," 42 *Bulletin of Atomic Scientists* (March 1986), pp. 14–15.

8. Executive Order 8381 (1940), *cited in* John Shattuck and Muriel Morisey Spence, *Government Information Controls: Implications for Scholarship, Science, and Technology* (Cambridge, Mass.: Harvard University, Office of Government, Community and Public Affairs, March 1988), p. 14.

During this same period, often at the behest of either the prestigious National Academy of Science or renowned individual scientists such as Leo Szilard, academic journals voluntarily refrained from printing anything that might be of assistance to wartime enemies of the United States. *For discussion see* Benson, "Overcoming Complacency," pp. 12–14.

9. Ibid., pp. 12–13.

10. In September 1985 the Reagan administration released National Security Directive 1985, which states that no restrictions may be placed on the reporting of unclassified federally funded research "except as provided in applicable United States statutes." NSDD 189, Sept. 21, 1985. However, according to Robert L. Park, president of the American Physical Society, since the "applicable statutes" are "numerous and elastic in their applicability," the directive is scarcely reassuring. Robert Park, *quoted in* Paul Strohm, "Government Restrictions on Academic Freedom," 72 *Academe* (Jan.–Feb. 1986), p. 42. The covering memorandum to agency heads was no more reassuring. Written by Robert McFarlane, then national security adviser to President Reagan, it reminded the agencies that the directive "preserves the ability to control unclassified information using legislated authority"—clearly a reference, Park points out, to the "applicable U.S. statutes" caveat. Ibid.

11. Richard N. Perle, "The Eastward Technology Flow: A Plan of Common Action," 31 *Strategic Review* (Spring 1984), p. 221.

12. Howard Morland, "The H-Bomb Secret: How We Got It, Why We're Telling It," 43 *The Progressive* (May 1979), p. 12.

13. Robert Pear, "Washington Feeling Insecure About Non-Secret Information," *The New York Times*, Aug. 30, 1987, p. E–5. *See also* American Library Association, "Less Access to Less Information By and About the U.S. Government" (Washington, D.C.: American Library Association, 1982), p. 82.

The fact that "bits and pieces" of unrelated information can be pieced together, as President Reagan noted in his directive, was illustrated by the way civilian scientists were able to discover the contents of the space shuttle Atlantis's payload. John Noble Wilford, discussing the December 3, 1988, launch of the shuttle, pointed out that although its payload was classified as "top secret," these scientists ultimately concluded that the Atlantis carried an intelligence-gathering satellite. "Why Everyone Knew about the Secret Shuttle Mission," *The New York Times*, Dec. 4, 1988, p. A–32.

These space experts reached their conclusions using what President Reagan would call the "mosaic theory" of knowledge, and what John E. Pike, an independent space policy specialist, called "open source deduction." Ibid. By rigorously studying unclassified information such as budget documents as well as Pentagon officials' testimony to Congress and their briefings to industry, "analysts string together bits of information and perceive patterns." Ibid. In addition, they pick up any gossip they can from aerospace circles, get together and compare their hunches, and finally arrive at an "educated guess."

Wilford observed that their accurate speculations must have been "discomfiting to the Pentagon and to those who insist that it is important for national security to classify as secret just about everything involving the military space program." Ibid. He added that these recent revelations raise questions about whether it is realistic to attempt keeping such missions secret, or even whether doing so is necessarily in the best interests of the country. John Pike expressed the same doubts, and pointed out that "to have intelligent discussions on whether military programs are worthwhile the public should know as much as the Pentagon and the Kremlin." Ibid.

14. Pear, "Washington Feeling Insecure," p. E–5.

15. Benson, "Overcoming Complacency," p. 14.

16. Carey and Carlucci, "Scientific Exchange," p. 139 (the Defense Department brochure is entitled "Soviet Military Power").

17. Inman in symposium, "Striking a Balance: Scientific Freedom and National Security," at the annual meeting of the American Association for the Advancement of Science, Washington, D.C., Jan. 7, 1982. (The full text of the talks is reprinted in *Aviation Week and Space Technology*, Feb. 8, 1982, p. 10.)

Scientists maintained that the federal government had not yet made its case for national security controls, prompting Admiral Inman to respond that "this reasoning is circular and unreasonable. . . . The specific details of why information must be protected are often even more damaging than the information itself." Ibid.

18. National Academy of Science, "Scientific Communication and National Security," National Academy of Science, Panel on Scientific Communication and National Security Committee on Science, Engineering and Public Policy 97 (hereinafter cited as *Corson Report*).

The *Corson Report* was written by high-level representatives from university faculties and administrations, former federal agency officials, and executives from high-technology firms. They were impaneled in 1982 to examine the academic research community's role in exporting militarily significant technology. Dale Corson, president emeritus of Cornell University, served as its chair. The panel released its report, officially known as the *National Academy of Science and Engineering Report*, on September 30, 1982. Christina N. Ramirez, "The Balance of Interests Between National Security Controls and First Amendment Interests in Academic Freedom," 13 *Journal of College and University Law* 179 (Fall 1986), pp. 181, 181 n.9.

A follow-up report was issued 18 months later. M. Wallerstein and L. McCray, *Scientific Communication and National Security: The Issues in 1984* (staff report to NAS [National Academy of Science] Committee on Science, Engineering, and Public Policy), p. 12; (hereinafter cited as *NAS Report Update*).

After being briefed at the highest level by national security agents and reviewing scores of bound volumes filled with classified and unclassified information, the Corson Committee concluded that the Soviet-bloc countries were indeed stealing huge amounts of crucial military technology from Western nations, and that their efforts to obtain scientific and technological information had expanded dramatically over the past decade. Moreover, Soviet intelligence agents had infiltrated many U.S. institutions, including its universities.

The Soviets' "prize catches" were acquired primarily from overt and covert intelligence activities, however, such as the legal and illegal purchase of U.S.-made equipment, and the Corson Committee observed that the academic research community was responsible for only an insignificant amount of this transfer—perhaps only 5 percent of the technology acquired from the West that by the Soviet's own estimation constituted its most significant acquisitions during the 1970s and early 1980s (*Corson Report*, pp. 17, 19, 99). The report pointed out that no representative of the U.S. intelligence agencies was able to offer evidence of specific damage to the country's national security stemming from leaks in the academic community (ibid., p. 19), and it concluded that "open scientific communication involving the research community" did not have serious "near-term" military implications. Ibid.

The panel accordingly agreed that university scientists might continue performing research beyond "basic scientific investigation" into "applications of technology with military relevance." This raised the possibility, of course, that the Soviet Union would eventually perceive the university campus as a "much better target of opportunity for the illegal acquisition of technology" (ibid., p. 23), and, as the panel pointed out, it is this potential threat that Admiral Inman and his colleagues in the intelligence and defense communities believe justifies stricter and broader application of the export control statutes (ibid., p. 54).

The Corson panel advised against classifying university research unless it is government-sponsored and likely to result within a short time in militarily useful products (ibid., p. 49). Noting that most universities refuse to undertake classified projects, it also recommended that in those circumstances where research data is very sensitive but classification nevertheless is unwarranted, two measures be implemented: One, written agreements should be entered into that prohibit nationals of certain countries from participating directly in research projects that receive government support; and two, designated manuscripts should be submitted simultaneously to the publishers and the federal contract officers with the proviso that an agency seeking modifications must do so within a 60-day period.

The panel concluded that no restrictions whatsoever, in terms either of access or dissemination, should be imposed on the vast majority of research, whether basic or applied (*NAS Report Update*, pp. 26–28). The policy of "security by secrecy" was difficult to administer and it unnecessarily disrupted the scientific community. The panel recommended that this country's national policy should be "security by accomplishment"—a policy that would secure the technological lead of the United States by fostering scientific productivity:

> In those few cases of government-sponsored research where national security considerations may require restrictions on publications, limitations on foreign access to facilities, or security classifications, the Panel believes that certain guiding principles and procedures should be followed. The provisions of [the export control laws] should not be invoked to deal with gray areas in government-funded university research. Rather, appropriate procedures should be incorporated in research contracts or other written agreements in those rare cases where some measure of control is required.

Ibid. As Christina Ramirez pointed out, the original NAS report was released in 1982 with what had been termed an "optimistic expectation" on the part of the research community for a resolution of the problems that had inspired the creation of the panel. *NAS Report Update, quoted in* Ramirez, "The Balance of Interests," p. 209. However, by January 1984, when an update of the panel's report appeared, "the optimism had evaporated," in large part because the government had imposed another series of restraints on the research community and "many scientists still [felt] they do not know their rights and obligations regarding dissemination of their research." Ibid.

19. Today the Department of Defense, and, to a lesser degree, the Department of Energy, provide major sources of funding for the university community—the Department of Defense providing such heady sums, in fact, that some

university administrators fear that scientists on their faculties are becoming unduly dependent on this single outlet. Joseph M. Ballantyne, "SDI and University Research: An Exchange of Views," 72 *Academe* (Sept.–Oct. 1986), p. 12.

20. 22 U.S.C. §2751–96 (1983).

21. 50 U.S.C. app. §2401 (1983).

22. Under the International Traffic in Arms Regulations (ITAR), which implement the Arms Export Control Act, information is "exported" whenever it is communicated overseas by "oral, visual, or documentary means," including "visits abroad by American citizens." 22 C.F.R. §125.03.

Under the Export Administration Regulations (EAR), which implement the Export Administration Act, "export" is defined as "(i) an actual shipment or transmission of technical data out of the United States;" or (ii) "any release of technical data in the United States with the knowledge or intent that the data will be shipped or transmitted from the United States." Data is also exported through "(i) visual inspection by foreign nationals . . . [or] (ii) oral exchanges of information in the United States or abroad of personal knowledge or technical experience acquired in the United States." 15 C.R.F. §379.1 (b)(2).

23. The Export Administration Regulations define "technical data" as:

> information of any kind that can be used, or adopted for use in the design, manufacturing, production, utilization or reconstruction of materials. The data may take a tangible form, such as a model, prototype, blueprint, or an operating manual; or they may take an intangible form such as technical service.

15 C.F.R. §379.1 (a). The International Traffic in Arms Regulations define "technical data" in much the same way, but they also include anything that "advances the state of the art," or "establishes a new art in an area of significant military applicability in the United States." 22 C.F.R. §125.01 (b).

24. 15 C.F.R. §399.1 (1984).

25. International Traffic in Arms Regulations, 22 C.F.R. §121.01 (1984).

26. 15 C.F.R. §387.1 (a)(ii) (1984); 50 U.S.C. app. §2410 (b)(1) (1983); 22 U.S.C. §2778 (c) (1983); 22 C.F.R. §127.03 (1984).

General licenses, or "exemptions," have generally been available for individuals whose research is considered "in the public domain." The International Traffic in Arms Regulations, for example, exempt information "in published form" or "sold at newsstands." 22 C.F.R. §125.11 (a)(1). *See United States* v. *Edler Industries, Inc.*, 579 F. 2d 516 (7th Cir. 1978).

The Export Administration Regulations also allow "correspondence, attendance at or participation in meetings" and "instruction in academic laboratories" to be included under a general license. 15 C.F.R. §379.3. Without a license, however, these academic activities can be undertaken only as long as they do not relate "directly or significantly to design, production, or utilization in industrial processes." Export Administration Regulations, 15 C.F.R. §379.3 (a).

27. 22 C.F.R. §§121.1–130.17 (1985).

28. Ibid. §124.3 (b)(1) (1985).

29. 50 U.S.C. app. §2401 (1983); *amended* 50 U.S.C. app. §2412.

30. 15 C.F.R. §§368.1–399.2 (1984).

31. 45 *Fed. Reg.* 65,014 (1980); Department of Defense, Office of the Under

Secretary of Defense Research and Engineering, *The Militarily Critical Technologies List* Oct. 1984 (Catalogue of Government Publications, Stock Number 85–12131).

32. *For discussion see* Edward Gerjuoy, "Control on Scientific Information Exports," 3 *Yale Law and Policy Review* 447, 454–55 (Spring 1985).

33. Colin Norman, "Administration Grapples with Export Controls," 220 *Science* (June 1983), p. 1023.

34. 42 U.S.C. §§2161–63 (1982).

35. Ibid. §2161 (b) (1982).

36. Ibid. §§2014 (x). A 1981 amendment to the Atomic Energy Act, moreover, authorizes the secretary of energy to "prescribe such regulations [with respect to atomic energy defense programs]... as may be necessary to prohibit the unauthorized dissemination of *unclassified* information." Ibid. §2013 (b) (emphasis added).

37. Mary M. Cheh, "The *Progressive* Case and the Atomic Energy Act: Waking to the Dangers of Government Information Controls," 48 *George Washington Law Review* 163, 171 n.49 (1980).

38. Defense Authorization Act of 1984, 10 U.S.C. 140c, and DoD 5230.24 and 5320.25. *See also* Robert Park, "The Muzzling of American Science," 72 *Academe* (Sept.–Oct. 1986), p. 19.

39. Irwin Goodwin, "Incident Over SPIE Papers Muddles Scientific Secrecy Issue," 38 *Physics Today* (June 1985), p. 55. *See also* Park, "The Muzzling of American Science," p. 23.

The Immigration and Naturalization Act also restricts academic exchanges by granting the Department of State almost total discretion to deny visas to anyone who would "endanger the security... of the United States," or to issue them visas that impose restrictions on their movements and activities while they are in this country. 8 U.S.C. §1182 (a)(27) (1982 and Supp. 11 1984).

40. Park, "The Muzzling of American Science," p. 29.

41. Ibid; *see also* Ramirez, "Balance of Interests," p. 191.

42. Park, p. 20.

43. Ibid.

44. Ibid.

45. Ramirez, "Balance of Interests," p. 189.

46. Gerjuoy, "Controls on Exports," p. 457 n.43.

47. Robert E. Sullivan and Nancy E. Bader, "The Application of Export Control Laws to Scientific Research at Universities," 9 *Journal of College and University Law* 451, 452 (1982).

48. Shattuck and Spence, *Government Information Controls*, p. 19.

49. Letter to Secretary of Defense Caspar Weinberger from the presidents of 12 scientific and engineering societies, Sept. 17, 1985; *cited in* Shattuck and Spence, *Government Information Controls*, p. 19. (Document on file at Harvard University, Office of Government, Community and Public Affairs.)

50. Shattuck and Spence, *Government Information Controls*, pp. 8–10.

51. *See* Ramirez, "Balance of Interests," pp. 216–19.

52. Other scientific and technical societies have "informally" barred foreign scientists from attending their meetings, including such prestigious groups as the Society of Manufacturing Engineers, the American Ceramics Society, and

the Society for the Advancement of Material and Process Engineering. Shattuck and Spence, *Government Information Controls*, p. 21.

53. Abrams, "The New Effort to Control Information," p. 27.

54. Joel Greenbert, "Science's New Cold War," 123 *Science News* (April 2, 1983), p. 218; Ramirez, "Balance of Interests," pp. 202–4.

55. Letter from M. Sardinas, Country Officer, Office of Chinese Affairs, Department of State (May 20, 1981). The letter read:

Dear Sir or Madam:

The Chinese scholar[s] at your institution is [are] part of an official United States-China exchange program which has sponsored more than 2,000 Chinese scholars and students to study in the United States to date. . . . The majority of these officially sponsored Chinese scholars are pursuing studies to acquire scientific or technical expertise urgently needed by China to achieve its modernization goals. The United States fully supports this effort. However, the United States government is concerned that none of these programs involve the transfer of technical data which is considered critical on export control or national security grounds. United States law and regulations require that the Department of State, together with the relevant United States agencies, examine in detail those programs which may involve the transfer of such technical data. . . . To be responsive to these concerns, the Department of State requests that you complete the enclosed questionnaire for the scholar[s] named above:

(Selected questions from questionnaire)

What is the scholar or student's full name?

How long will the scholar or student be at your institution? What major subject areas will be involved in the scholar or student's program? . . .

(Include information such as research problems and specific experiments).

How will this program be conducted? For example, will the scholar do individual research or joint laboratory research? What research method and procedures, instruments . . . or specialized equipment may be used during the course of the study program? Will student have access to specialized library collections? Specialized laboratory facilities? Do the procedures or results of the scholar's research program have applications to the production or processing of advanced materials? If so, how? Do the procedures or results have application to the design, development, manufacture, or reconstruction of any specific end item . . . ? How? Do you [the host professor] or your institution have any contacts with industry or government organizations? If so, please list them and indicate whether the foreign visitor will have any access to contract activities.

Quoted in Abrams, "The New Effort to Control Information," p. 26 (hereinafter cited as State Department Letter).

56. Ramirez, "Balance of Interests," p. 202.

57. State Department Letter. *See also NAS Report Update*, p. 9.

58. Ibid. The restriction was required because the assigned reading material for the course included unclassified technical data that appears on the Munitions Control List, and thus cannot be "exported" without a license.

59. These universities, while acknowledging the imperatives of national security, have nevertheless resented government-imposed restrictions, either because they require them to undertake police activities which they consider the government's responsibility, or because they consider such restrictions inimical to academic freedom. *For discussion see* John Shattuck, *Federal Restrictions on the Free Flow of Academic Information and Ideas* (Cambridge, Mass.: Harvard University, Office of Government, Community & Public Affairs, July 1985), pp. 18–19;

Ramirez, "Balance of Interests," pp. 202–4; Kim McDonald, "Three Universities Warn Pentagon on Censorship," 28 *Chronicle of Higher Education* (April 4, 1984), p. 18.

60. Shattuck, *Federal Restrictions on the Free Flow of Ideas*, p. 18. *See also Corson Report*, pp. 180–81.

61. Office of the Undersecretary of Defense for Research and Engineering, *Defense Science Board Task Force Report on University Responsiveness to National Security Requirements*, (Jan. 19, 1982), pp. 2–8. *Cited in* Gerjuoy, "Controls on Scientific Information Exports," p. 464.

62. Michael G. Finn, "Foreign National Scientists and Engineers in the U.S. Labor Force 1972–1982," *cited in* Park, "The Muzzling of American Science," p. 22.

63. Ibid.

64. *For discussion see* Shattuck, *Federal Restrictions on the Free Flow of Ideas*, pp. 8–11. Prepublication review agreements, which are lifelong in effect, had been signed by 150,000 individuals as of January 1986. Strohm, "Government Restrictions," p. 42.

65. National Aeronautics and Space Administration, Federal Acquisition Regulation, April 1, 1984, *quoted in* Shattuck, *Federal Restrictions on the Free Flow of Ideas*, p. 10.

66. Ibid.

67. Ibid., p. 8.

68. Ibid., p. 9.

69. *For discussion see* Gina Bari Kolata, "NSA Asks to Review Papers Before Publication," 215 *Science* (March 19, 1982), p. 1485; G. Kolata, "Prior Restraints on Cryptology Considered," 208 *Science* (June 27, 1980), pp. 1442–43.

70. 42 U.S.C. §2274 (1982). According to Harold Relyea, "Information in this category is [said to be] 'born classified,' i.e., it is subject to official secrecy protection from the moment of its creation, regardless of where located, and can be removed from its privileged status only by affirmative determination of the government." "National Security Controls and Scientific Information," Library of Congress Congressional Research Service (June 13, 1983). *See also* Harold Relyea, "National Security and Information," 4 *Government Information Quarterly* (1987), p. 11; Robert A. Rosenbaum, Morton J. Tenzer, Stephen H. Unger, William Van Alstyne, and Jonathan Knight, "Academic Freedom and the Classified Information System," 219 *Science* (Jan. 21, 1983), p. 257.

71. *See* Gerjuoy, "Controls on Scientific Exports," pp. 462–63.

72. David E. Sanger, "Computer Work Bends College Secrecy Rules," *The New York Times*, Oct. 16, 1984, pp. A-1, D-5. *Cited in* Gerjuoy, "Controls on Scientific Exports," pp. 462–63. Edward Gerjuoy points out, however, that "there is a genuine difference . . . between prepublication requirements imposed by the government and those negotiated by university and industry in their joint research ventures." Ibid. A violation of a law, of course, can be punishable by a criminal penalty, whereas breaches of a contract entered into with private industry results at most in the payment of damages.

73. Natalie Robins, "Library Follow-Up," 246 *The Nation* (June 25, 1988), p. 885.

74. Ibid.

75. Herbert Mitgang, "The F.B.I.'s War on Spies in the Stacks," *The New York Times*, June 26, 1988, p. E–6.

76. Linda Greenhouse, "F.B.I. Defends Library Monitoring Program," *The New York Times*, July 4, 1988, p. A–17.

77. Mitgang, "The F.B.I.'s War," p. E–6.

78. Ibid.

79. American Library Association, "Less Access to Less Information By and About the U.S. Government," p. 84.

80. Herbert Mitgang, "Book Notes," *The New York Times*, Aug. 31, 1988, p. C–22.

81. Ibid.

82. Mitgang, "The F.B.I.'s War," p. E–6.

83. Greenhouse, "F.B.I. Defends Program," p. A–17.

84. Herbert Mitgang, "Library Spy Hunt Is Curbed by F.B.I.," *The New York Times*, Nov. 11, 1988, p. A–24.

85. Ibid.

86. Ibid.

87. *See New York Times* v. *Sullivan*: "Even a false statement may be deemed to make a valuable contribution to public debate, since it brings about 'the clearer perception and livelier impression of truth, produced by its collision with error.' " 376 U.S. 255, 279 n.19 (1964), *quoting* John Stuart Mill, *On Liberty* (Oxford: Blackwell, 1947), p. 15.

For discussion see Franklyn S. Haiman, *Speech and Law in a Free Society* (Chicago: University of Chicago Press, 1981), pp. 182–208.

88. *See, for example, U.S.* v. *Marchetti*, 466 F. 2d 1309 (4th Cir.), *cert. denied*, 409 U.S. 1063 (1972) (CIA may enforce prepublication review pursuant to contractual agreements with its employees in order to implement its statutory mandate to "protect intelligence sources and methods from unauthorized disclosure"); *Snepp* v. *U.S.*. 444 U.S. 507, 511 (1980) (per curiam) (although Snepp, a former CIA employee, wrote a book that divulged no classified information, he nevertheless violated his contractual agreement with the agency by not providing it with "an opportunity to determine whether the material he proposed to publish would compromise classified information sources").

See also Alfred A. Knopf, Inc., v. *Colby*, 509 F. 2d 1362 (4th Cir.), *cert. denied*, 421 U.S. 992 (1975).

89. *New York Times* v. *U.S.* (The Pentagon Papers case), 403 U.S. 713 (1971).

90. This author is indebted to James R. Ferguson, whose writings on the relationship between technological information and the First Amendment have provided valuable background information and an analytic framework for this discussion. *See*, in particular, "National Security Controls on Technological Knowledge: A Constitutional Perspective," 10 *Science, Technology, and Human Values* (1985), p. 87; "Scientific Freedom, National Security, and U.S. Competitiveness," *Issues in Science and Technology* (Fall 1986), p. 106; "Scientific Freedom, National Security, and the First Amendment," 221 *Science* (1983), p. 620.

Additional material for this discussion was supplied by Richard N. Perle, "Technology Security, National Security, and U.S. Competitiveness," *Issues in Science and Technology* (Fall 1986), p. 106; Edward Gerjuoy, "Controls on Scientific Exports," pp. 468–78.

91. In *U.S.* v. *Edler Industries, Inc.*, the Seventh Circuit Court of Appeals affirmed the constitutionality of the International Traffic in Arms Regulations (ITAR), which restrict the transmission of any commodities and "technical data" having military utility. 579 F. 2d 516 (1978). According to the court, ITAR's licensing requirements did not constitute prior restraint, nor were they unduly broad, since they exempted information in the public domain. Significantly, however, the court's decision was also influenced by the fact that it considered the information controlled by ITAR roughly analogous to commercial speech, and for reasons examined in *Ohralik* v. *Ohio State Bar Association* the Supreme Court has concluded that the constitutionality of government-imposed restrictions on commercial speech should be assessed with a less stringent standard than similar restrictions on so-called "pure speech":

> Expression concerning purely commercial transactions has come within the ambit of the [First] Amendment's protection only recently. In rejecting the notion that such speech is wholly outside the protection of the First Amendment . . . we were careful not to hold that it is wholly undifferentiable from other forms of speech.
>
> We have not discarded the common sense distinction between speech proposing a commercial transaction, which occurs in an area traditionally subject to government regulation, and other varieties of speech. To require a parity of constitutional protection for commercial and noncommercial speech alike could invite dilution, simply by a leveling process, of the force of the Amendment's guarantee with respect to the latter kind of speech. Rather than subject the First Amendment to such a devitalization, we instead have afforded commercial speech a limited measure of protection, commensurate with its subordinate position in the scale of First Amendment values, while allowing modes of regulation that might be impermissible in the realm of noncommercial expression.

436 U.S. at 455.

92. At a recent international symposium on optical engineering, the Department of Defense prohibited several scientists from delivering unclassified papers on topics ranging from microelectronics to infrared technology lest foreign adversaries acquire enough information on these critical subjects to develop more sophisticated weapons. The department's precautions may have been excessive, but they were not foolhardy: as Thane Gustafson points out, "technological leaks" have resulted in many "sudden and disastrous military give-aways." *Quoted in* S. H. Unger, "The Growing Threat of Government Secrecy," 85 *Technology Review* (Feb.–March 1982), p. 30.

93. The examples are from Ferguson, "Scientific Freedom, National Security, and the First Amendment," pp. 620–23.

94. 467 F. Supp. 990 (1979).

95. *For discussion see* Morland, "The H-Bomb Secret," p. 12.

96. Ramirez, "Balance of Interests," pp. 222–23.

97. Erwin Knoll, " 'Born Secret': The Story Behind the H-Bomb Article We're Not Allowed to Print," 43 *Progressive* (May 1979), p. 15.

98. 467 F. Supp. at 993.

99. Knoll, " 'Born Secret,' " p. 16. In 1950 the government succeeded in squelching another article on the hydrogen bomb, although in this case without having to institute a lawsuit. The editors of *Scientific American* had not submitted this article, written by Hans Bethe, to the Atomic Energy Commission for review because they assumed that it contained no information that was not already in

the public domain. The commission managed to obtain a copy, however, and urged the editors to delete specified sections. The latter reluctantly did so, and at the same time destroyed all the original copies of the Bethe article. Mary M. Cheh, "The *Progressive* Case and the Atomic Energy Act: Waking to the Dangers of Government Information Controls," 48 *George Washington Law Review* 163, 176–77 (1980). Cheh points out that "Dr. Bethe's position in the *Scientific American* incident is somewhat ironic considering that he filed an affidavit on behalf of the government in the *Progressive* case." "The *Progressive* Case and the Atomic Energy Act," p. 176.

100. 283 U.S. 697 (1931).

101. 403 U.S. 713 (1971).

102. For discussion *see* Chapter 2.

103. *New York Times* v. *U.S.*, 403 U.S. at 725–27 (Brennan, J., concurring).

104. As Justice Brennan explained, the government must convince the Court that substantial danger is both likely and imminent before it will agree to suppress communication:

> The entire thrust of the Government's claim throughout these cases [involving its applications for prior restraint] has been that publication of the material sought to be enjoined "could" or "might," or "may" prejudice the national interest in various ways. But the First Amendment tolerates absolutely no prior judicial restraints of the press predicated upon surmise or conjecture that untoward consequences may result . . . only governmental allegation and proof that publication must inevitably, directly and immediately cause the occurrence of an event kindred to imperiling the safety of a transport already at sea can support even the issuance of an interim restraining order.

403 U.S. at 725–27 (concurring opinion). *See also* Joint Brief of Appellants Knoll, Day, and Morland in *U.S.* v. *Progressive*, No. 79–1429, U.S. Court of Appeals for the Seventh Circuit, pp. 13, 15, 23–25, 26–28, 29–34.

105. 42 U.S.C. at §2014 (x).

106. 467 F. Supp. at 991. This argument presages the one President Reagan used in a 1984 directive in which he compared information to a mosaic: bits of information, innocuous in themselves, "can reveal highly classified and other sensitive information when taken in the aggregate." *See* Robert Pear, "Washington Feeling Insecure about Non-Secret Information," *The New York Times*, August 30, 1987, p. E–5.

107. Knoll, " 'Born Secret,' " pp. 15–16.

108. *U.S.* v. *Progressive, Inc.*, 467 F. Supp. 990 (W.D. Wisc. 1979).

109. Ibid. at 993.

110. Ibid.

111. Ibid. at 994.

112. 467 F. Supp. at 995.

113. Ibid. at 996.

114. *For discussion see* Ramirez, "Balance of Interests," p. 224 n.376.

115. Philip Taubman, "U.S. Drops Efforts to Bar Publication of H-Bomb Articles," *The New York Times*, Sept. 18, 1979, p. A–1; *appeal dismissed*, 610 F. 2d 819 (7th Cir. 1979).

116. 467 F. Supp. at 995.

117. National Academy of Science, Panel on Scientific Communication and

National Security Committee on Science, Engineering and Public Policy, "Scientific Communication and National Security" (Washington, D.C.: National Academy Press, 1982), p. 97.

118. Letter to *The New York Times*, May 27, 1973, *cited in* Samuel H. Day, Jr., " 'Scientists of Conscience': How the *Progressive* Managed to Find a Few," 43 *Progressive* (May 1979), p. 33.

119. *Quoted in* John Shattuck, paper presented at the Sept. 17, 1984, Washington, D.C., conference, *Free Trade in Ideas: A Constitutional Imperative*, organized by the American Civil Liberties Union and the Fund for Free Expression; published proceedings p. 31. (Proceedings available from the American Civil Liberties Union, 122 Maryland Ave., N.E., Washington, D.C., 20002.)

120. Park, "The Muzzling of American Science," p. 19.

121. National Academy of Science, Committee on Science, Engineering and Public Policy, *Working Papers of the Panel on Scientific Communication and National Security* 38–41 (1982), p. 45.

122. Ibid., 38–41; p. 40.

123. *For discussion see* Gerjuoy, "Controls on Scientific Exports," p. 464.

124. Mark Popovsky, *Science in Chains: The Crisis of Science and Scientists in the Soviet Union Today* (London: Collins and Harvill Press, 1980), pp. 66, 70, 82, *quoted in* Gerjuoy, "Control on Scientific Exports," p. 466.

125. Testimony of Robert L. Park, director of the Office of Public Affairs, American Physical Society, before a hearing of the Committee on Government Operations, U.S. House of Representatives, Feb. 25, 1987. *Cited in* John Shattuck and Muriel Morisey Spence, *Government Information Controls: Implications for Scholarship, Science and Technology* (Cambridge, Mass.: Harvard University, Office of Government, Community, and Public Affairs, July 1985), p. 26.

126. Gerjuoy, "Controls on Scientific Exports," p. 19.

127. Ibid.

128. Knoll, " 'Born Secret,' " p. 13.

129. John Buell, "On Science and Secrecy," 43 *Progressive* (May 1979), pp. 34–35. The consequences of the "secrecy mystique" were also confirmed in June 1989 by a congressional committee, which had recently concluded a three-year investigation of the country's nuclear weapons plants. The committee released a report of its findings in which it concluded that the myriad safety breakdowns at these plants were a direct result of their managers' "devotion to secrecy." Michigan Representative John D. Dingell, chairman of the House Energy and Commerce Subcommittee on Oversight and Investigations, which undertook the study, wrote a letter to accompany his panel's report in which he said that "obsessive secrecy and lack of outside oversight have been hallmarks of the nuclear weapons program since its beginning as the wartime Manhattan Engineering District" in the early 1940s. "Report Cites Secrecy as a Cause of Problems at Nuclear Plants," *The New York Times*, June 19, 1989, p. A–12.

According to the report, because of unchallenged secrecy the Department of Energy and its contractors were free to ignore health and safety standards: "This penchant for secrecy and the classified nature of the process of making nuclear weapons contributed to a mind-set of emphasizing production at the expense of health and safety." Ibid.

130. *Quoted in* Samuel H. Day, Jr., " 'Scientists of Conscience,' " 43 *Progressive* (May 1979), p. 28. Einstein's letter reads in its entirety:

Through the release of atomic energy, our generation has brought into the world the most revolutionary force since prehistoric man's discovery of fire. This basic power of the universe cannot be fitted into the outmoded concept of narrow nationalism. For there is no secret and no defense; there is no possibility of control except through the aroused understanding and insistence of the peoples of the world.

We scientists recognize our inescapable responsibility to carry to our fellow citizens an understanding of the simple facts of atomic energy and its implications for society. In this lies not only security but our only hope—we believe that an informed citizenry will act for life and not death.

Conclusion

The United States is outspoken in its support for the 1948 Universal Declaration of Human Rights, which asserts in Article 19 that each individual is entitled "to hold opinions without interference and to seek, receive and impart information through any media and regardless of frontiers."[1] In 1975 the United States endorsed another international agreement, the Helsinki Accords, which morally obligates participating states to "facilitate freer movement and contacts" between people of the world, and encourages them to "administer flexibly" their respective provisions for exit from and entry into their territories.[2] Most recently, in January 1989, the United States was 1 of 33 nations, including the Soviet Union, to sign yet a third human rights agreement, this time pledging to "take every opportunity offered by modern means of communication . . . to increase the freer and wider dissemination of information of all kinds."[3]

After the 1989 agreement was signed, several U.S. officials expressed concern that the Soviet Union might breach its terms.[4] However legitimate, their concern was too narrowly focused, since this country has itself failed to honor many of its own commitments. The chairman of the commission established by Congress to implement the Helsinki Accords, for instance, testified in 1987 that certain U.S. laws and administrative policies "contradict the very spirit" of these accords.[5]

The chairman could have been referring to the Beirut Agreement, which, according to the United States Information Agency, vests its agents with authority to discriminate against any domestic film that "depicts America in an unfavorable light" by effectively denying this film the trade concessions it needs to survive in the export market,[6] or to the Foreign Agents Registration Act, which provides officials at the Department of Justice with license to stigmatize controversial foreign films by labeling them "political propaganda" and to saddle their distributors with oppressive registration and reporting requirements.[7]

The chairman could also have been referring to a series of export control acts, which were initially drafted to restrict the transfer of militarily useful technology,[8] but which, in a peculiar metamorphosis, now prohibit scientists, academicians, and scholars from publicly disseminating vast categories of unclassified research.

In signing the Helsinki Accords, the United States pledged to promote "freer movement and contacts between people of the world," so the chairman could have been referring to provisions in the Immigration and Nationality Act that contravene this objective. These provisions allow government authorities to exclude from the country not only criminals and bomb-wielding terrorists but also people such as Hortensia Allende, because she participated in disarmament marches, and former NATO General Nino Pasti, because he campaigned against the deployment of cruise missiles in Europe.[9]

The chairman could have been alluding to the Trading with the Enemies Act, under whose terms the Treasury Department effectively prohibits most Americans from traveling to Cuba;[10] or to a series of executive fiats that similarly forbid them to visit any country on the president's "enemies list."[11] Finally, he could have been thinking about a State Department policy, sanctioned by the Supreme Court in 1981,[12] providing for the revocation of the passport not only of anyone whose actions manifestly threaten U.S. security, but also of any individual whom the government suspects of wanting to visit West Berlin or San Salvador, for instance, in order to criticize this country's environmental record, or its maneuvers in Central America.[13]

Any one of these policies contravenes not only the Universal Declaration and the Helsinki Accords, but also the First Amendment to the Constitution, and, woven together, they comprise what law professor Burt Neuborne and American Civil Liberties Union attorney Steven Shapiro call a "nylon curtain" designed "to keep foreign ideas out and American citizens in."[14]

The U.S. curtain, however porous, is nevertheless an anomaly for a nation whose human rights record is, in general, exemplary, and Neuborne and Shapiro are anxious to distinguish the United States from totalitarian countries enshrouded by iron curtains: "We don't have a Berlin Wall. No captive peoples are imprisoned behind our borders."[15] Most foreign books and periodicals circulate freely, they could have added, and aliens enjoy almost as much access to the domestic media as do citizens.[16] Most Americans have to endure only a long line before receiving passports, moreover, and although foreigners must undergo ideological grillings before receiving United States visas, the vast majority do eventually receive them. However, while satisfaction is warranted, smugness is not: Its estimable record notwithstanding, America's nylon curtain remains in place, an appendage more appropriate to an insecure and xenophobic country than to a powerful and self-confident one. The question is, why do Americans tolerate this invisible screen that dims their view of the rest of the world?

Perhaps Americans tolerate the screen for the same reason they tolerate any hypocritical practice: because of their human capacity to divorce ideals from operative biases.[17] This capacity is particularly apparent in dealing with First Amendment issues, where most Americans see no inconsistency between their professed attachment to free speech and free press and their willingness to abide policies that undermine both.

An editorialist for the *Sequent* provides a case in point. The *Sequent* is a national newspaper dedicated to conservative principles, staffed by and addressed to citizens who proclaim a deep allegiance to the United States Constitution. However, in a recent issue this writer excoriated Margaret Randall, a Mexican national seeking permanent residence in the United States, because she had in the past expressed emphatic support for certain left-wing governments.[18] Deportation was too good for her, he asserted; like a World War II collaborator, she deserved to be prosecuted for treason.[19]

Such "cognitive dissonance" is not the sole reason why citizens tolerate practices that handicap so-called "transborder speech." Although Americans are themselves defrauded whenever the government limits the stock of information from which they may draw, many nevertheless regard these practices as pardonable because they appear to affect primarily foreigners, aliens whose claim to constitutional protection they are apt to consider presumptuous and even suspect.

Americans abide these practices, moreover, because they are invariably justified on the grounds of national security. A Cuban epidemiologist may not deliver a paper at a New York City symposium, the government claims, nor may a delegation of citizens visit Havana, for reasons of national security. The phrase itself has become a talisman, used to legitimate all sorts of government restrictions, from the necessary to the unnecessary to the indefensible, and it operates as if by magic to quell dissent and encourage acquiescence.

Finally, although most of these policies violate the First Amendment, at least as it has traditionally been interpreted, the public tolerates them because the Supreme Court tolerates them. In the domestic context the Court regards the First Amendment with a solicitousness that approaches reverence, but in any context where national borders are involved, it tends to sustain government policies even when they flout the amendment's basic principles. Authorities have only to claim that these practices promote "foreign relations," or, better yet, protect "national security," and the Court becomes as acquiescent as the public. With a lame reference to its own incapacities, its inability to act decisively or anticipate events "still in the womb of time," the Court proceeds to support government officials whenever they ban foreign travel, brand foreign films, or bar foreign speakers.[20]

The Court permits public authorities to curtail domestic speech under extraordinary circumstances, and there are, of course, occasions when restrictions on transborder speech should similarly be allowed: when the government can make at least a credible showing that the admission of a given individual—the shah of Iran, for instance—could damage foreign relations or national security in more than a remote or conjectural way; or when it acts to prevent private citizens from visiting a war zone, or physicists from sharing data on advanced laser technology with their Libyan colleagues.[21] Such occasions are few, however, and the Court is surely capable of distinguishing them from the myriad other situations in which restrictions serve only to spare public leaders discomfort or challenge. The Court's failure to make such distinctions exhibits not "admirable self restraint," as it claims, but simple dereliction.

The American Library Association recently concluded that "America's informed citizenry is a population at risk," primarily because of its heavy reliance on domestic sources of information that are increasingly subject to government manipulation.[22] The risk is compounded to the extent that Americans are denied access to competing voices from foreign sources, and thus not only members of the Court, but citizens themselves, are guilty of dereliction when they tolerate policies that screen out or silence these voices.

Notes

1. G.A. Res. 217A (111), U.N. Doc. A/810 (1948), p. 71. *For discussion see* Stephen R. Barnett, "U.S. Regulation of Transborder Speech," 9 *Comm/ent* 635, 643–45 (Summer 1987).

2. Conference on Security and Cooperation in Europe: Final Act, August 1, 1975, *reprinted in* 14 *International Legal Materials* 1292 (1975).

3. Robert Pear, "35 Nations Issue East-West Accord Assuring a Broad Range of Rights," *The New York Times*, Jan. 17, 1989, pp. A–1, A–12.

4. Ibid.

5. United States Congress, Committee on the Judiciary, *Exclusion and Deportation of Aliens*, Hearing before the Subcommittee on Immigration, Refugees and International Law of the House Committee on the Judiciary, 100th Cong., 1st Sess. 125 (1987) (testimony of Steny H. Hoyer, Chairman of the Helsinki Commission).

6. Agreement for Facilitating the International Circulation of Visual and Auditory Materials of an Educational, Scientific, and Cultural Character, January 12, 1967, 17 U.S.T. 1579, T.I.A.S. No. 6116, 197 U.N.T.S. 3. *For discussion see* Chapter 4.

7. *For discussion see* Chapter 3.

8. *For discussion see* Chapter 5.

9. Immigration and Nationality Act of 1952, ch. 477, 66 Stat. 163 (codified at 8 U.S.C. §1101–1524 (1982). *For discussion see* Chapter 1.

10. Act of October 6, 1917, ch. 106, 40 Stat. 411 (1917), 50 U.S.C. app. §1 (1968); *see* C.F.R. §515.201 (b); 47 *Federal Register* 17030, 32060 (1982).

11. *For discussion see* Chapter 2.

12. *See Haig* v. *Agee*, 453 U.S. 280 (1981).

13. *See* oral argument of Solicitor General Wade H. McCree, Jr., *quoted in Haig* v. *Agee*, 453 U.S. at 319 n.9 (Brennan, J., dissenting). *For discussion see* Chapter 2.

14. Burt Neuborne and Steven Shapiro, "The Nylon Curtain: America's National Border and the Free Flow of Ideas," 26 *William and Mary Law Review* 719, 720 (1984–1985).

15. Ibid.

16. *For discussion see* Barnett, "Transborder Speech," pp. 643–45.

17. This phenomenon was described most trenchantly in Gunnar Myrdal's 1944 classic *An American Dilemma: The Negro Problem and Modern Democracy* (New York: Harper and Brothers Publishers, 1944). Although Myrdal was referring specifically to the discrepancy between Americans' avowed commitment to equality, on the one hand, and their treatment of fellow citizens of African descent, on the other, the capacity that he described to distinguish their abstract commitments from their day-to-day attitudes on concrete issues applies as well to conflicts involving First Amendment values:

> [Many mutually inconsistent] attitudes are blended into none too logical a scheme which, in turn, may be quite inconsistent with the wider personal, moral, religious, and civic sentiments and ideas of the Americans. Now and then, even the least sophisticated individual becomes aware of his own confusion and the contradiction in his attitudes. Occasionally he may recognize, even if only for a moment, the incongruence of his state of mind and find it so intolerable that the whole organization of his moral precepts is shaken. *But most people, most of the time, suppress such threats to their moral integrity together with all of the confusion, and ambiguity, and inconsistency which lurks in the basement of man's soul.*

An American Dilemma, p. xli (emphasis supplied).

18. "Writers Protest Deportation Case," *The New York Times*, November 14, 1986, p. A–27.

19. Ibid.

20. *For discussion see* Elizabeth Hull, *Without Justice for All: Constitutional Rights of Aliens* (Westport, Conn.: Greenwood Press, 1985), pp. 147–54.

Alexander Bickel speculated on the reasons for the Court's reluctance to challenge federal policies in areas relating to foreign affairs:

> The Court's [apprehension arises from its] sense of lack of capacity, compounded in unequal parts of the strangeness of the issue and the suspicion that it will have to yield

more often and more substantially to expediency than to principle; the sheer momentousness of it, which unbalances judgment and prevents one from subsuming the normal calculations of probabilities; the anxiety not so much that judicial judgment will be ignored, as that perhaps it should be, but won't.

"The Passive Virtues," 75 *Harvard Law Review* 40, 75 (1961).

21. *See Near* v. *Minnesota*, 283 U.S. 697 (1931); *New York Times* v. *United States*, 403 U.S. 713 (1971); *United States* v. *Progressive*, 467 F. Supp. 990 (1979). *For discussion see* Chapter 5.

22. Eileen Cooke, Director of the American Library Association's Washington, D.C. office, *quoted in* Herbert Mitgang, "Group Assails U.S. Information Flow," *The New York Times*, May 12, 1988, p. C–33. *See also* American Library Association, "Less Access to Less Information By and About the U.S. Government: A 1981–1987 Chronology," American Library Association, Washington, D.C., Office (February 1988). (Report available from the American Library Association, 110 Maryland Avenue, N.E., Washington, D.C., 20002.)

Bibliography

"*Abourezk* v. *Reagan*: Curbing Recent Abuses of the Executive Immigration Power." *Cornell International Law Journal* 21 (Winter 1988): 147.

Abraham, Lt. General James A. "SDI and University Research: An Exchange of Views." *Academe* 72 (Sept.–Oct. 1986): 9.

Agar, Herbert. "A Prayer for the New President." *Saturday Review of Literature* 36 (January 17, 1953): 8.

Agee, Philip. *Inside the Company: CIA Diary*. New York: Stonehill, 1975.

———. *On the Run*. Secaucus, N.J.: Lyle Stuart, 1987.

American Law Division, Congressional Research Service. "The Foreign Agents Registration Act." Senate Foreign Relations Committee Print 1977, 95th Congress, 1st Session.

American Library Association. *Less Access to Less Information By and About the U.S. Government*. Washington, D.C.: 1988.

Antonini, Thomas J., Fantozzi, Michael L., and Pruss, Lynn Marie. "*Harvard Law School Forum* v. *Shultz*: When Exclusion of Aliens Under the Immigration and Naturalization Act Conflicts with the First Amendment Rights of United States Citizens." *Journal of College and University Law* 14 (Summer 1987): 153.

Ballantyne, Joseph M. "SDI and University Research: An Exchange of Views." *Academe* 72 (Sept.–Oct. 1986): 9.

Barnett, Stephen R. "United States Regulation of Transborder Speech." *Comm/ent* 9 (Summer 1987): 635.

Benda, Susan R. and Morton Halperin. "Forbidden Writers—The Foreign Threat in Literary Garb." *College English* 47 (November 1985): 690.

Benda, Susan R. "Ideology No Longer a Basis for Visa Denials." *First Principles* 13 (Feb.–March 1988): 9.

Benson, Sumner. "Overcoming Complacency." *Society* 23 (July–August 1986): 14.

Bernstein, Barton J. "Nuclear Deception: The U.S. Record." *Bulletin of Atomic Scientists* 40 (Aug.–Sept. 1986): 42.

Bickel, Alexander. "The Passive Virtues." *Harvard Law Review* 75 (1961): 40.

———. *The Least Dangerous Branch*. Indianapolis, Ind.: Bobbs-Merrill, 1962.

Black, Charles. *Structure and Relationship in Constitutional Law*. Baton Rouge, La.: Louisiana State University Press, 1969.

Bolmer, John E., II. "The Public Forum Doctrine and *Haig* v. *Agee*." *Hastings Constitutional Law Quarterly* 10 (Fall 1982): 187.

Boudin, Leonard B. "Constitutional Right to Travel." *Columbia Law Review* 56 (1956): 47.

Buell, John. "On Science and Secrecy." *Progressive* 43 (May 1979): 34.

Burr, Steven. "Immigration and the First Amendment." *California Law Review* 73 (1985): 1889.

Carey, W. D. and Carlucci, Frank. "Scientific Exchange and U.S. National Security." *Science* 215 (Jan. 8, 1982): 139.

Chafee, Zechariah, Jr. *Three Human Rights in the Constitution of 1787*. Lawrence, Kans.: University of Kansas Press, 1956.

Chalk, Rosemary. "Continuing Debate over Science and Secrecy." *Bulletin of Atomic Scientists* 42 (March 1986): 14.

Cheh, Mary M. "The *Progressive* Case and the Atomic Energy Act: Waking to the Dangers of Government Information Controls." *George Washington Law Review* 48 (1980): 163.

Chirico, Guy W. "The Right to Travel and Presidential Emergency Authority: The Supreme Court Lowers the Standard of Review in *Regan* v. *Wald*." *Albany Law Review* 49 (Summer 1985): 1001.

Christ, Roxanne E. "The Beirut Agreement: A License to Censor?" *Loyola of Los Angeles International and Comparative Law Journal* 7 (1984): 255.

Cole, David. "Deportation of a Poet." *Nation* 246 (June 25, 1988): 892.

Congressional Research Service, American Law Division. *The Foreign Agents Registration Act*. Senate Foreign Relations Committee Print 1977, 95th Congress, 1st Session.

Cooper, Phillip J. "The Supreme Court, the First Amendment, and Freedom of Information." *Public Administration Review* 46 (Nov.–Dec. 1986): 622.

Day, Samuel H., Jr. " 'Scientists of Conscience' (How the *Progressive* Managed to Find a Few)." *Progressive* 43 (May 1979): 28.

Delgado, Richard. "The Language of the Arms Race: Should the People Limit Government Speech?" *Boston University Law Review* 64 (1984): 961.

Donner, Frank J. *The Age of Surveillance: The Aims and Methods of the American Intelligence System*. New York: Knopf, 1980.

Doob, Leonard. *Public Opinion and Propaganda*. Hamden, Conn.: Shoe String Press, 1966.

Dorfman, Anne. "Neutral Propaganda: Three Films 'Made in Canada' and the Foreign Agents Registration Act." *Comm/ent* 7 (Spring 1985): 435.

Dworkin, Ronald. *Taking Rights Seriously*. Cambridge, Mass.: Harvard University Press, 1977.

Edgar, Harold, and Benno C. Schmidt, Jr. "*Curtiss-Wright* Comes Home: Executive Power and National Security." *Harvard Civil Rights–Civil Liberties Law Review* 21 (Summer 1980): 349.

Emerson, Thomas. "Toward a General Theory of the First Amendment." *Yale Law Journal* 72 (1963): 877.

———. *System of Freedom of Expression*. New York: Random House, 1970.

———. "Legal Foundations of the Right to Know." *Washington University Law Quarterly* 1 (1976): 1.

Esakoff, Sharon. "U.S. Censorship of Educational Films for Distribution Abroad." *Cardozo Arts and Entertainment Law Journal* 3 (1984): 403.

"Fade-Out: Censor." *Nation* 246 (June 11, 1988): 812.

Farber, Daniel. "National Security, the Right to Travel, and the Court." *Supreme Court Review* 1981 (1982): 263.

Ferguson, James R. "Scientific Freedom, National Security, and the First Amendment." *Science* 221 (August 1983): 620.

———. "National Security Controls on Technological Knowledge: A Constitutional Perspective." *Science, Technology, and Human Values* 10 (1985): 87.

"The First Amendment Right to Gather State-Held Information." *Yale Law Journal* 89 (1980): 923.

Flynn, Patrick Allen. "The Constitution Abroad: The Operation of the Constitution Beyond the Continental Limits of the U.S." *Texas Law Review* 32 (1953): 58.

Friendly, Fred W. *The Good Guys, The Bad Guys, and the First Amendment*. New York: Random House, 1976.

Gallagher, Hugh Gregory. *Advise and Obstruct: The Role of the United States Senate in Foreign Policy Decisions*. New York: Delacorte Press, 1969.

Gerjuoy, Edward. "Controls on Scientific Information Exports." *Yale Law and Policy Review* 3 (Spring 1985): 447.

Glicksman, Maurice. "Institutional Openness and Individual Faculty Academic Freedom." *Academe* 72 (Sept.–Oct. 1986): 16.

Goldman, Patti. "Combatting the Opposition: English and United States Restrictions on the Right of Access to Governmental Information." *Hastings International and Comparative Law Review* 8 (Spring 1985): 249.

Goldstone, James, Jennifer M. Granholm, and Robert J. Robinson. "A Nation Less Secure: Diminished Public Access to Information." *Harvard Civil Rights–Civil Liberties Law Review* 21 (1986): 409.

Goodwin, Irwin. "Incident Over SPIE Paper Muddles Scientific Secrecy Issue."*Physics Today* 38 (June 1985): 55.

Gordon, Charles, and Rosenfield, Harry N. *Immigration Law and Procedure*. New York: M. Bender, 1966.

"Government Exclusion of Foreign Political Propaganda." *Harvard Law Review* 66 (1955): 1393.

Greenbert, Joel. "Science's New Cold War." *Science News* 123 (April 2, 1983): 218.

Gunther, Gerald. "Forward: In Search of Evolving Doctrine on a Changing Court: A Model for a Newer Equal Protection." *Harvard Law Review* 86 (1972): 1.

Haberman, David P. "Governmental Speech in the Democratic Process." *Washington University Law Quarterly* 65 (1987): 209.

Haiman, Franklyn S. *Speech and Law in a Free Society*. Chicago: University of Chicago Press, 1981.

Halperin, Morton. "We Need New Intelligence Charters." *The Center* 18 (May–June 1985): 51.

Halperin, Morton, and David N. Hoffman. *Top Secret: National Security and the Right to Know*. Washington, D.C.: New Republic Books, 1977.

Hand, Learned. *The Bill of Rights*. Cambridge, Mass.: Harvard University Press, 1958.

Harrington, Mary Keenan. "*Regan* v. *Wald* and the Grandfather Clause of the Trading with the Enemies Act: A Lesson in Explicit Vagueness." *Pace Law Review* 5 (1985): 693.

Hellman, Lillian. *Scoundrel Time*. Boston: Little, Brown, & Co., 1976.

Homonoff, Howard B. "The First Amendment and National Security: The Constitutionality of Press Censorship and Access Denial in Military Operations." *New York University Journal of International Law and Policy* 17 (Winter 1985): 369.

Hull, Elizabeth. *Without Justice for All: The Constitutional Rights of Aliens*. Westport, Conn.: Greenwood Press, 1985.

Jaffe, Louis. "The Right to Travel: The Passport Problem." *Foreign Affairs* 35 (1956): 17.

James, Raymond C. "The Right to Travel Abroad." *Fordham Law Review* 42 (1974): 838.

"Judicial Review of Visa Denials: Reexamining Consular Nonreviewability." *New York University Law Review* 52 (1977): 1137.

Jussim, Daniel. "Terrorizing the Constitution." *Civil Liberties* (Spring 1987): 3.

Kaiser, Charles, Lucy Howard, Thomas M. De Frank, Stuart A. Seidel, and Nancy Stadtman. "An Off-the-Record War." *Newsweek* 102 (Nov. 7, 1983): 52.

Kalven, Harry. *A Worthy Tradition: Freedom of Speech in America*. New York: Harper and Row, 1988.

Kalven, Jamie. "U.S. Visa Policy: The Machinery of Exclusion." *Bulletin of Atomic Scientists* 43 (May 1987): 21.

Karp, Walter. "Liberty under Siege: The Reagan Administration's Taste for Autocracy." *Harper's* 271 (Nov. 1985): 53.

Kinoy, Arthur. *Rights on Trial*. Cambridge, Mass.: Harvard University Press, 1983.

Knoll, Erwin. "Born Secret." *Progressive* 43 (May 1979): 12.

Kolata, Gina Bari. "NSA Asks to Review Papers Before Publication." *Science* 215 (March 19, 1982): 1485.

———. "Prior Restraints on Cryptology Considered." *Science* 208 (June 27, 1982): 1442.

Konvitz, Milton R. *Civil Rights in Immigration*. Ithaca, N.Y.: Cornell University Press, 1953.

Lacayo, R. "Placing a Lock on the Borders." *Time* 128 (Dec. 29, 1986): 68.

Langenberg, Donald N. "Secret Knowledge and Open Inquiry." *Society* 23 (July–August 1986): 9.

Lasswell, Harold, and Ralph Casey. *Propaganda, Communication, and Public Opinion*. Princeton, N.J.: Princeton University Press, 1946.

Laursen, Thomas E. "Constitutional Protection of Foreign Travel." *Columbia Law Review* 81 (1981): 902.
Lewis, Anthony. "National Security: Muting the 'Vital Criticism.' " *U.C.L.A. Law Review* 34 (1987): 1687.
Lutz, Eugene Clark. "President Carter's Attempt to Halt Travel to Iran and the Constitutional Right to Travel." *Syracuse Journal of Law and Commerce* 9 (Spring 1982): 115.
McDonald, Kim. "Three Universities Warn Pentagon on Censorship." *Chronicle of Higher Education* 28 (April 4, 1984): 18.
McIntire, E. "The Denial of Visas Under Sections 212 (a)(27) and (28), The Ideological Exclusionary Clauses of the Immigration and Nationality Act: A Documentation of Nine Cases Prepared for Congressman Barney Frank." (August 15, 1983, unpublished report available from the office of Congressman Barney Frank, 1030 Longworth Building, Washington, D.C., 20515.)
Madison, James. *The Writings of James Madison*. Edited by Gaillard Hunt. New York: Putnam's, 1910.
Madison, James, Alexander Hamilton, and John Jay. *The Federalist*. New York: Dutton, 1948.
Meiklejohn, Alexander. *Free Speech*. New York: Harper and Row, 1949.
———. *Self-Government*. New York: Harper and Row, 1960.
———. "The First Amendment Is an Absolute." *Supreme Court Review* 1961 (1962): 245.
Mill, John Stuart. *On Liberty*. Oxford: Blackwell, 1947.
Miller, Page Putnam. "Status Report on the Freedom of Information Act." *PS* 21 (Winter 1988): 87.
Mills, C. Wright. *Power, Politics and People*. New York: Ballantine, 1953.
Miranda, Carlos Ortiz. "Rethinking the Role of Politics in United States Immigration Law: The Helsinki Accords and Ideological Exclusion of Aliens." *San Diego Law Review* 25 (1987–1988): 301.
Mohr, James W. "Opening the Floodgates to Dissident Aliens." *Harvard Civil Rights–Civil Liberties Law Review* 6 (December 1980): 141.
Moore, John Norton. "The 'Greatest Threats' Are External." *Center* 18 (May–June 1985): 46.
Morland, Howard. "The H-Bomb 'Secret.' " *Progressive* 43 (May 1979): 24.
Mowat, Farley. *My Discovery of America*. New York: Atlantic Monthly, 1985.
Myers, Jennifer S. "Passport Controls: Revocation of Passports for National Security Reasons." *Harvard International Law Journal* 23 (Spring 1982): 163.
Myrdal, Gunnar. *An American Dilemma: The Negro Problem and Modern Democracy*. New York: Harper and Brothers Publishers, 1944.
Nader, Ralph. "Knowledge Helps Citizens, Secrecy Helps Bureaucrats." *New Statesman* 111 (Jan. 10, 1986): 12.
National Academy of Science, Panel on Scientific Communication and National Security Committee on Science, Engineering and Public Policy. "Scientific Communication and National Security." Washington, D.C.: National Academy Press, 1982.
"National Security Interest and Civil Liberties." *Harvard Law Review* 85 (1972): 1130.

Neuborne, Burt, and Steven R. Shapiro. "The Nylon Curtain: America's National Border and the Free Flow of Ideas." *William and Mary Law Review* 26 (1984–85): 719.

Norman, Colin. "Administration Grapples with Export Controls." *Science* 220 (June 1983): 1021.

———. "To Catch a Spy." *Science* 222 (Nov. 1983): 904.

Park, Robert L. "The Muzzling of American Science." *Academe* 72 (Sept.–Oct. 1986): 19.

"Passport Refusals for Political Reasons: Constitutional Issues and Judicial Review." *Yale Law Journal* 61 (February 1952): 171.

"Patricia Daniloff." *Nation* 243 (November 1, 1986): 428.

Perle, Richard N. "The Eastward Technology Flow: A Plan of Common Action." *Strategic Review* 31 (Spring 1984): 221.

———. "Technology Security, National Security, and U.S. Competitiveness." *Issues in Science and Technology* 3 (Fall 1986): 106.

Perry, Michael J. "Modern Equal Protection: A Conceptualization and Appraisal." *Columbia Law Review* 79 (1979): 1023.

Plakins, Ava Marion. "Heat Not Light: The Foreign Agents Registration Act after *Meese* v. *Keene*." *Fordham International Law Journal* 11 (Fall 1987): 184.

"Plugging the Leak: The Case for a Legislative Resolution of the Conflict between the Demands of Secrecy and the Need for an Open Government." *Virginia Law Review* 71 (June 1985): 801.

Popovsky, Mark. *Science in Chains: The Crisis of Science and Scientists in the Soviet Union Today*. London: Collins and Harvill Press, 1980.

Powe, Scot. "Espionage, Leaks, and the First Amendment." *Bulletin of Atomic Scientists* 42 (June–July 1986): 8.

"Public Bombs, and Minds Born Secret." *Progressive* 43 (Spring 1979): 23.

Ramirez, M. Christina. "The Balance of Interests between National Security Controls and First Amendment Interests in Academic Freedom." *Journal of College and University Law* 13 (Fall 1986): 179.

"*Regan* v. *Wald*: The Supreme Court Defers to Presidential Authority in Matters of Foreign Policy by Upholding Travel Restrictions to Cuba." *Georgia Journal of International and Comparative Law* 15 (1985): 83.

Relyea, Harold. "National Security and Information." *Government Information Quarterly* 4 (1987): 11.

Robins, Natalie. "Library Follow-Up." *Nation* 246 (June 25, 1988): 885.

Robinson, Nancy S. "Silenced Screens: The Role of the United States Information Agency in Denying Export Certificates to American Films." *New York University Journal of International Law and Politics* 17 (1978): 77.

Rosenbaum, Robert A., Morton J. Tenzer, Stephen H. Unger, William Van Alstyne, and Jonathan Knight. "Academic Freedom and the Classified Information System." *Science* 219 (January 21, 1983): 257.

———. "The Enlargement of the Classified Information System." *Academe* 69 (Jan.–Feb. 1983): 9a.

———. "Government Censorship and Academic Freedom." *Academe* 69 (Nov.–Dec. 1983): 15a.

Rosenberg, Howard L. "For Our Eyes Only." *American Film* (July–August 1983): 40.

Saltzburg, Stephen A. "The Reach of the Bill of Rights Beyond the *Terra Firma* of the United States." *Virginia Journal of International Law* 20 (1980): 741.

Scanlan, John A. "Why the McCarran-Walter Act Must be Amended." *Academe* 73 (Sept.–Oct. 1987): 5.

Schapiro, Mark. "The Excludables." *Mother Jones* 7 (Jan. 1986): 29.

Schwartz, Bernard. *The Reins of Power: A Constitutional History of the United States*. New York: Hill and Wang, 1963.

Schwartz, Murray L., and James C. N. Paul. "Foreign Communist Propaganda in the Mails: A Report on Some Problems of Federal Censorship." *University of Pennsylvania Law Review* 107 (1959): 621.

"Secrecy and the Public's Need to Know." *Center* 18 (May–June 1985): 15.

Shapiro, Martin. *Freedom of Speech: The Supreme Court and Judicial Review*. Englewood Cliffs, N.J.: Prentice-Hall, 1969.

Shattuck, John. *Federal Restrictions on the Free Flow of Academic Information and Ideas*. Cambridge, Mass.: Harvard University, Office of Government, Community, and Public Affairs, July 1985.

Shattuck, John, and Muriel Morisey Spence. *Government Information Controls: Implications for Scholarship, Science and Technology*. Cambridge, Mass.: Harvard University, Office of Government, Community, and Public Affairs, March 1988.

Sheehan, Neil. *A Bright Shining Lie: John Paul Vann and America in Vietnam*. New York: Random House, 1988.

Shiffrin, Steven. "Government Speech." *U.C.L.A. Law Review* 27 (1980): 565.

Simons, Howard. "Secrecy and the Public's Right to Know." *The Center* 18 (May–June 1985): 15.

Steele, Richard D. *Steele on Immigration Law*. Rochester, N.Y.: The Lawyers Co-Operative Publishing Co., 1985.

Strohm, Paul. "Government Restrictions on Academic Freedom." *Academe* 72 (Jan.–Feb. 1986): 42.

Sullivan, Robert E., and Nancy E. Bader. "The Application of Export Control Laws to Scientific Research at Universities." *Journal of College and University Law* 9 (1982): 451.

Teller, Edward. "Kicking the Secrecy Habit." *Progressive* 43 (May 1979): 33.

Tilner, Mitchell C. "Ideological Exclusion of Aliens: The Evolution of a Policy." *Georgetown Immigration Law Journal* 2 (Summer 1987): 1.

Tribe, Laurence. *American Constitutional Law*. Mineola, N.Y.: Foundation Press, 1978.

TRB. "Something to Declare." *The New Republic* 189 (October 17, 1983): 8.

Turner, Stansfield. "Intelligence and Secrecy in an Open Society." *Center* 19 (March–April 1986): 2.

Tussman, Joseph. *Government and the Mind*. New York: Oxford University Press, 1977.

Unger, S. H. "The Growing Threat of Government Secrecy." *Technology Review* 85 (Feb.–March 1982): 30.

United States Commission on Civil Rights. *The Tarnished Golden Door: Civil Rights Issues in Immigration*. Washington, D.C.: U.S. Government Printing Office, 1980.

United State Congress. *Report of the Congressional Committee Investigating the Iran-*

Contra Affair with Supplemental, Minority, and Additional Views. 100th Congress, 1st Sess., H. Report No. 100–433 and S. Report No. 100–216 (November 1987).

United States Congress. House Committee on Science and Technology. Hearings before the Subcommittee on Science, Research and Technology and the Subcommittee on Investigations and Oversight of the House Committee on Science and Technology. 97th Congress, 2nd Sess. (1982).

United States Congress. House Judiciary Committee. *Canadian Films and the Foreign Agents Registration Act*. Oversight Hearings before the Subcommittee on Civil and Constitutional Rights of the House Judiciary Committee, 98th Congress, 1st Sess. (1983).

United States Congress. House Judiciary Committee. *Exclusion and Deportation Amendments of 1983*. Hearing before the Subcommittee on Immigration, Refugees, and International Law. 98th Congress, 2nd Sess. (June 28, 1984).

United States Congress. House Subcommittee on Immigration, Refugees, and International Law of the Committee on the Judiciary. *Hearings on Exclusion and Deportation Amendment of 1983*. June 28, 1984. 98th Cong., 2nd Sess. H. R. 4509 and H. R. 5227. Washington, D.C.: U.S. Government Printing Office, 1984.

United States Department of Defense. Report of the Defense Science Board Task Force on Export of U.S. Technology. Office of the Director of Defense Research and Engineering. *An Analysis of Export Control of U.S. Technology—A DoD Perspective*. Washington, D.C.: U.S. Government Printing Office, 1976.

Walzer, Michael. *Obligations: Essays on Disobedience, War, and Citizenship*. New York: Harper and Row, 1970.

Wasserman, Jack. *Immigration Law and Practice*. 3d ed. Philadelphia, Pa.: American Law Institute, American Bar Association Committee on Continuing Professional Education, 1979.

Whelan, Charles M. "Passports and Freedom of Travel: The Conflict of a Right and a Privilege." *Georgetown Law Journal* 41 (1952): 63.

Whitton, John Boardman, and Arthur Larson. *Propaganda: Towards Disarmament in a War of Words*. Dobbs Ferry, N.Y.: Oceana Publications, 1963.

Wilson, David. "Federal Control of Information in Academic Science." *Jurimetrics Journal* 27 (Spring 1987): 283.

Wise, David. *The Politics of Lying: Government Deception, Secrecy, and Power*. New York: Random House, 1973.

Woodcock, George. "On Being 'Inadmissible.' " *New York Review of Books* 31 (September 27, 1984): 42.

Wurtzell, Judy. "First Amendment Limitations on the Exclusion of Aliens." *New York University Law Review* 62 (April 1987): 149.

Yudof, Mark. *When Government Speaks: Politics, Law, and Government Expression in America*. Berkeley: University of California Press, 1983.

Zoglin, Richard. "Questions of National Security." *Time* 127 (June 2, 1986): 67.

Index

About the Author

ELIZABETH HULL is associate professor of political science at Rutgers University, Newark. She has written many articles on immigration and constitutional issues, and a book entitled *Without Justice for All: Constitutional Rights of Aliens*.

www.ingramcontent.com/pod-product-compliance
Ingram Content Group UK Ltd.
Pitfield, Milton Keynes, MK11 3LW, UK
UKHW021907150926
475560UK00003B/223

9 780275 930431